KU-765-535

7000
YEARS OF
JEWELLERY

EDITED BY HUGH TAIT

THE BRITISH MUSEUM PRESS

L B OF GREENWICH LIBRARIES	BL
017217040	
Bertrams	23.03.07
739.27	£20.00

© 1986, 2006 The Trustees of the British Museum
Published by The British Museum Press
A division of The British Museum Company Ltd
38 Russell Square, London WC1B 3QQ

www.britishmuseum.co.uk

First published 1986
First published in paperback 1989
Reprinted 1995, 1996, 2001
Third edition 2006

ISBN-13: 978-0-7141-5032-1

ISBN-10: 0-7141-5032-0

Designed by Roger Davies
Cover design by Andrew Shoolbred

Set in Palatino by Goodfellow and Egan
Printed in Italy by Milano Stampa

Half-title illustration Helios brooch by Castellani, *c.* 1860, inspired by a Hellenistic Greek ornament (see p. 189)

Frontispiece Portrait of Lady Layard, wife of the archaeologist Sir Austen Henry Layard who discovered the ancient Assyrian city of Nimrud. As a present for his bride on their wedding in 1869, Layard had a number of Assyrian cylinder seals made up into a necklace, bracelet and earrings in Victorian gold settings by Phillips Brothers, London. The portrait was painted in 1870 by Vincente Palmaroli y Gonzalez (1834–96), and the jewellery was bequeathed to the British Museum by Lady Layard in 1912

Above Turquoise eagle brooch, one of twelve presented by Prince Albert to the bridesmaids at his wedding to Queen Victoria in 1840 (see p. 187)

Opposite Gold and agate Egyptian-style pendant made by Phillips Brothers, London, 1863–70. This is a version of a jewel owned by Princess Alexandra, based on an ancient piece acquired in Egypt by the Prince of Wales (later Edward VII) and given to her in 1862, a year before their marriage

Abbreviations
D diameter
H height
L length
W width

7000

Greenwich Council
Library & Information Service

IN HOUSE
QUALITY
SYSTEMS

Blackheath Library
Old Dover Road, SE3 7BT
020 8858 1131

Please return by the last date shown		
30/03/07.	−9 MAR 2009	1 4 JUL 2021
2 6 APR 2007	2 2 OCT 2009	Ch. 17 Aug 21
17/5/07	7.12.09.	
	8. 1. 10	3 1 AUG 2021
−8 JUN 2007	3 0 JUL 2012	3 1 AUG 2021
	−4 JAN 2013	1 9 APR 2022
2 9 SEP 2007	1 8 MAY 2013	
26/1	2 8 FEB 2014	
	2 0 OCT 2014	
−9 JUN 2008	Thank You!	
−5 FEB 2009	1 9 APR 2017	

To renew, please contact any Greenwich library

| Issue: 02 | Issue Date: 06.06.00 | Ref: RM.RBL.LIS |

GREENWICH LIBRARIES

3 8028 01721704 0

CONTENTS

List of Contributors *page 6*

Preface *7*

Introduction *11*

1 **The Middle East:** 5000–2000 BC *23*

2 **The Middle East, Eastern Mediterranean and North of the Alps:** 2000–1400 BC *33*

3 **Egypt:** 1500–900 BC *42*

4 **Europe and Western Asia,** 1400–600 BC *48*

5 **Phoenician, Greek, Etruscan and Persian Lands:** 850–325 BC *57*

6 **China, Celtic Europe, Mexico and Peru:** 600 BC–AD 600 *70*

7 **The Mediterranean, Parthia, India, Egypt, Roman Britain and Byzantium:** 325 BC–AD 600 *84*

8 **Europe, China, Korea and Japan:** AD 300–1000 *101*

9 **Mayan Central America:** AD 600–1000 *121*

10 **Central and South America:** AD 500–1500 *127*

11 **Europe, Islam, China, Korea and Java:** AD 1000–1500 *135*

12 **Europe:** AD 1500–1700 *150*

13 **China, India, Tibet and Mongolia:** AD 1500–1850 *167*

14 **West Africa:** AD 1500–1800 *177*

15 **Europe:** AD 1700–1950 *183*

16 **Amulets** *194*

17 **Cameos in Jewellery** *216*

18 **Functional Finger-rings** *227*

Select Glossary *241*

References for the illustrations *244*

Bibliography *250*

Further reading *251*

Index *253*

THE CONTRIBUTORS

Carol Andrews *Ancient Egypt*

Nigel Barley *Africa (Benin)*

David Buckton *The Late Roman and Byzantine Empires*

Elizabeth M. Carmichael *Central and South America*

John Cherry *Medieval Europe*

Christopher Entwistle
The Late Roman and Early Byzantine Empire

Reynold Higgins *The Greek and Roman world*

Catherine Johns *Roman Britain*

Dafydd Kidd *Early Medieval Europe*

Ian Kinnes *Bronze Age Europe*

Robert Knox *India (Buddhist amulets)*

Malcolm McLeod *Africa (Asante)*

John Picton *Africa (Benin)*

Jessica M. Rawson *The Far East*

Judy Rudoe *18th-century to 20th-century Europe*

Anthony Shelton *Central and South America*

Ian Stead *Iron Age Europe*

Hugh Tait *Renaissance to 17th-century Europe*

Rachel Ward *Islam and Mughal India*

Leslie Webster *Anglo-Saxon and Viking England*

Wladimir Zwalf *India and Tibet*

PREFACE

The aim of this book is to bring together jewellery from all the major phases of man's history. The selection, made entirely from the collections of the British Museum, ranges in date from about 5000 BC to the middle of the twentieth century. The scope extends beyond Europe and the ancient cultures of Western Asia to India, Tibet and the Far East and includes certain areas of Africa and America. Owing to the accident of survival and archaeological rediscovery and of opportunity for acquisition, some areas and periods are necessarily more richly represented than others.

Jewellery for personal adornment is the main theme, but, in addition, amuletic (protective) jewellery – in so far as it can be specifically recognised – is treated separately. The use of cameos in jewellery and the role of finger-rings are two further aspects singled out for individual consideration, partly because both have histories peculiar to themselves.

I am deeply grateful to my colleagues in the eight Departments who have given so generously and unsparingly of their time and expertise and who have written on the items from the collections in their care.

I would also like to express my appreciation of the work of David Gowers of the Photographic Service, who has photographed all the jewellery specially for this book, using great patience and imagination to capture the intricate and elusive detail of these tiny objects. The great wealth of the Museum's collections was first revealed in the exhibition *Jewellery Through 7000 Years* of 1976 and its accompanying catalogue. My thanks now go to Celia Clear of British Museum Publications for suggesting that this material might be the basis of a new survey and to Jenny Chattington for all her invaluable work in the production of this book.

HUGH TAIT
May 1986

Note on the present edition
A few revisions have been made in the sections on Celtic Europe, Roman Britain, cameos and finger rings to take account of new research and discoveries. The section on Europe AD 1700–1950 has been completely rewritten with new illustrations and includes numerous acquisitions made by the British Museum since 1990. Sadly, Hugh Tait died in 2005.

INTRODUCTION

Jewellery was man's answer to the profound human need for self-adornment and, consequently, is one of the oldest forms of decorative art. For the past seven thousand years its history – albeit interrupted and incomplete – can be traced from the centres of the earliest known civilisations in Mesopotamia (Iraq) and Egypt to its universality in modern times. This panoramic survey of personal jewellery highlights both the inventiveness of man's imagination and, at the same time, the basic, almost primitive qualities that remain consistent factors throughout the long story.

Man's recognition of the intrinsic beauty of certain materials and minerals, especially gold, has led to their constant use in totally unconnected civilisations separated by vast barriers of time and space. That these basic materials were from the earliest times fashioned to beautify the human form seems beyond doubt, but at what stage jewellery began to serve man's superstitious need to protect himself from the multitude of frightening ills that could befall him and were beyond his comprehension cannot be established; in the absence of supporting archaeological or written evidence, the little carved stone pendants representing animals and objects which have been found in Mesopotamia and date from about 3000 BC cannot be regarded as amulets with certainty but, like so much jewellery through the ages, they were probably worn for both decorative and amuletic purposes.

466–8

Again, no date can be put on the first use of jewellery to proclaim the wearer's wealth and social status. While man was making jewellery from objects that were available for all to wear, such as local shells or pebbles, it could have no such function; but clearly at some very early stage in man's history relatively scarce materials began to be selected and fashioned for this purpose. The seven-thousand-year-old necklace excavated at Arpachiyah (modern Iraq) incorporates obsidian, a natural volcanic black glass that must have been extremely rare and, certainly, must have been brought a vast distance, perhaps from the mountainous area far to the north around Lake Van (modern Turkey). The obsidian would not have been easy to chip away, or to polish and drill, with the tools available then. Even the cowrie-shells that form part of the necklace had to be brought from the coasts of the Persian Gulf or the Red Sea and so were probably a curiosity for those living in the vicinity of Arpachiya.

18

The special qualities of obsidian that led to it being a coveted luxury among the peoples of the alluvial plains of Mesopotamia could not compare, however, with the almost indestructible gleaming brilliance of gold. Once metalworking techniques had been discovered, gold became a much-desired element in the creation of

1 This portrait of Robert Dudley, Queen Elizabeth I's favourite (1532[?]–88) is dated 156[?], the last figure being illegible; however, it was probably painted c. 1560–5, when he was striving for the hand of the Queen in marriage. In 1564 he was created Earl of Leicester and this portrait, probably by Steven van der Muelen, conveys the confidence of those years, when his influence at court was steadily increasing; it also records the bejewelled attire of this Elizabethan celebrity, who was in close touch with the artistic trends in the leading centres on the Continent.

jewellery, though in some periods silver was the more highly prized of the two precious metals. During the formative early period of Egypt's history (*c.* 3000 BC) a simple form of gold jewellery incorporating stones or rare minerals was undoubtedly being made, but so little has survived or been recovered that its use, its quality and its extent are still conjectural. The oldest and most spectacular examples are to be found not in Egypt, but further to the east, in ancient Babylonia (Iraq), where, on the site of the Biblical city of Ur of the Chaldees, the mass interments – the so-called Royal Tombs, especially the tomb of Queen Pu-abi – have yielded a fantastic profusion of gold jewellery dating from about 2500 BC, when Ur was the most powerful city-state in Mesopotamia. These discoveries, made between 1922 and 1934, proved the existence of jewellery of very high quality and diversity: hair ornaments in sheet gold, cut to resemble flowers; earrings and complicated gold chains and necklaces of cornelian, lapis lazuli, agate and gold; even finger-rings inlaid with lapis lazuli within a fine scale pattern of gold cells.

Two of the most important techniques in the history of jewellery, filigree and granulation, were sparingly and hesitatingly used in the making of this royal jewellery from Ur; at the present these pieces are the earliest recorded use of these techniques, but their unsure application suggests that the Sumerians may have been experimenting with their introduction. It is important to remember that all the metals used, together with the cornelian and lapis lazuli, must have been imported by the Sumerians, and yet they had craftsmen who had developed a skilful handling of both gold and silver. Their successful production of gold wire led them to create fine 'loop-in-loop' chains, some filigree work, in which the patterns formed by the gold wires could be left as openwork or soldered to a background, and occasionally inlay work, as in the lapis lazuli bead which has gold wire inlaid into incised lines. The Sumerians had a marked liking for the vivid combination of the intense blue of the lapis

2 A detail from the so-called Standard of Ur, from one of the Sumerian royal graves (*c.* 2500 BC). The function of this unique object, a hollow rectangular box, is unknown. Its sides are covered with brightly coloured mosaics of shell, red limestone and lapis lazuli. The long sides depict scenes from Sumerian life: on one side is the king, banqueting amid his nobles and receiving tribute. The other side, part of which can be seen here, shows the king and his army advancing into battle, and this includes an early illustration of the use of wheeled chariots. The Sumerians, by the mid-3rd millennium BC, had developed techniques of decoration that were to become extremely important in the history of jewellery, such as filigree, granulation and, as shown here, inlay work.

lazuli and the deep yellow of the burnished gold, but normally the jewellery was made entirely of gold with 'cells' or 'cloisons' on the surface ready to receive the shaped pieces of lapis lazuli. Exceptionally, pieces of Sumerian gold jewellery have been found decorated with granulation – minute spherical grains of gold, arranged in decorative patterns and soldered to the gold background – but the attempts at this technique are crude and, perhaps, indicative of a primitive stage in its evolution.

The Sumerians, with their knowledge of writing and the engraved seal, of the wheel, and of the skills required to smelt and fashion metals into weapons, utensils and ornaments, were able to make great progress towards establishing a settled social order when most peoples of the world were still living in a primitive state. It is, therefore, not surprising to find the art of the Sumerian goldsmith spreading widely over the lands of Western Asia and northwards to the Mediterranean areas of Turkey, where, on the site of Homer's Troy, fine gold jewellery dated about 2500–2300 BC was excavated. The movement may have continued westwards, for in the islands of southern Greece, the Cycladic Islands and in Crete gold jewellery of a slightly later date and less spectacular nature has been found.

Although the tenuous thread is now broken, there was probably a fairly continuous development in different parts of the Eastern Mediterranean and in Western Asia. In the Nile valley, where one of the more stable cultures of ancient history was developing simultaneously, jewellery had by the Twelfth Dynasty (c. 1900 BC) begun to play a most important role, having already acquired elaborate amuletic, social and decorative functions. From the earliest times, both in Mesopotamia and Egypt, the production of substitutes for the more valuable and rare materials seems to have been a surprisingly well-established feature of the jewellery trade – and, indeed, to have persisted more or less without a break to the present day. Even the obsidian necklace from Arpachiya included a perforated clay bead, apparently made in imitation of the obsidian, and in Egypt the attractive green glazed steatite beads of the Badarian culture (c. 4000 BC) have been found in the graves of men, usually in the form of massive bead girdles. The Egyptians went on to produce beads and other elements of jewellery in cheaper materials, like the blue glazed composition (or faience) with a quartz base, and, by the New Kingdom period, multicoloured glass. One of the New Kingdom pictorial records of a jeweller's workshop – a wall-painting from a Theban tomb of the late fifteenth century BC – shows the metalworkers and the beadmakers working side by side, using the bow-drills for the hardstones and then threading the beads to form a magnificent large collar; and, no doubt, some of the workshops incorporated substitute materials for those who could not afford, or were not entitled to wear, the best quality jewellery.

The Minoan culture on the island of Crete reveals in its jewellery strong influences from both the Egyptian and the Western Asiatic civilisations. From about 1700 BC Cretan jewellery has survived in sufficient quantity to state that the techniques of filigree, granulation and repoussé work had been most successfully mastered and combined with novel designs, so that when, about 1550 BC, the

14

3

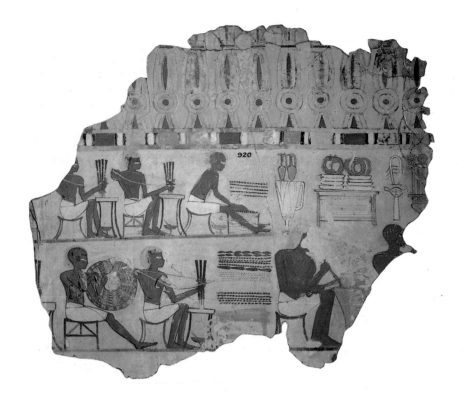

3 A wall-painting from the tomb of Sobkhatpe at Thebes (New Kingdom, *c*. 1420 BC), with a scene inside a jewellers' workshop. In the upper register two men are at work with bow-drills, used for making the perforations in hardstone beads, using an abrasive kept in the bowls at their feet. Another polishes the surface of a cornelian string; finished strings of cornelian beads are deposited before him. The lower register also shows a man drilling, with completed strings, in front of him; a man next to him threads beads to form a broad collar. In the same workshop a goldworker (bottom right) sits at his brazier with a blow-pipe and a pair of tongs; the products shown above include two gold jugs, four gold *shebyu*-collars (see 67) and a number of silver vessels.

Minoan culture was transplanted to the Greek mainland and the city of Mycenae rose to power, the Mycenaeans seem to have adopted Minoan jewellery forms and techniques. After the fall of Knossos (*c* 1450 BC) the Mycenaeans became the undisputed heirs of the Minoan cultural heritage and their jewellery reflects this continuity, but it also begins to develop a character of its own.

In Northern Europe the absence of written evidence makes the subject more difficult to trace, but by about 2000 BC the craft of metalworking had been introduced. Though a few splendid items of gold jewellery, like the gold lunula, have survived from the period about 1800–1500 BC – contemporary with the construction of Stonehenge – it is not until the succeeding centuries that the development of jewellery during the European Bronze Age becomes more easy to chart. Although there is nothing yet excavated which might be identified as a 'palace' of a chieftain, the quantity of metalwork, both weapons and ornaments, found in the burials indicates the privileged status of these leaders. Their metalworkers, using both gold and bronze, produced jewellery of good quality and bold design. The trading contacts that provided the impetus had been established with the Eastern Mediterranean by about 2000 BC and brought jewellery, such as faience beads, into Central Europe, whilst gold, tin and amber were exported to the Mycenaean world. The increased wealth of these chieftains manifested itself in the pursuit of purely decorative jewellery, often using for the first time local materials like jet, which could be fashioned and polished but which required different skills from those of the metalworker. Significantly, the ornamental motifs on the Melfort jet necklace are not unlike those used by the goldworker who had made the Irish lunula, and no doubt reflect the dominant role of the craft of the metalworker in this field.

Towards the period 1100–1000 BC there is evidence of widespread disruption, which affected not only the higher civilisations to the south-east, including the Mycenaeans and the Hittites, but also the flourishing barbarian Bronze Age society in Central Europe. The Urnfield culture, which emerged subsequently, has been regarded as 'proto-Celtic', whereas the peoples of the Hallstatt culture (*c.* 700–500 BC) and the succeeding La Tène culture are accepted as fully Celtic. The Celts were never a nation in the usual sense of the word but they established a stylistic tradition that persisted in parts of Europe throughout the Roman period and reappeared in the succeeding centuries before the emergence of medieval society in Western Europe. Unlike much of the earlier jewellery from the Eastern Mediterranean, Mesopotamia and Egypt, with their very hot climates, Celtic jewellery was often essentially functional – pins and brooches, for example. Nevertheless, the ornamentation lavished on it is often remarkable for its inventiveness and complexity. Perhaps the single item of jewellery most readily associated with the Celts is the torc. These massive neck-pieces and armlets, with their very distinctive circlet shapes and terminals of varying design, may have their ancestry in Asian sources and it is interesting to see that they are not wholly unknown even in Egypt.

88

Celtic craftsmen were using red enamel, as well as red coral inlay, to decorate their bronze jewellery as early as 400 BC. Enamel is a glass material; usually one or more different coloured vitreous glazes are fired and fused onto the surface of the metal, but there are several different ways of applying the enamel. Among the earliest putative examples of the art of cloisonné enamelling are six gold finger-rings that were found in a Mycenaean tomb at Kouklia (Cyprus) dating from thirteenth century BC, for, instead of gemstones, a fused glass is to be seen in the cloisons of the gold bezels. Minoan and Mycenaean jewellery of this period has very occasionally been found with a dark blue enamel fused into the repoussé depressions in sheet gold, but the true cloisonné enamelling on a gold sceptre from a royal tomb at Kourion Karloriziki (Cyprus), probably made some two hundred years after the six rings, is at present the last evidence of the technique being used until Roman times. Although some examples of gold jewellery with 'dipped' (that is, a simple 'encrusted') enamelling provide evidence that this elementary form of enamelling was practised in the Greek world in the third century

186

BC, it would seem that neither the Greek nor the Roman jewellers depended on the art of enamelling for their polychrome effects. In contrast, the jewellery of the Kuban (near the Caucasus) and of the Celtic West, along the borders of the northern provinces of the Roman Empire, was often enriched with both cloisonné and champlevé enamelling. The latter technique is the reverse of cloisonné enamelling, in which the surface of the object is built up with tiny walls to form cells into which the enamel can be fused; with the champlevé technique the enameller gouges out channels or troughs in the surface of the metal object and fills them with enamel but leaves the ridges of metal between the channels to form the outline of the design and keep one coloured enamel from running into a different coloured enamel in an adjacent area. On Celtic bronze jewellery, throughout the Roman period, champlevé enamelling was

214

carried out, even in those Celtic areas which had become the northern provinces of the Roman Empire. Although the Romans noted that 'the barbarians in the ocean pour these colours into bronze moulds, that the colours become as hard as stone preserving the designs' (according to the Greek philosopher, Philostratus, writing in the second century AD), they do not seem to have adopted it. They do, however, seem to have acquired a taste for colour in their jewellery, especially for polished gemstones of different hues and for cameos – no doubt from their contacts with Western Asia – and this legacy was to have a lasting effect on the history of European jewellery.

The inlaying of jewellery with richly coloured stones, especially garnets, was a striking feature of the Migration period (fourth to eighth centuries AD) following upon the collapse of the Roman Empire. This practice, combined with the re-emergence of Celtic champlevé enamelling and an obsessive use of surface ornamental detail, made Northern European jewellery of this period among the most colourful and the most intricate.

Gold cloisonné jewellery was to reach remarkable artistic heights for the first time in the Eastern Roman Empire, certainly by the sixth century AD in the workshops of the Byzantine court. The jewellers in Constantinople developed the art and, from the sixth to the twelfth centuries, they produced expressive miniature figural scenes using a brilliant range of translucent and opaque colours. The Western goldsmiths, especially during the Ottonian period (c. 936–1002 AD), strove to rival these achievements, though very little of the enamelled jewellery has survived.

To the east of Byzantium, in the lands of Islam (after c. 700 AD), the jewellers were apparently content to carry on the tradition of the Eastern Roman Empire and the Sasanian Empire (third to seventh centuries AD). By the eleventh to twelfth centuries, if not before, an increased use of silver for jewellery can be seen, particularly in Islamic Persia and, with it, the adoption of the decorative use of niello – a compound of silver, lead, copper and sulphur, the composition varying considerably. Niello is fusible at a low temperature and is applied to metal (usually silver) in much the same way as enamel, though it is not a vitreous substance. The Islamic craftsmen frequently used silver but often applied a fired gilding to parts, if not all, of the object. The combination of parcel-gilt silver and black nielloed ornament could be very attractive.

A scarcity of gold in Western Europe in the late Anglo-Saxon and Viking period led to the increased production of silver jewellery, often with extremely high artistic nielloed ornament, even depicting complex figural compositions, as on the 'Fuller' Brooch of the ninth century AD. The continuation of this fashion in England in the late twelfth century is well documented by the Lark Hill hoard (deposited in c. 1180) with its six silver finger-rings, one of which still retains its nielloed ornamentation. Contemporaneously a similar taste for silver jewellery with elaborate niello decoration can be observed in the workshops at Kiev (modern USSR), which had close links with both the Byzantine court and the peoples of Northern Europe.

In China the early stages in the development of jewellery are obscure, but the working of jade seems to be an ancient tradition.

4 A detail of the donor figure in a Chinese painting from Dunhuang (10th century AD). The woman is wearing a splendid silk robe, and her jewellery includes hair ornaments, gold earrings and several necklaces.

458–62 Pendants in the form of animals, carved in jade and turquoise, have survived from the Shang and early Zhou periods (thirteenth to tenth centuries BC) and are thought to have had amuletic properties. In ancient China jade was not only highly regarded as a beautiful stone, but from early times it was thought to possess special qualities of a quasi-magical or spiritual nature and no doubt its rarity and the difficulty of getting supplies made it a most precious material – rather as gold has become in the Mediterranean lands.

The most common item of Chinese jewellery worn by men to have survived from the centuries before Christ is the belt-hook, and the carving of the early jade belt-hooks is of the highest order, both technically and artistically. Jewellery for women was also functional, being principally concerned with the adornment of the hair, and took the form of both pins and combs. To some extent earrings were worn in the earlier periods; a beautiful painting of a Chinese lady
4 shows the simple gold earring which so effectively contrasts with the strong black quality of the hair. The painting also helps to illustrate the Chinese love of richly coloured and elaborately patterned fabrics for their dress and costume. There was almost no place for jewellery on the body when clothed in such a profusion of colour and design. In the period between about AD 500 and 1000 the Japanese seem to have worn jewellery to a very limited extent, mainly beads, but thereafter there is no evidence that jewellery played any significant part in their adornment. In China the hair ornaments become more delicate and elaborate, and by the Ming dynasty head-dresses for women had become fragile and intricate creations of pierced and finely worked gold.

Before the Ming dynasty the use of gemstones was rare in Chinese
373 jewellery but, as a pair of openwork plaques demonstrate, cabochon gems in crude settings began to enrich the surfaces and contribute to a polychrome effect. In India and Burma, the source of so many of the gemstones for the ancient world and for the medieval courts of Western Europe, there had been a long history of gem-studded jewellery, for both men and women. At the court of the Mughal emperors in the sixteenth and seventeenth centuries AD, for example, the dominance of large and unspoilt gemstones is well documented, though it was the European gem-cutters of the seventeenth and eighteenth centuries who completely transformed the appearance of jewellery, introducing elaborate cuts and creating a dazzling impression as the many facets reflected the light in a range of colours.

As in China, some of the ancient civilisations of Central and Southern America, especially the Olmec, the Maya and the Aztec, were producing jade as well as gold jewellery. The present state of knowledge concerning the histories of the ancient cultures of America before the arrival of the Spaniards in the sixteenth century is too incomplete to permit of any form of precise dating. Consequently chronological sequences are very approximate, but it is interesting to note that much of the jewellery is designed to embellish parts of the human face, not only earrings but nose-ornaments, lip-pieces and ear-flares. The large gold pectoral ornaments display the greatest
291 variety of skills, having anthropomorphic or zoomorphic subjects executed in relief, with openwork, filigree and applied elements cast

as a rule by the *cire-perdue* (lost-wax) process. The functions of this jewellery are totally undocumented but much of it may have served more than a purely decorative purpose. With the Spanish conquests stretching from Peru in the south to Mexico in the north, the production of this remarkable jewellery came abruptly to an end.

Back in Europe, the late medieval experiments with enamelled gold 'sculptural' jewellery incorporating figures (*émail en ronde bosse*), led to the perfection of a distinctive new class of three-dimensional jewellery by goldsmiths like Cellini and Caradosso. By the mid-sixteenth century the Spanish court, enriched by the New World and its gold and emeralds, was leading Europe into its last great epoch of formal ostentatious display, in which the art of the goldsmith–jeweller played such a vital role. Jewellery was now being designed on an international scale by artists and men who were not practising goldsmiths. The princes of Northern Europe, wishing to keep abreast with the latest fashions of the Renaissance courts of Italy, expected their court artists to provide drawings and designs for jewellery in the new styles – and Hans Holbein at the 347 English court of Henry VIII was no exception. The contemporary development of the art of engraving provided a means for mass reproduction of these designs and they were soon being distributed throughout the goldsmiths' and jewellers' workshops of Europe. This rapid dissemination of styles brought about a greater unity in European jewellery and it is only rarely that the nationality of court jewellers of the sixteenth century can with certainty be identified. Furthermore, the leading goldsmiths and jewellers also moved from one court to another, according to the chance of patronage, and a constant exchange of ideas on techniques and styles was thereby fostered.

The role of the gifted artist in the creation of jewellery went even further, for during the period from the late sixteenth to the end of the eighteenth century, miniaturists like Nicholas Hilliard and Jean Petitot often provided the major element in the jewel – the portrait – and demanded that it should be an integrated part of the design and colour scheme of the jewel into which it was set. No finer example than the famous 'Lyte' Jewel has survived and, by a miracle of good fortune, it has reached us complete with its unbroken pedigree, its royal history and a contemporary panel-painting of its first owner, proudly wearing it in 1611. Few personal jewels can offer us such a richly documented story. Although the gift of gold chains to reward loyal service had been the standard practice since the Middle Ages and was to die out only in the eighteenth century, when, significantly, the gold snuff-box took the place of jewellery, grateful monarchs have rarely given to humble subjects a present more exquisite in form than the 'Lyte' Jewel.

Throughout the seventeenth century the miniaturist, often working in the delicate technique of enamel-painting on enamel, provided the most artistic of pictorial jewellery, though often his contribution was relegated to the backs, especially if precious gemstones were 368 being used. Eighteenth-century jewellery with its emphasis on faceted diamonds spawned a new category – glass pastes. In France, 417 by 1740, Georges-Frédéric Strass had so perfected his glass compound

5 The 'Lyte' Jewel, opened to reveal the miniature of King James I painted in 1610 by Nicholas Hilliard, the court limner. He was the first English-born artist to occupy the post, which he held under Queen Elizabeth I and, again, under her successor. In his technical *Treatise* he stresses the importance of relating the miniature to its jewelled setting, especially in terms of colour, but it remains doubtful if he himself was ever a practising goldsmith.

that his name became a synonym for paste-set jewellery, made in imitation of precious stones. Indeed, some of the most technically brilliant calibré-cutting is to be found in the best quality paste-set jewels and, inevitably, famous deceptions were perpetrated. The love of semi-precious stones, particularly garnets and rock-crystals, continued, especially in elegant rococo settings, and a new fashion for jewels composed of finely graduated seed-pearls, often fused to create a quasi-sculptural effect, was established before 1800.

Jewellers of the nineteenth century frequently drew inspiration from past epochs, and some of their finest efforts went into the production of jewellery in the 'archaeological' style, like the Pompeian 434 necklace made by Eugène Fontenay for the Maison Boucheron about 1870 and the coin-set and medallic *'bulla'* pendants and so on. Both 437–9 neo-Gothic and neo-Renaissance jewellery had their vogue, but much of the most engaging jewellery of the Victorian era is light- 424–9 hearted, with its sentimental and even realistic observations of nature, occasionally rendered with a touch of humour.

During the second half of the century the reopening of the trading ports of Japan after several centuries of total inaccessibility and isolation led to a craze for jewellery ornamented with Japanese motifs and even imitating certain metalworking techniques, such as 440–3 *shibuichi* work, which depended on inlays of gold, silver and copper for its effects. Tiffany & Co in New York and Arthur Lasenby Liberty in London were in the forefront of this movement. But 444–8 European jewellery in the Art Nouveau style at the turn of the century is often the most imaginative and original, both in design and in its use of varied materials. Furthermore, it was particularly sculptural, and many gifted artists were working in this medium. The avant-garde jewellers of the inter-war years exploited the development of the machine age in their designs. At the same time, the widespread use of platinum, a strong metal that can be used in a very thin gauge, had given jewellery yet another quality, enabling large stones to be held in minimal settings.

Crowns and sceptres, mitres and crosiers, rings of investiture and high office, and so on, are all jewels made specifically to denote rank and, as such, have been deliberately excluded from this survey. Whilst some of the jewellery described here dating from prehistoric and early times may have been worn for that purpose, the evidence is inconclusive. Personal jewellery from the earliest periods was undoubtedly already being used as an indication of status and, even in medieval Europe, this attitude was still so strongly held that laws and decrees were proclaimed both in England and on the Continent controlling the freedom of the individual in this respect and permitting only certain classes of society to wear certain categories of jewellery.

The use – or misuse – of jewellery by man is an elusive subject, but no matter whether a piece of jewellery was originally chosen for its amuletic purpose, its attractiveness or its social cachet, it probably always had one special quality: it could be used as a form of currency, almost as an investment. Few branches of the decorative arts have such diverse and complex uses – or, indeed, such a long history.   HT

6 A goldsmith's workshop by Alessandro Fei (1543–92). One of the oil-paintings on panel made for the *Studiolo* of the Grand Duke Francesco de' Medici between 1570 and 1575 by Giorgio Vasari and his school. The *Studiolo* was a room in the Palazzo Vecchio in Florence, where the paintings concealed the cupboards behind, in which the Grand Duke kept his mineral specimens, rock-crystal objects, jewels, gold, silver, and so on. It was his *Kunstkammer*, with no natural source of light and with secret staircases linking it to the private rooms of the palace. The paintings on each of the four walls were intended to relate to one of the Four Elements; this painting of a goldsmith's workshop appears to portray the Florentine court craftsmen at work in the Casino San Marco. It shows many different aspects of the normal goldsmiths' work, from the preparatory drawings and designs pinned up for their guidance to the furnaces for casting and annealing. There are two standing men hammering out dishes, while another sits chasing a silver basin. In the foreground sits the master goldsmith working on the Medici Grand Ducal crown and holding it with his left hand; the design for the crown is pinned up where he can refer to it at a glance (see detail, pp. 8–9). On the extreme left there is another crown and a coronet, with a papal triple tiara cut off by the picture frame. Behind, at a separate table, a small group of men are mounting precious gemstones, though rings and gems are also awaiting mounting on the work-bench in the foreground. On the shelf to the right the finished objects are apparently temporarily displayed out of harm's way. This valuable document is securely dated and offers a unique visual record less than ten years after Cellini's *Trattato dell' oreficeria* had been published in Florence (1568).

CHAPTER ONE

The Middle East

=5000–2000 BC=

Western Asia

Beads are among the commonest objects found in excavations at prehistoric villages in Western Asia, and presumably were used for the same general range of decorative purposes as they are today, especially for jewellery and for sewing onto clothes. Brightly coloured and unusual raw materials were naturally the most popular, and the demand for these was probably a significant factor in the development of the extensive trade or exchange networks which already existed long before 5000 BC.

One material which travelled widely was obsidian, a translucent volcanic glass from Turkey which was primarily used for making sharp blades and tools, but its appearance or value invited use in jewellery too. A necklace from northern Iraq, dated about 5000 BC, includes obsidian beads, as well as others made from cowrie-shells that were filled with red ochre. The shells must have come from the sea, so the necklace combines elements that originated many hundreds of miles apart. Another feature of this necklace is that there is one bead that has the shape of the obsidian ones but is made of dark clay: apparently there had been one obsidian too few, and this was a substitute that brought the total to seven. The invention and manufacture of substitute materials, imitating scarce and expensive varieties of natural stone, played an important part in the story of jewellery in the ancient world just as it does today.

A vast amount of jewellery was found in graves in the Sumerian city of Ur, in what is now southern Iraq. Necklaces used about 3000 BC consist largely of beads made from locally available materials such as shell, though there are also examples of glazed faience, a shiny imitation stone which could be made in several colours and which is one of the forerunners of glass. The most impressive discoveries, however, were made in some tombs dated about 2500 BC. These were mass interments, each with one principal body surrounded by many others; they are usually regarded as royal graves, in which the king or queen was accompanied to the next world by an appropriate retinue of soldiers and attendants. The men and women buried there were wearing Sumerian court dress, or a special variety of dress suitable for these strange ceremonies.

The position of the jewellery on the skeletons enabled the excavator, Sir Leonard Woolley, to reconstruct the approximate appearance of many pieces, even though the strings and materials holding them together had long since perished. The men, normally identified by the weapons they held, often wore headbands consisting of three large beads at the front with a gold chain behind; the purpose of these may have been to keep head-cloths in position, like the

Left 7 Sumerian court jewellery from Ur (*c.* 2500 BC). The jewellery is from several bodies, but the general effect must be approximately correct. It includes: a hair ornament with three gold rosette finials fixed to modern shafts; gold hair-ribbons; three head-dresses of lapis lazuli and cornelian beads, with gold or gold and lapis lazuli pendants; a pair of gold earrings; a gold and lapis lazuli choker; three necklaces with beads of gold, lapis lazuli and cornelian; and a silver dress-pin with a lapis lazuli head. Jewellery of this kind was worn by many of the attendant women buried side by side in the royal graves. H (total) 65cm

Below 8 A pendant of white shell from a royal grave at Sumerian Ur (*c.* 2500 BC). Large animal pendants like this were rare outside the royal graves. This bull, with its vertical perforation, was either used as part of a head-dress or attached to a dress-pin. L 3.5cm

18

29

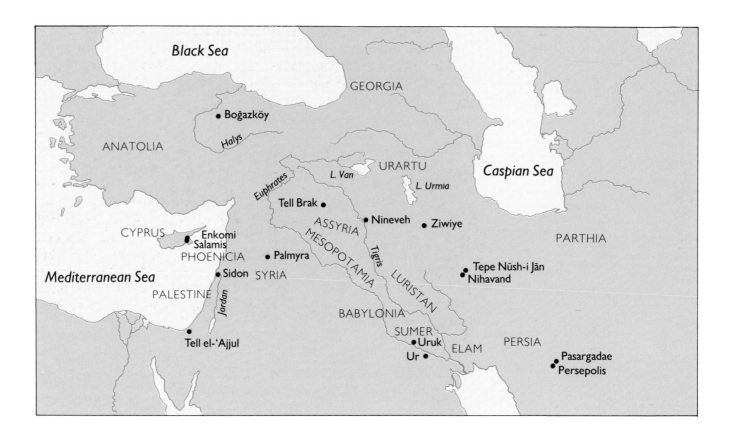

twisted cords worn by modern Arabs. The jewellery of the women
was much more elaborate, and included head-dresses of golden
flowers and foliage, huge crescent-shaped earrings, chokers around
the neck, magnificent loose necklaces, large dress-pins to fasten the
clothes, and various other rings, pins and beads whose exact function
is seldom known. Finger-rings also occur in the Ur graves, and
subsequently elsewhere in Western Asia, though they play a relatively minor part in the history of jewellery before the invention of
the signet-ring. A grave later than the royal burials contained the
body of a man with a rich collection of jewellery, including a lapis
lazuli cylinder-seal mounted in gold. Seals of this kind, which could
be rolled on damp clay, were the standard form of signet in southern
Mesopotamia from the Sumerian period until the middle of the first
millennium BC. Such seals were sometimes attached to large toggle-
pins, an arrangement which accounts for the statement in a Babylonian text that Rimush, a king of about 2300 BC, was 'murdered
with cylinder-seals'.

The main materials used in Sumerian jewellery were gold, silver,
deep blue lapis lazuli, and translucent red cornelian. All four seem
to have been abundant at Ur, though they must have been imported
into southern Iraq, which is exceptionally fertile but has no mineral
resources of these kinds. The precious metals may have come
mainly from the highlands of Turkey and Iran. The source of lapis
lazuli is likely to have been in the far north-east of modern Afghanistan, and some at least of the cornelian originated in India and was
sent by sea across the Indian Ocean to the port of Ur. Agate, a stone
with bands of varying shades, the use of which distantly fore-

9 Map of part of the Near East, showing
the location of the principal cultures
and the main sites mentioned in the
text.

Right Beads and pendants from
Sumerian Ur (*c.* 2500 BC). The three
lower strings of gold, lapis lazuli and
plain cornelian beads and pendants
were all found together in the royal
grave PG 580 and have been arbitrarily
restrung. The top string (**10**) includes
cornelian beads that have been stained
or etched with white lines; this
technique was probably invented in the
region of the Harappan civilisation
(modern India and Pakistan), where
these beads are likely to have
originated.

The spiral motif seen on some of the
gold pendants was not new even in
2500 BC and was to have a long
subsequent history (see **116**). Similar or
related designs were employed on the
jewellery of Troy and in Bronze Age
Europe (see **95**, **96**, **108**). One of these
pendants has a flat double spiral made
from a single piece of wire (**12**), whilst
another is three-dimensional,
consisting of two lengths of gold wire,
the four ends of which are coiled into
cones (**11**). Two smaller gold pendants

on **11** have a single cone of gold wire, and the two adjacent lapis lazuli pendants are carved to imitate this shape. Similarly, in **13** the lapis lazuli leaf-shaped pendants imitate the gold ones. L (**13**) 18cm

shadows the development of the cameo, is rare in the royal graves at Ur but is more common a few hundred years later.

Great care was evidently taken by the Sumerians to alternate and balance the different colours of stone and metal. While the shapes and ornamentation are relatively restrained, the workmanship is excellent and serves to remind us that traditions of making fine jewellery existed and survived through many periods for which we do not have such lavish evidence. There are examples of small-scale inlay and of filigree, a technique that was later to become extremely popular; there is also some granulation work, though it is not particularly fine. One bead is made of lapis lazuli inlaid with gold wire, a reversal of the normal arrangement whereby gold is inlaid with stones: this piece is somewhat later than the rest, and the gold caps at either end of it are characteristic of the later part of the third millennium. Many items of jewellery that are comparable, in style and technology, with those from Ur have been excavated elsewhere in Western Asia, though different areas had their local traditions.

JER

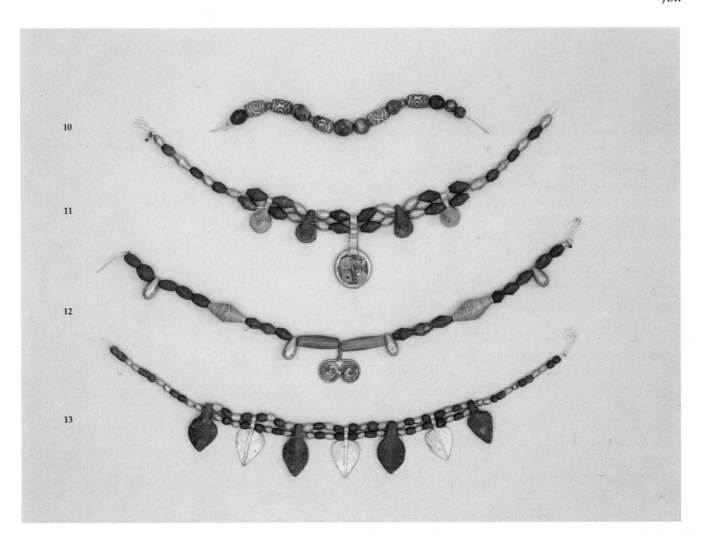

25

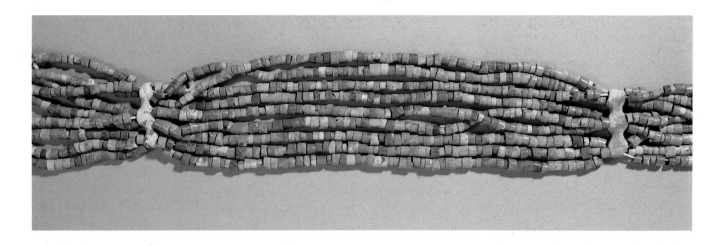

Egypt

In Egypt during the Predynastic and Early Dynastic Periods (c. 3100–2686 BC) some of the standard forms of Pharaonic jewellery and the techniques of its manufacture were evolved. As early as the Badarian Period (c. 4000 BC) natural pebbles and bone had been supplemented by finely worked beads and pendants of cornelian, lapis lazuli, jasper, felspar, turquoise and alabaster. The uneven, generally biconical borings of these beads confirm that small pointed flints were used for making the perforations. But by far the most common material was steatite, glazed blue or green in imitation of turquoise or semi-precious green stones. Its most characteristic use was for the small beads that were made up into the massive girdles typical of the period. Spacer-beads, used to separate the rows, made their first appearance in these multi-stranded girdles, and continued in use in necklaces, bracelets and collars. The use of Red Sea shells, of copper and turquoise (the latter only obtained from Sinai during the Dynastic Period), and of lapis lazuli (Egypt's only source was Afghanistan) argues far-reaching contacts beyond the narrow geographical confines of the Badarian culture in Middle Egypt. However, the ivory employed was probably from the hippopotamus, rather than the elephant, and therefore available locally.

The succeeding Naqada I culture (c. 3500 BC) in general reproduced the bangles, necklaces and bracelets of the Badarian Period but forehead ornaments are new. Another innovation was the production of beads of minute size, and a new material was introduced: glazed composition, a quartz sand core coated with vitreous alkaline glaze whose green or blue colouring shows that, like glazed steatite, it was originally thought of as a substitute for semi-precious stones.

During the Naqada II Period (c. 3200 BC) the shapes of beads became much more regular and, as stone beads were made with greater ease, the use of shell in jewellery became ever more restricted. Gold makes an appearance as thin strips turned up into beads or as foil over a core: a diadem incorporating gold beads is unique for the time.

The jewellery of the Nubian A-group people (c. 3200–3000 BC) was generally simple in form and material; that of the partly contemporary Early Dynastic Period in Egypt shows far greater assurance in

14 Detail of a girdle made of bright-green glazed steatite beads. The girdle, 131cm long, was found lying over the knees of a man in a grave of the Predynastic Egyptian Badarian culture at Mostagedda (c. 4000 BC). The bone spacer-beads separating the rows are among the earliest known.

22, 23

24

20

manufacturing techniques. A type of bracelet worn by royalty in the First Dynasty (*c.* 3100–2890 BC) was composed of rectangular beads known as *serekhs*. These occur in various materials: gold and turquoise *serekhs* were found on the arm of a queen of King Djer, and blue glazed composition *serekhs* have been excavated from a First Dynasty mastaba tomb at Giza. Necklaces of the period seem to have been formed from a single string of beads; it was not until the beginning of the Old Kingdom and the Fourth Dynasty (*c.* 2613–2494 BC) that the broad collar (*wesekh*), composed of many strands of beads with terminals and spacers, came into being. By this time anklets and diadems, girdles and belts, bangles and bracelets were all in use. Invariably inlaid, they were often made of silver (always more highly prized than gold) and electrum (a naturally occurring compound of gold and silver), as well as of gold or copper. A new material is Egyptian blue, a copper calcium tetrasilicate, used as a pigment throughout Egyptian history. The Old Kingdom saw a considerable increase in the number of materials used, glazed composition became ever more common and beads and amulets of gold more numerous and often quite large. 471

The First Intermediate Period (*c.* 2181–2040 BC) was a time of civil war and disruption from which jewellery of only the poorest materials and crudest workmanship might have been expected. Yet a surprising range of materials was employed in jewellery and precious metals were not unknown: although they date towards the end of the period, the gold bangle and gold and silver bracelet-spacers are not unique. Diadems made for purely funerary use continued to be produced during this time: they consisted of metal headbands with 37, 38 ornamented discs attached.   CA

Above **15** An Egyptian ivory *serekh* bracelet bead from the tomb of King Djer at Abydos (1st Dynasty, *c.* 3000 BC). The *serekh* is a rectangular frame, at the bottom of which is a design of recessed panelling like that found on façades of early brick tombs and on false doors, dating from the Old Kingdom. On top perches the falcon of Horus. The frame usually contains the Horus name of the king, but this example has only a dotted design. The bead is pierced from side to side with two holes for threading. H 1.6cm

Below Egyptian bangle and bracelet of the First Intermediate Period. The bangle (**16**) is made from two pieces of gold wire, knotted in the centre to produce a reef-knot and soldered at the ends into loops. It is one of two such bangles from a grave at Mostagedda (*c.* 2100 BC), and was found on the body of a woman, who wore one on each wrist. The knot-clasp amulet based on the reef-knot became one of the most popular amulets of the Middle Kingdom.

The bracelet (**17**), found at Matmar, is also from a female burial (*c.* 2070 BC). The four rows of cornelian beads are joined by four spacer-bars, one of gold, the others of silver. The remaining beads are of gold, cornelian and green glazed composition. L (**17**) 14cm

16

17

18 A necklace of the Halaf period (*c.* 5000 BC) from Arpachiyah, Iraq. It consists of flakes of obsidian (polished on one side), one bead of dark unbaked clay, cowrie-shells with their backs removed and one black stone pendant or whetstone. The shells originally held red pigment, and there are traces of bitumen around the outside. L (largest obsidian) 5.8cm

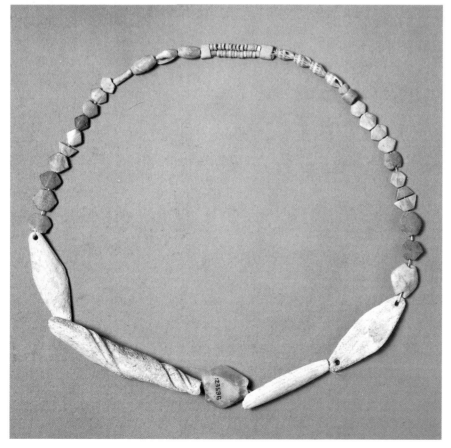

19 A necklace of beads made from shell, mother-of-pearl, stone and faience (*c.* 3000 BC). This necklace comes from a grave of the Jamdat Nasr period at Ur; the people buried in these graves generally used locally available materials of this kind for their jewellery. L (largest shell) 8.67cm

20, 21 Jewellery from Predynastic Egypt. The outer string, a gold and hardstone diadem (**20**), comes from the undisturbed burial of a woman of the Naqada II culture (*c.* 3200 BC) at Abydos. The hardstone sections consist largely of chips and beads of turquoise and garnet, but with some jadeite and malachite. The beaded part of the diadem was worn at the front of the head and was held in place by a string which disappeared under the tresses. It seemed to hold a piece of cloth like a veil over the face.

The garnet and cornelian bead necklace (**21**), of which a detail is shown here (centre), is from a grave of the Nubian A-Group (*c.* 3100 BC) at Faras. The beads are arranged in two separate groups of garnet and cornelian; the section of cornelians was apparently worn at the back of the neck. L (**20**) 31.2cm

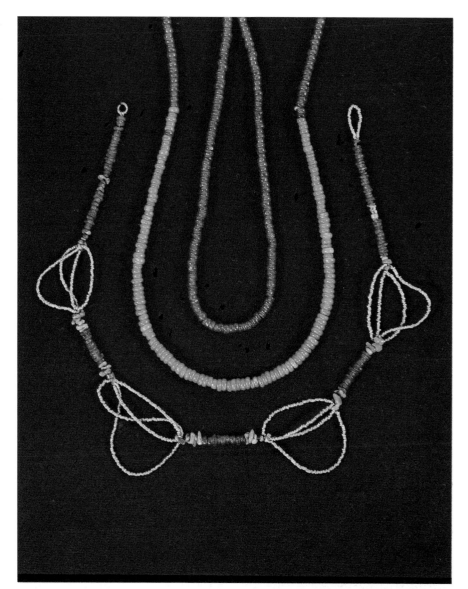

Jewellery from Predynastic Egypt. The ivory bangles (**22, 23**) are from a grave of the Badarian culture (*c.* 4000 BC) at Mostagedda. They were found with three other similar examples on the wrists of a child aged about three. They are typical of the kind of bangle common in this period, which seems to have been worn by males only.

The shell forehead ornament (**24**), also from Mostagedda, was excavated from a woman's grave, dating to the Naqada I culture (*c.* 3500 BC); it was found lying in front of the woman's eyes. Other examples have been found in male burials. These ornaments were probably charms, and may have been used as tribal or class distinctions. D (**23**, external) 5.5cm

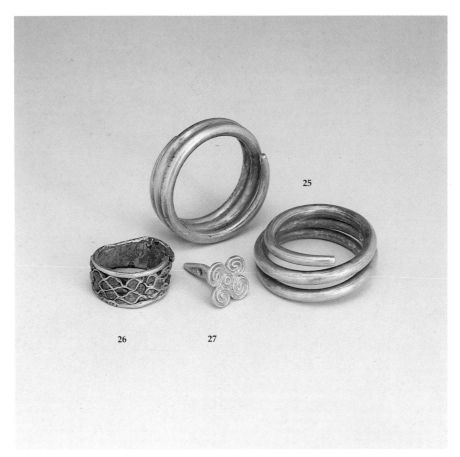

Jewellery from Queen Pu-abi's tomb at Ur (*c.* 2500 BC). The gold spiral rings (**25**) were found by the queen's skull, and it is thought that tresses of hair were passed through them. They can hardly have been earrings, as Pu-abi already had a pair of these, but spiral rings were sometimes found close to the ears and may have served various functions.

The gold finger-ring (**26**), with lapis lazuli inlay in cloisons, was one of ten rings worn by Pu-abi.

The gold toggle-pin (**27**) apparently belonged to a spare head-dress which was placed beside Pu-abi's body. The quadruple spiral motif incised on its head is similar to that already seen in **11** and **12**. D (**25**) 3.61cm, 3.58cm

28 Head-dress ornaments from the grave of a man at Sumerian Ur (*c.* 2500 BC). The larger of the three gold roundels is inlaid with cornelian and lapis lazuli; the string of beads (attached by loops inserted between the sheet-gold backing and the outermost wire rings) are cornelians, with quadruple lapis lazuli and gold spacers. The double rosette pattern of the two other roundels, both in openwork filigree, may also once have held inlay. D (cloisonné disc) 4.5cm

Beads from Sumerian graves at Ur. **29** is a headband (*c.* 2500 BC), with beads of lapis lazuli, cornelian and chalcedony attached to a gold chain made by the 'loop-in-loop' method. This was found around the head of one of Queen Pu-abi's male attendants. Very similar headbands were regularly worn by men in the royal graves.

The gold and lapis lazuli beads (**30**) are slightly later in date (*c.* 2300–2100 BC), and have been arbitrarily restrung. The central lapis lazuli bead, with its gold caps, is unusual in having gold wire inlaid in a spiral around it. L (**30**) 24cm

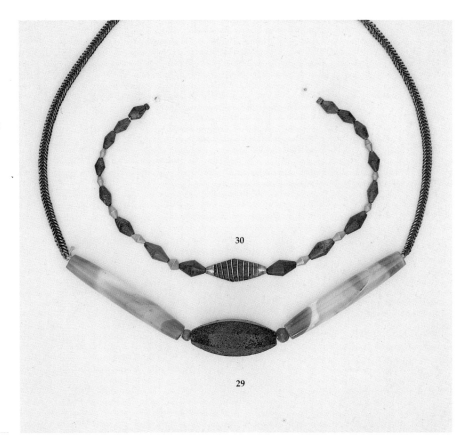

31–36 Sumerian jewellery from Ur (*c.* 2100 BC). This jewellery was excavated from a grave containing the single body of a man. His rich jewellery suggests that he was a person of considerable importance. His lapis lazuli cylinder-seal with gold mounts (**31**) is carved with two scenes of combat between heroes and animals (for an impression of the seal see **572**, on p.229). There had once been an inscription, but it was erased in antiquity, which indicates that the man in the grave was not the seal's original owner.

The plain sheet-gold frontlet (**32**) was one of six worn on the man's head. The gold spiral earring or hair-ring (**33**) is made of sheet metal, probably hammered over a bitumen core, and was originally one of a pair. The necklace (**34**) is of cornelian and hollow gold beads. The gold pendant of a goat (**35**) was originally hung from a necklace. The pair of hollow bracelets (**36**) are made of hammered sheet gold. D (**36**, largest) 8.9cm

Egyptian headband ornaments from two graves of the First Intermediate Period at Matmar, each containing the burial of a child aged about three. The 11 rosettes (*c.* 2150 BC) are of green glazed composition and have slit-shaped perforations radiating from the centre (**37**). Of the 15 rosettes originally discovered, 4 have remained in Cairo.

The copper disc (**38**) is worked in repoussé, the hollows inlaid with thin slivers of cornelian and green and black glazed composition mounted on a bed of cement. The disc (*c.* 2100 BC) was found wrapped in a piece of cloth behind the neck of the child, but it was probably intended to be sewn onto a cloth headband or attached to a metal diadem. D (**38**, max. extent) 4.8cm

39 An early 4th-Dynasty (*c.* 2660 BC) painted limestone statue of Prince Rahotep and his wife Nofret, from their tomb at Maidum (Egypt). Nofret is portrayed wearing a headband, painted white, with coloured ornaments in the form of rosettes and flowers. This apparently represents a silver headband with appliqué ornaments, like **37** and **38**. She is also wearing a broad collar of hardstone beads with tear-drop pendants. Rahotep is adorned more simply, with a single bead string and an amulet pendant.

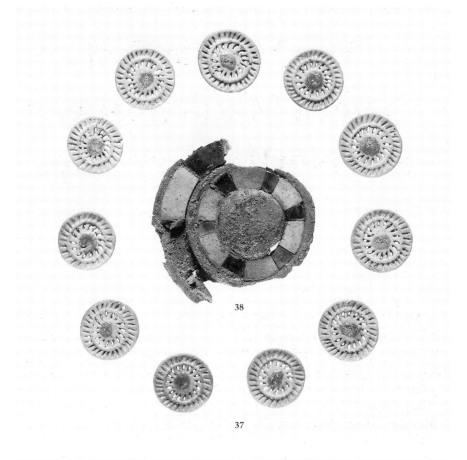

38

37

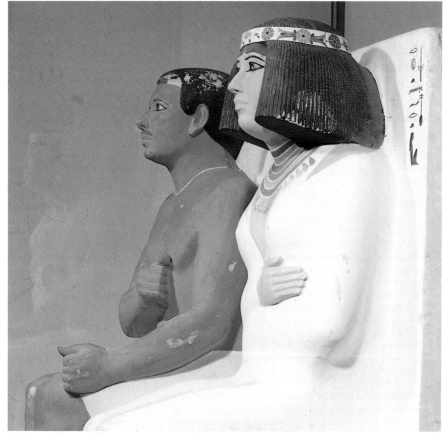

CHAPTER TWO

The Middle East Eastern Mediterranean and North of the Alps

2000–1400 BC

Egypt

The Middle Kingdom (*c.* 2040–1730) marks a high point in the art of the Egyptian jeweller. Goldworking in every technique was carried out. True *ajouré*, cutting out from sheet metal, is typified by an openwork plaque, which also demonstrates one of many examples of chasing, a technique whereby the metal is worked from the front so that the details are indented into the surface. The technique of repoussé is also used: here the metal is worked from behind with a punch so that the details stand out in relief at the front.

Two other techniques to come into prominent use at this time are inlaying in cloisons and granulation. Inlaying of a simple kind had been practised occasionally since the Early Dynastic Period. A copper headband disc of First Intermediate Period date is inlaid with cornelian and glazed composition but the settings are not true cloisons – a network of cloisons or cells into which each inlay is fitted individually. An inlaid ornament in the form of a winged scarab shows an advance in skill over other pieces, although the cloisons comprising the body and head were probably each made all in one, folded up in a mould, rather than from single pieces of metal soldered together to form a box. Moreover, the wing inlays are not fitted into cloisons at all, but are still fixed side by side by means of cement. Nevertheless, this piece gives some idea of the excellence reached in the making of contemporary inlaid pectorals. Fully developed cloisonné work is to be seen in another contemporary piece, an amuletic string with a lotus-flower pendant. The pendant has inlays of blue and green glass and of cornelian set into cloisons of silver arranged in a design representing three lotus flowers.

The technique of granulation consists of soldering minute spherical grains of metal on to the metal surface. The form of decoration first occurs in the Near East at Ur (*c.* 2600 BC), but there is no example from Egypt earlier than the reign of Ammenemes II (*c.* 1929–1895 BC): a hollow cylindrical amulet-case ornamented with designs in granulation probably dates from this period.

Silver continued to become more common during this period, although it was still rare and was more highly valued than gold.

40 An Egyptian gold oyster-shell pendant of the 12th Dynasty (*c.* 1950–1800 BC). The upper surface is inscribed with the name Senusert (Sesostris) in a cartouche. Orthographic peculiarities cast doubt on the authenticity of the inscription, but although the inscription may be a later addition, the shell itself may still be authentic, as uninscribed metal oyster-shells were a popular amulet in the Middle Kingdom. The shell represented is probably *Avicula (Meleagrina) margaritacea.* H 4.9cm

Cornelian, amethyst, garnet, lapis lazuli, green felspar, jasper and turquoise were the lapidary's favourite stones. Bracelets made from brightly coloured beads separated by spacers were popular, as were *wesekh*-collars of cylinder- and disc-beads. Strings of metal-capped beads, often graded in size, first appear now. Another characteristic type of Middle Kingdom jewellery was the metal oyster-shell amulet. Uninscribed oyster-shells are fairly common at this period, and were intended to ensure the good health of the wearer; those inscribed with royal names may have been a military decoration.

Beadmakers and workers in precious metals worked side by side: wall-paintings of the Middle Kingdom and the New Kingdom show almost identical scenes of men drilling and threading beads alongside metalworkers with tongs and blowpipes.

may have been for sewing the ornament to clothes or for suspension, perhaps to be worn as a pectoral.

Also from the 12th Dynasty (*c*. 1795 BC) is the gold openwork plaque (**43**), representing King Ammenemes IV (Makherure), offering a vase of unguent to Atum, god of the setting sun, who carries an *ankh*-amulet in his right hand and a *was*-sceptre in his left. Although this plaque is usually described as a pectoral, there are only three pins on the reverse and no rings for suspension; it is more likely to have been the covering for a cylindrical amulet or some form of appliqué decoration.

The two gold spacers-bars with reclining cats (**44**) are from a bracelet said to be from the tomb of Queen Sobkemsaf at Edfu (17th Dynasty, *c*. 1650 BC). Each is a flat box with twelve gold tubes running through its width for threading, with a similar inscription roughly incised between horizontal lines on the base referring to the King Nubkheperre Inyotef and his wife Sobkemsaf.

Below **41** A *wesekh*-collar of glazed composition from Egypt's 11th Dynasty (*c*. 2020 BC). Each of the terminals has a ridge along the underside pierced by six holes through which the thread holding the beads is knotted. The purplish colour of the outermost row of beads comes from oxide of manganese and is not common until the 18th Dynasty. L (outermost row) 41.6cm

Top right Egyptian royal jewellery of the Middle Kingdom. The winged scarab (**42**) is of electrum richly inlaid with cornelian, green felspar and lapis lazuli (12th Dynasty, *c*. 1885 BC). In its forefeet it holds a sun-disc and in its back feet a *kha*-sign flanked by two papyrus heads. The design represents the prenomen of Sesostris II (Khakheperre). Tubes soldered to the underside of the wings

The gold finger-ring with a lapis lazuli scarab (**45**), perhaps from Thebes, is also associated by its inscription with Nubkheperre Inyotef; the name 'Inyotef' is inscribed on the base of the funda. The scarab is held in position on its gold mount by one of the thin twisted gold wires which are wound round the shank.

The gold-mounted heart scarab of green jasper (**46**) belonged to King Sobkemsaf II (17th Dynasty, *c.* 1640 BC). The scarab has a human face on its rounded back and gold legs attached to the mount. Around the edge and on the base of the mount are roughly chased hieroglyphs from Chapter XXXB of the *Book of the Dead*: 'Spell for preventing the heart from opposing the deceased'. Tomb-robbers brought to trial *c.* 1125 BC confessed to having robbed the tomb of King Sobkemsaf at Thebes and having stolen jewellery and amulets from the mummy, as recorded in the Abbott papyrus, in the British Museum. L (**46**, mount) 3.6cm

Bottom right Bead jewellery of the Egyptian Middle Kingdom. The metal-capped beads are from the 12th Dynasty (*c.* 1900–1800 BC). The 40 amethyst beads (**48**) have gold-foil caps and an uninscribed amethyst scarab in the centre.

The 39 spherical glazed composition beads (**47**) are capped with discs of silver. With this string is a stamped gold knot-clasp amulet, characteristic of this period. It is made in two halves, which are joined by inserting a raised flange on the underside of one half into a groove cut into the underside of the other.

The bracelet (**49**), dated *c.* 2000–1800 BC, is made from beads of amethyst, cornelian, lapis lazuli, green felspar and turquoise. Four of the five spacer-bars are of electrum; the fifth, and largest, is gilded silver (probably modern). H (spacers, **49**) 1.8cm

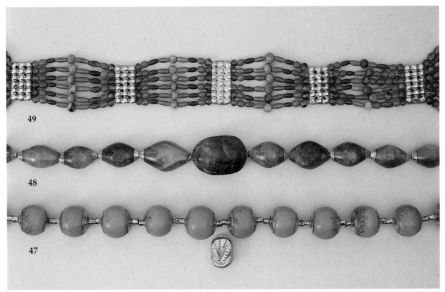

During the troubled Second Intermediate Period (c. 1786–1567 BC) graves again contained jewellery of the poorest materials; it was not until just before the beginning of the Eighteenth Dynasty that gold returned in any quantity. Gold cats, like those on the royal bracelet spacers, may have an honorific significance. A contemporary scarab-ring looks back to the Middle Kingdom for its gold mounting-plate and forward to the New Kingdom for its twisted-wire shank decoration and added gold legs.   CA

44

45

Western Asia

In Western Asia, after the great wealth of Sumerian Ur, the excavated jewellery of the centuries after 2000 BC may seem relatively impoverished. From Turkey, homeland of the Hittite Empire, comes a small necklace of solid gold, but a pair of earrings from Ur are more typical of the kind of jewellery used in areas which did not have their own supplies of precious metals. A small amount of gold has been worked with great skill to produce a highly decorative effect as

50 A pair of gold earrings from Ur, dating to the Old Babylonian Period (*c.* 1900 BC). The lower edges have embossed spikes and at either end are circular filigree cloisons and granulation. H (larger) 3.33cm

51 A Hittite necklace (*c.* 1700–1500 BC). Each of the gold hawk pendants, which are strung on gold wire, originally had three disc pendants attached, but several are now missing. W 13.1cm

economically as possible. The miniature techniques of filigree and granulation are now well established.

One area which was often a centre of innovation was the east coast of the Mediterranean, where goods and merchants from Turkey, Mesopotamia and Egypt came together. Craftsmen here were able to amalgamate skills and fashions of diverse origins. Some of the finest examples come from tombs and hoards excavated at Tell el-'Ajjul in southern Palestine. Some of the pendants found here are made of thin curving sheets of gold fastened together back to back, giving an air of solidity to objects that are really hollow. We also have inlays of glass, once brilliantly coloured, that was used instead of turquoise or lapis lazuli.   JER

52–55 A group of gold pendants, from Tell el-'Ajjul, Palestine (*c.* 1600 BC). **52** (bottom) is made from two sheets of gold soldered together back to back; the join is covered by wire to which clusters of granules are attached. The convex front sheet is decorated with filigree and granulation.

53 (right) is more crudely worked than **52**, and has granulation attached to bosses on the surface.

54 (left) is of sheet metal cut into the shape of a hawk, with granulated and filigree decoration.

55 (top) is in the shape of a winged disc with an oval above and small discs at the angles of the wings, all originally inlaid with blue glass. Underneath is a stylised animal head with horns. w (**52**) 4.57cm

Minoan and Mycenaean Jewellery

In the Eastern Mediterranean the Bronze Age civilisation of Crete – named 'Minoan' by its discoverer, Sir Arthur Evans – flourished between about 3000 and 1100 BC. Although its origins can be traced to western Asia Minor, it soon developed, in its new home, into a unique and brilliant culture. The first thousand years, from 3000 to 2000 BC, exhibit a gradual development towards the full Minoan culture.

From 2000 BC the island was ruled from a number of palaces, the most important of which were Knossos in the north and Phaestos in the south. Their rulers were in fruitful contact with their neighbours in Egypt, Syria and the Hittite lands. About 1700 BC these palaces were all destroyed by a terrible earthquake, but were immediately rebuilt on a similar but grander plan, in the form in which we see their ruins today. Then, about 1450 BC, all the palaces except that at Knossos were destroyed, this time, it seems, by invading Mycenaeans, who established themselves at Knossos and ruled all Crete from there. Crete now became a second-rate power, part of the great Mycenaean Empire, until the Minoan/Mycenaean world collapsed, for reasons which are unclear, about 1100 BC.

The art of making gold jewellery was practised from about 2400 BC. Tombs in Crete of this date have yielded diadems, hair ornaments, beads and bracelets of sheet metal, and quite elaborate chains, chiefly of the loop-in-loop variety. These forms derive ultimately from Babylonian prototypes, of which there are excellent examples from Ur in the British Museum. Cretan jewellery of this type is not represented in the British Museum but can be seen in the Archaeological Museum at Heraklion and the Metropolitan Museum in New York.

About 2000 BC the more sophisticated techniques of filigree and granulation were introduced from Western Asia. A rich source of Minoan jewellery of this period is the so-called Aegina Treasure, a large collection of personal ornaments and gold plate acquired in 1892 and believed to come from the island of Aegina.

Minoan jewellery gives place about 1450 BC to Mycenaean. The Mycenaean culture, which takes its name from the key site of Mycenae, was to a large extent a mainland Greek offshoot of the Minoan culture. The principal difference in the jewellery of the two cultures is that the Mycenaean is more plentiful but less adventurous in content than the Minoan. Rightly did Homer call Mycenae 'rich in gold'. The Mycenaeans obviously had a more plentiful source of gold to draw on, but this source has not yet been identified.

Nearly all of the surviving pure Mycenaean jewellery examples are to be found in Greek museums, but the British Museum does have a large collection of jewellery from Cyprus, part Mycenaean and part Oriental, chiefly from the Museum's excavations at Enkomi at the end of the last century. This jewellery comprises for the most part simple funerary diadems and mouthpieces, earrings of several forms, with occasionally beads and pendants of higher quality.

The Minoan/Mycenaean world ended about 1100 BC, and gold jewellery of any quality was thereafter very scarce in Greek lands until shortly after 900 BC.   RH

57 A detail of a Minoan gold pectoral, said to be from the island Aegina (17th century BC). At each end is a similar human head in profile; the eyes and eyebrows were formerly inlaid. Below hang 10 small pendant discs. w (complete) 10.8cm

56 A Minoan gold repoussé pendant, said to be from the island of Aegina (17th century BC). It shows a Nature god standing on a field with lotuses, holding in either hand a water-bird. the two curved objects behind him are probably composite bows. H 6cm

Right **58** A Minoan gold repoussé
earring, said to be from the island of
Aegina (17th century BC). The hoop is
in the form of a double-headed snake; it
frames a pair of monkeys and a pair of
greyhounds. Pendants of owls and
discs hang from the circumference on
chains, and cornelian beads are
threaded in various places. D (hoop)
6.5cm

Below A group of gold Cypro-
Mycenaean jewellery excavated at
Enkomi (Cyprus) in 1896. The two pairs
of earrings are dated to the 14th or 13th
century BC. One pair (**59**) is of 'leech'
shape. The other pair (**60**) has hoops of
thin wire; from each of these is
suspended a stylised head of a bull.

The necklace and pendant date from
the 14th century BC. The necklace (**61**)
has 16 double shield-shaped gold
beads, with other beads of gold and
cornelian.

The hollow gold pendant (**62**) is in the
form of a pomegranate and is decorated
with fine granulation. H (**62**) 3.6cm

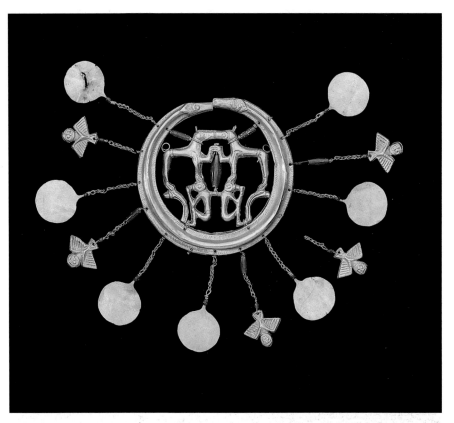

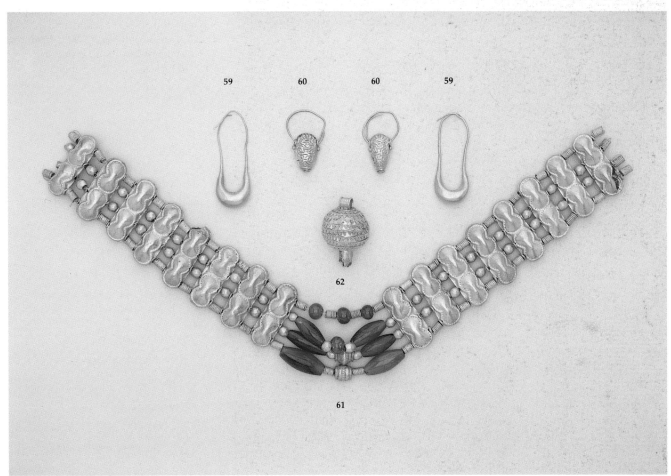

63 A pair of Early Bronze Age gold earrings (*c.* 2100–1800 BC), excavated at Boltby Scar Camp, North Yorkshire (England). These earrings, of the 'basket' type, have repoussé decoration around the edges consisting of spaced bosses flanked by ridges. L (larger) 3.2cm

North of the Alps

As early as 4000 BC the prosperous farming communities of the Balkans had established a precocious copper and gold technology, seen most spectacularly in the remarkable Varna cemetery (Bulgaria). From here the knowledge spread slowly westward, taking advantage of new ore sources around the Danube basin. Nevertheless, most jewellery continued in traditional materials with only a few examples of simple sheet-copper trinkets and rare gold necklets reflecting new circumstances. The British Isles – with rich resources of alluvial gold – were to provide the major stimulus to a taste for spectacular personal display. Initially gold and copper were employed, but the latter was soon to be supplanted by the more resilient bronze.

The range of products focuses upon personal prestige, occurring either as grave-offerings with high-ranking individuals or as hoards reflecting status through accumulation of wealth. Ornaments of sheet gold, such as basket-shaped earrings or the crescent-shaped necklets known as lunulae, had traced or embossed motifs borrowed from contemporary Beaker pottery. Amber, jet and shale were also employed in the conspicuous display of the control of rare resources and the craftsmen who worked them with exceptional skill. Notable here are the spacer-plate necklaces, where complex stringing produced the crescentic visual effect of the lunulae, an effect enhanced by the punched decoration of the plate components. Bronze objects must be cast, so this material was normally employed for the relatively simple forms of axes and daggers, again as status indicators, since the technology of complex moulds for elaborate objects had yet to be developed. Occasionally, however, techniques were adapted from goldworking to beat out ingots into bronze sheet for bangles and neck-rings.

The emergence and consolidation of ranked societies over this period is thus marked by personal display to reinforce the institution of chieftainship, power being expressed by the use of rare resources and the control of skilled craftsmen. These circumstances are evident across Western Europe at the same time and, although there are few direct links between these essentially rural communities, the social processes taking place within them are comparable.   IK

Top right **64** A jet necklace of the North British Early Bronze Age (*c.* 1800–1500 BC), found at Melfort, Argyll (Scotland). This incomplete necklace is made up of: a small triangular toggle; 2 triangular terminals; 6 trapeze-shaped spacer-plates; 51 barrel-shaped beads of various dimensions. The spacers and terminals are decorated in pointillé technique in two styles. The terminals have triangular motifs, and three of the spacers are ornamented in similar styles with filled triangles and plain lozenges. The other spacers have plain zigzags reserved against filled triangles.

The necklace components are made from two varieties of jet. One is generally well preserved with a shiny polish and is black in colour; 22 of the barrel-shaped beads, the triangular toggle and 3 of the spacers are of this variety. The other variety has a crazed surface, is poorly preserved and is brown in colour. The fact that the beads are of two different types of jet and that the beads of each type have different designs suggests that parts of two necklaces were put together before burial. The largest spacer is 5 × 2.4cm

Bottom right **65** An Irish gold lunula of the Early Bronze Age (*c.* 1800–1500 BC). Its geometric ornament, chased and scored, is arranged in zones and is symmetrical about a vertical axis. The outer edge was trimmed down in antiquity, removing most of the outer ornamental border. When the terminals are overlapped to close the ring (possibly fastened with a thong), the lunula becomes conical, both inner and outer edges forming near-true circles, and rides well on the base of the neck. W 23.7cm

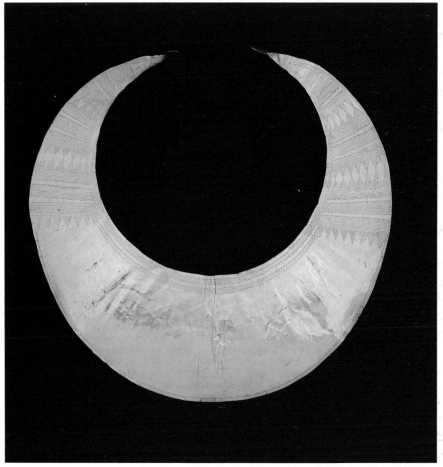

CHAPTER THREE

Egypt

1500–900 BC

66 A detail from an 18th-Dynasty wall-painting from the tomb of Nebamun at Thebes (c. 1400 BC), with a scene of a banqueting and musical entertainment. The female musicians wear gold earrings, bangles and armlets, and broad collars of beads and gold. The dancing girls wear gold earrings, bangles, broad collars of beads and gold, and gold girdles.

In form and technique jewellery of the New Kingdom (c. 1567–1085 BC) is generally similar to that of the Middle Kingdom except that coloured glass, now produced in quantity for the first time, is often used in imitation of stone for beads and inlays. Glass earplugs are found in shapes identical to glazed composition plugs of a similar date. It was during this time that both earplugs and earrings become far more common, worn by men as well as women. Like the torc, which was almost unknown in Egypt before Coptic times (88 is a very rare example), the earring was a new form of jewellery which first appeared during the latter part of the Second Intermediate Period among the Pan-Grave people, who were Nubian in origin although they settled in Egypt. Varied forms now include leech shapes and open hoops, some with suspension loops.

One of the most popular types of earring worn during the Eighteenth Dynasty (c. 1567–1320 BC) was made from a number of tubes of triangular section; these were evidently worn by women rather than by men, often with a pair to each lobe. Other types of earring were worn by stretching the flesh of the lobe so as to pass through the open end, but most entailed piercing of the ear. The glass earplugs are pierced through the length of their shafts as though for stringing, but the holes are probably due to the method of manufacture, although they may have been worn as earring pendants on a thin metal ring.

A heavy gold *shebyu*-collar, made from strings of closely threaded disc-beads, and hollow gold *awaw*-bangles, few of which have survived in this material, can be seen depicted on the black granite torso of an official of late Eighteenth-Dynasty date. These, like the gold flies, were honorific decorations, first awarded during the Eighteenth Dynasty. The gold flies may originally have been awarded as purely military decorations, but probably came to be available for any courtier to wear.

Broad collars show considerable variations, especially during the Amarna Period, when floral elements of multicoloured glazed composition became popular. Large numbers of flat-backed highly coloured date-palm leaves, poppy petals, mandrake fruits, bunches of grapes, lotus flowers and petals, daisies, corncockles and multiple jasmine blossoms were turned out from open moulds and strung together to form the characteristic collars which imitated garlands of real flowers.

Gold floral and inlaid elements and beads of stone and glass originally from collars have been combined in a double string with distinctive ribbed beads ('nasturtium-seed' beads) which came almost certainly from a girdle. All were found in a royal Eighteenth-Dynasty burial. Other loose gold and stone beads and pendants and a scarab have been restrung in the fashion of contemporary late Eighteenth-Dynasty royal jewellery. A pair of royal gold inlaid

Below Gold *shebyu*-collar and *awaw*-bangles from Egypt's 18th Dynasty (*c.* 1500–1320 BC). The collar (**67**) consists of three rows of gold ring-beads strung tightly together (some *shebyu*-collars had four strings). The gold chains attached to each terminal were made by the loop-in-loop method.

The bangles (**68**) were made from a strip of thin sheet gold beaten into shape on a wooden ring; the two ends were soldered together to form a three-sided hoop with an open face on the inside, onto which a strip of thin sheet gold was soldered at the top and bottom of the hoop. D (**68**): external 11.9cm, internal 8cm

The granite torso of a late 18th-Dynasty official (**69**) is shown wearing a *shebyu*-collar and *awaw*-armlets.

bracelets date to the very end of the New Kingdom, but their tradition can be traced back to the Middle Kingdom. The technique used on these bracelets of decorating a surface with cut-out and chased figures surrounded by inlay is found in the early Eighteenth Dynasty. An inscription inside each of the bracelets notes that they were made for Prince Nemareth, a son of the founder of the Twenty-second Dynasty, Sheshonq I.

Finger-rings now occur in considerable numbers. Early in the period rings with a swivelling rectangular bezel came into fashion. A massive gold ring with a glass cylinder bezel dates from the Eighteenth Dynasty, but this type is rare in this period. The most popular types are those with a metal shank and a scarab as the bezel, often set in a swivelling mount. A distinctive feature of many of the rings of this period is the decoration of gold wire wound round the shank; the wire passes through the swivelling bezel to hold it in place. Other forms of finger-ring include elaborate examples made completely of glazed composition in openwork designs. New are solid metal stirrup shaped rings used as signet-rings and often imitated in glazed composition.

By the later stages of the New Kingdom there is a marked increase in the use of amulets and figures of deities as decorative elements in jewellery. Indeed, scarcely any jewellery except such elements have survived from the succeeding impoverished period. CA

94

82

83

81

491, 492

84

474–5

Top right **79** Egyptian beads and pendants from the 18th-Dynasty Tomb of the Three Princesses at Thebes (*c.* 1480 BC). The single drop pendant is inlaid with cornelian, green glazed steatite and decayed glass or glazed composition. The small beads of the outer string are gold, cornelian and blue glass. On the inner string the groups of three beads (of gold, flanked by lapis-lazuli, blue glass and green felspar) are separated by cornelian, red jasper, green felspar and turquoise-blue glass. Separating the two strings are gold *nefer*-signs. L (outer row) 65.5cm

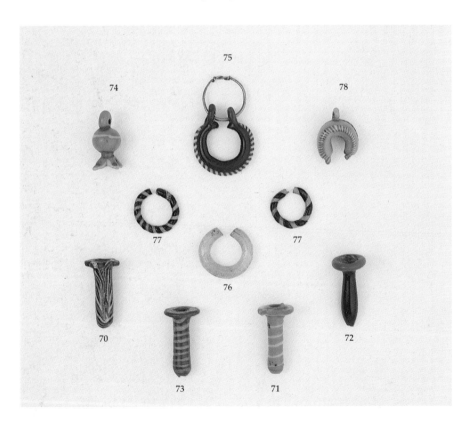

Left A group of Egyptian glass ear ornaments of the 18th and 19th Dynasties (*c.* 1400–1300 BC), a selection of the wide variety of types worn in this period. **74** and **78** are earring pendants, probably worn suspended from the ear-lobe on a wire ring. Although a wire ring is now threaded through the loops of another example (**75**), this would originally have been worn with a bar passing through the loops and the ear-lobe. The other penannular rings (**76**, **77**) were worn by stretching the lobe so that it could pass between the open ends of the rings; **77** comes from a child's burial.

The remaining specimens, like their counterparts in glazed composition, are earplugs in the shape of papyrus-columns (**70, 71, 73**) and a palm-column (**72**).

All of these ear ornaments, except **76**, are made from canes of coloured glass decorated with threads of glass in contrasting colours. H (**70, 73**) 2.8cm

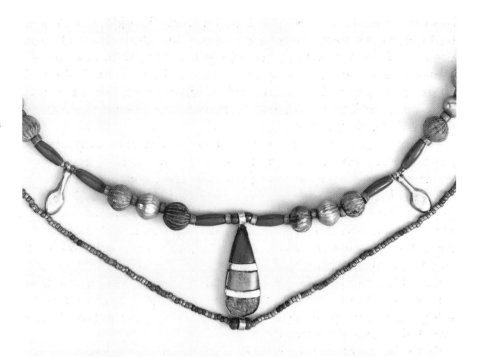

Bottom right A group of Egyptian gold jewellery. The pair of identical gold fly pendants (**80**) date from about 1550–1300 BC. They are of gold foil moulded over a core; suspension rings are soldered to the heads.

Typical of the early part of the 15th century BC is **81**, a gold signet-ring with a green glazed scarab (18th Dynasty, *c.* 1500–1450 BC). The shank is made from gold foil folded over wire, and the scarab is inscribed with the prenomen of Queen Hatshepsut, flanked by hieroglyphic signs.

82 is a gold swivel signet-ring, set with a thin plaque of dark blue glass, engraved with great virtuosity on both faces; each refers to Tuthmosis III, the successor of Hatshepsut.

83, a massive gold ring with a swivelling cylinder-shaped bezel of blue glass imitating lapiz lazuli, is also from the 18th Dynasty (*c.* 1400 BC). The shank is cast solid and beaten out towards the ends. Gold wire is wound round one end of the shank, then passes through the bezel and is finally wound round the other end of the shank.

The gold stirrup-shaped signet-ring (**84**) is from the time of Akhenaten (18th Dynasty, *c.* 1379–1362 BC). It was cast by the *cire-perdue* or lost-wax process. Its oval bezel is deeply incised with a central seated figure – probably Akhenaten himself – holding a *maat*-feather, flanked by a ceremonial fan and an *ankh*-sign, with a uraeus-flanked sun-disc at the top and signs for Lord of the Two Lands below.

Also from the Armarna period (*c.* 1380–1350 BC) is the gold frog swivel-ring (**85**); the base of the bezel is inscribed with a scorpion. This ring was probably worn as an amulet by a woman, for the frog was the emblem of Heqat, goddess of childbirth and fertility. The scorpion is a symbol of Selkit, one of the four protecting goddesses of the dead.

86 is one of a pair of hollow gold earrings – the other is in Cairo – found during the excavation of Tomb 56 in the Valley of the Kings near Thebes. It is inlaid with a cartouche containing the name of Queen Tausert, one of the last rulers of the 19th Dynasty (*c.* 1209–1200 BC). Most of the inlay material is missing but what remains appears to be decomposed glass. D (**83**, external) 3.1cm

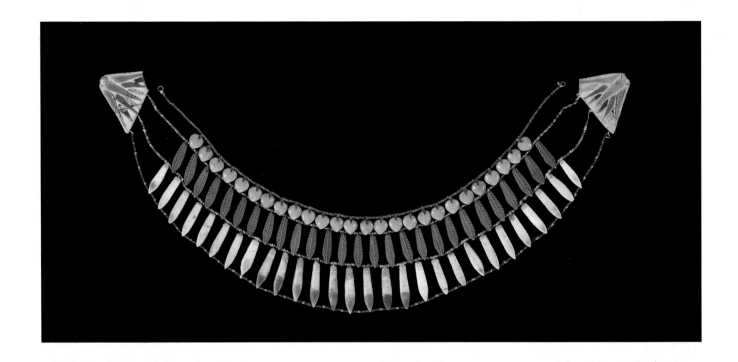

Above **88** An Egyptian gold torc (*c.* 1400–1200 BC), composed of thin gold disc-beads strung tightly together on thick cord. The cord is original. At each end is a gold cup with a hole in the base through which the cord passes. This torc, unlike its Celtic counterpart, has the appearance of the scaly body of a snake. D (external) 15.1cm

Above right A group of Egyptian earrings (*c.* 1500–1200 BC). The leech-shaped earring (**89**) was made from a piece of sheet electrum, folded over a shaped core; the joins are

masked by wire notched to imitate beading. This type of earring appears usually to date to the late 18th Dynasty.

The penannular earring (**90**) is identical in form to the glass earring (**75**), and is formed from two circles of sheet gold, raised by beating and soldered together. Along the outside edges the line is masked by applied 'rope braid' decoration.

The ribbed earrings (**91**) are made from five tubes of sheet gold, triangular in section. The central tube is extended for inserting into the ear-lobe. D (**90**, external) 3.4cm

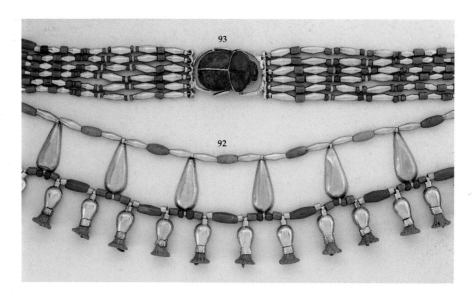

Top left **87** An Egyptian collar of glazed composition beads and pendants excavated at Amarna (18th Dynasty, *c.* 1380–1350 BC), characteristic of the type of jewellery popular during this period. The rows consist of mandrake fruit (top), date-palm leaves (middle) and lotus petals (lower). The lotus-shaped terminals are inlaid with red, yellow, blue and green glazed composition to indicate petals. L (total) 52cm

Below **94** A pair of Egyptian gold bracelets inscribed for Prince Nemareth, son of Sheshonq I, founder of the 22nd Dynasty. The bracelets (*c.* 940 BC) are inlaid with lapis lazuli and blue glass. On each a framed panel contains a raised gold figure of Harpocrates seated on a lotus, with traces of red inlay between the tips of the lotus flowers. The remaining part of each bracelet is decorated with a chevron pattern formed of gold alternating with inlays. H 4.2cm

Above Beads and pendants of the 18th Dynasty (*c.* 1370–1350 BC). The necklace (**92**) is composed of beads of green glass and gold (in the upper row), and cornelian, red jasper, blue glazed composition and gold (in the lower row). The corncockle pendants in the lower row have blue glazed composition flowers with serrated edges and gold calyxes.

The bracelet (**93**) is strung from a collection of gold, cornelian and glazed composition beads and gold pendants, with a lapis lazuli scarab set in gold; the scarab's feet hold a bar at either end with six rings for threads. L (scarab, **93**) 2.8cm

CHAPTER FOUR

Europe and Western Asia

1400–600 BC

North-west Europe

This period represents the culmination of earlier metalworking traditions. From their firm foundation new techniques developed to enlarge and diversify the range of products.

As earlier methods of beating out and embossing sheet gold reached their apogee, exemplified by the gold cape from Mold (Wales), now in the British Museum, casting, bar-twisting and making wire began to offer new decorative possibilities. The twisted torc could be produced either by the torsion of bars or strips, or by casting to imitate twisting; the latter technique allowed the production of bronze versions. Wire became especially prominent with the invention of the fibula or safety-pin brooch, whose range of decorative possibilities greatly exceeded the usual dress-pins which it would finally supplant. Whilst repoussé and chasing continued as basic ornamental techniques, an improved casting technology, especially involving complex clay moulds, increasingly concentrated attention upon the elaboration of shape as a prime concern. As well as gold and bronze, amber and shale continued in popularity, with the range now extended by glass, technologically still restricted to bead production. Body ornaments – neck-rings, beads, bracelets and earrings – were now joined by a new emphasis on clothing and hair fittings.

In Britain such materials are commonly found in hoards which

Above **96** A bronze brooch of the North European Middle Bronze Age (*c.* 12th century BC) from Holstein (Germany). This is one of the earliest types of brooch in Europe. It is constructed in two parts: the head-spiral, bow, catch and foot-spiral are made from a single piece of wire. The pin, which may have been cast in a mould, was threaded on before the head-spiral was coiled up. The bow and catch are ornamented with grooving in imitation of twisted work. L 7cm

Left **95** A bronze arm-ring of the Central European Middle Bronze Age (*c.* 13th century BC). It is decorated with geometric chased or scored ornament on the hoop, and has chased nicks on the spiral terminals. D (max) 12.2cm

Right Three cast-bronze dress-pins. **97** (*c.* 13th century BC) and **99** (*c.* 7th century BC) are from Hallstatt (Upper Austria). The latter is provided with a ferrule to protect its point, shaped to match the elaborately modelled head of the pin.

98, from Ramsgate, Kent (England), dates to *c.* 1200–1000 BC (North French Middle Bronze Age). It is pierced horizontally, probably to secure it to clothing. This is one of a small group of pins imported from north-east France into south-east England, together with a group of arm-rings decorated with similar chased ornament L (**99**) 39.7cm, D (head, **97**) 5.5cm

Below Part of a hoard of bronzes from a mound at Hollingbury Hill, Sussex (England), dating to the British Middle Bronze Age (12th century BC). The arm-rings (**100**, *right*), each wrought from a single bar, belong to a group of four 'Sussex loops' found in the hoard. The coiled finger-ring (**101**, *left*) is one of three in the hoard, which also included a torc and a palstave. The hoard came to light within the ramparts of the later hillfort of Hollingbury, which probably developed from an earlier palisaded settlement with which the hoard of bronzes may well be associated. The arm-rings and the finger-rings are of types only found in south-eastern England, although similar finger-rings occur in contemporary Northern Europe, where the type may have originated. D (max., of arm-rings) 8.3cm

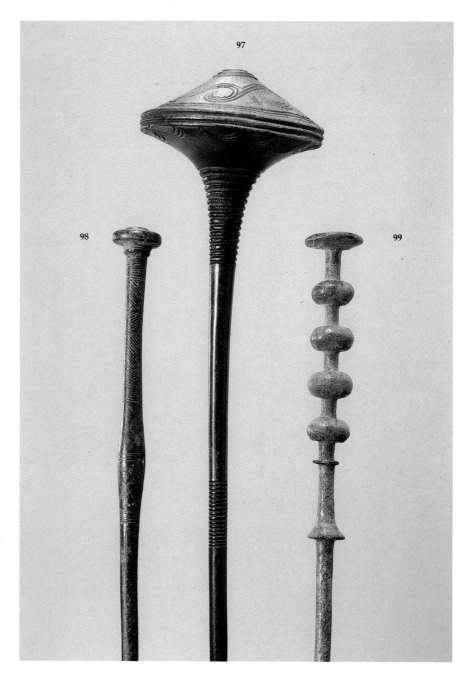

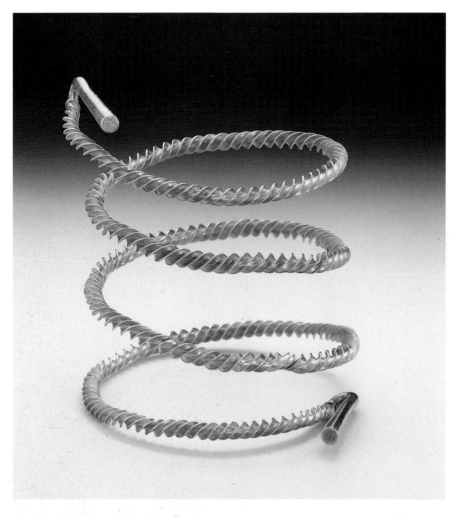

Left **102** A gold torc of the Middle Bronze Age (*c.* 1200–900 BC), found on the borders of Glamorgan with Brecknockshire (Wales) in 1838. It is made from a twisted bar of cruciform section and is wound into 3½ coils. This is an example of the 'Tara' type of torc, found in Britain, Ireland and northern France. Although it is generally held that all those found outside Ireland were exported from there, the Irish specimens are never found coiled up, but the British usually are, and a difference in use is likely: in Ireland they were worn about the neck, in Britain about the arm. L 11.6cm

Bottom left **103–7** Gold jewellery of the Middle and Later Bronze Age.

From left to right: **103** is of a type variously interpreted as 'ring-money' (a form of currency) or, by analogy with contemporary Egyptian rings of the same design, as hair-rings. It is made from sheet gold wrapped around a copper (-alloy) ring. This example, from Fuaraig Glen, Glen Avon, Banffshire (Scotland), is of Later Bronze Age date (*c.* 1200–800 BC) and was probably imported into Scotland from Ireland.

The gold 'lock-ring' (**104**), found at Cheesburn in Northumberland (England) is of the Late Bronze Age (8th–7th century BC) and is an Irish type imported into Britain. It is uncertain exactly how such rings were used.

The 'sleeve-fastener' (**105**) is of the same period, and was found near Tara Hill, Co. Wexford (Ireland). This type is found outside Ireland only in western Scotland. It is conventionally considered to have been used like a modern cuff-link, with the hoop projecting outside the sleeve; however, such a use is precluded on certain specimens owing to the size of the terminals, which are sometimes very large and sometimes very small. It may simply have been used as a special-purpose currency.

The two earrings (**106**, **107**), each made from a twisted bar of gold, belong to a small group of earrings from Western Europe apparently influenced by contemporary designs in the Near East. Both date from about 1200–1000 BC: **106** appears to have been found in Ireland, although its precise find-place unknown; **107** is from Dinnington, Northumberland (England).w (max., **103**) 3cm

Above **108** Suite of jewellery made of gold wire (*c.* 11th–9th century BC), found on the banks of the Danube between Duna-Földvár and Paks (Hungary). This is one of the finest groups of gold-wire jewellery of the Late Bronze Age discovered in Central Europe. It comprises:

a) a pair of brooches, each made in several parts. A single wire forms the large foot-spiral, the catch, bow, head, the spring and pin. Four further lengths of wire with spiral terminals are attached to the bow.

b) a four-armed piece with spiral terminals. The central plate has a slot for attaching to a rod; it would probably have been mounted with similar pieces to form a pectoral ornament.

c) a pair of loop-pendants, each with two spiral terminals and a twisted loop. w (**b**) 11.9cm

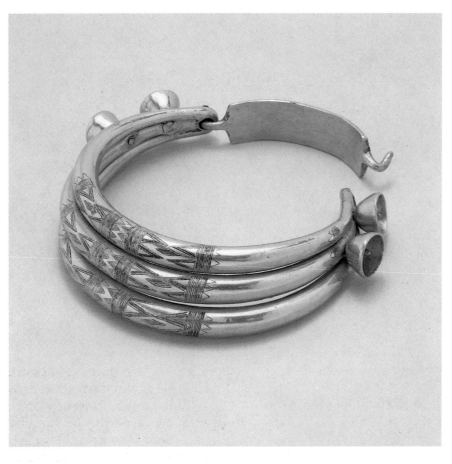

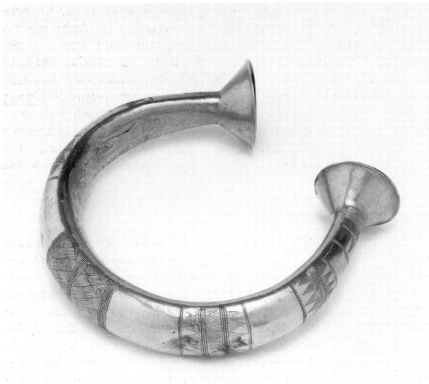

109 A gold collar found near Sintra in Portugal (*c.* 7th century BC). The Sintra collar is the finest Late Bronze Age neck-ring from Iberia, with features of the design reflecting both local traditions and connections as far afield as southern Scandinavia. Its chevron and zigzag ornament is chased; each of the four lotus-like cups is attached to the central bar by a spike-headed rivet. The small size of the collar suggests that it was designed for a child or woman. D 13.1cm

110 Hollow gold bracelet of the Late Bronze Age (8th–7th century BC), found at Morvah, Cornwall (England). This item is from a hoard of six gold bracelets, two like this one, the other three of different types. W 8.3cm

111 A gold 'dress-fastener' of the Later Bronze Age (8th–7th century BC). The conical terminals have four chased grooves on the outside. This is an Irish type characteristic of the final phase of the Bronze Age. Precisely how these objects were used is uncertain; and it has been suggested that they may have been designed as currency rather than jewellery. W 11.7cm

give little clue to actual wear, but grave-finds in parts of Western Europe have shown ornate arrangements, especially those concerned with hair and head-dress fittings. Pins and, later, brooches could be used in complex ways on clothing and in Ireland the penannular 'dress- and sleeve-fasteners' seem to have had a comparable role. 105, 111

Wealth and rank still seem to have been critical to the use of jewellery as personal ornament and, perhaps, as currency in social transactions, such as gift-giving and bride-wealth. Although the basic forms are widely shared, varying only with local fashion, some specific types are not merely of unusual appearance but have been found only within a restricted area: the 'Sussex loop' arm-ring is a good example in suggesting the use of ornaments to signify particular ethnic identity. This type has been found only in Sussex, 100 southern England, normally in pairs, in hoards assigned to a period of the southern British Middle Bronze Age when large numbers of personal ornaments (arm-rings, bracelets, finger-rings, pins and torcs) were hoarded. IK

Western Asia

An unusual development in jewellery is represented by the bronze pins of Luristan, dated about 1000–700 BC. Luristan is a mountainous region of south-western Iran, and the pins and other Luristan bronzes are typically decorated with monsters and contorted figures at first sight reminiscent of the patterns used by the nomadic tribes of Central Asia, some of which were infiltrating Iran during this period. In fact, however, the Luristan motifs mostly seem to be stylised versions of ones that were at home in the old centres of civilisation in Mesopotamia and Elam (southern Iran). Pins had been employed to fasten clothes since at least the Sumerian period (see 7), and were to remain indispensable until they were superseded by the brooch or safety-pin (fibula). Some of the pins from

Luristan, however, reach an extraordinary size, and it is probable that these were not really designed for wearing at all, but were manufactured specifically as votive jewellery, for dedication in temples.

A gold belt fragment of about the eighth century BC, from central Iran, would once have been sewn on to a cloth or leather backing. Decorated belts of this kind were used principally in the kingdom of Urartu and its provinces. The stylised animals embossed on its surface are likely to have some connection with the art of the Scythians or related tribes: comparable stylised animals recur on later metalwork from what is now the southern USSR. A characteristic of the nomadic style was to take animal motifs and distort them in such a way that the shape of the animal was secondary both to the shape of the object it was decorating and to the general decorative effect. Jewellery incorporating distorted animals is found over a long

117

Four dress-pins from Luristan, in the western part of modern Iran (*c.* 1000–700 BC). All, except **113**, are of cast bronze. The head of **112** represents a lion; that of **114** is in the shape of a winged monster, while the disc-shaped head of **115** is decorated with a pattern of arcaded buds and pomegranates. **113** is an iron pin with a cast head of base silver, representing a hero wrestling with two animals. L (longest, **115**), 41.45cm, D (head) 12.3cm

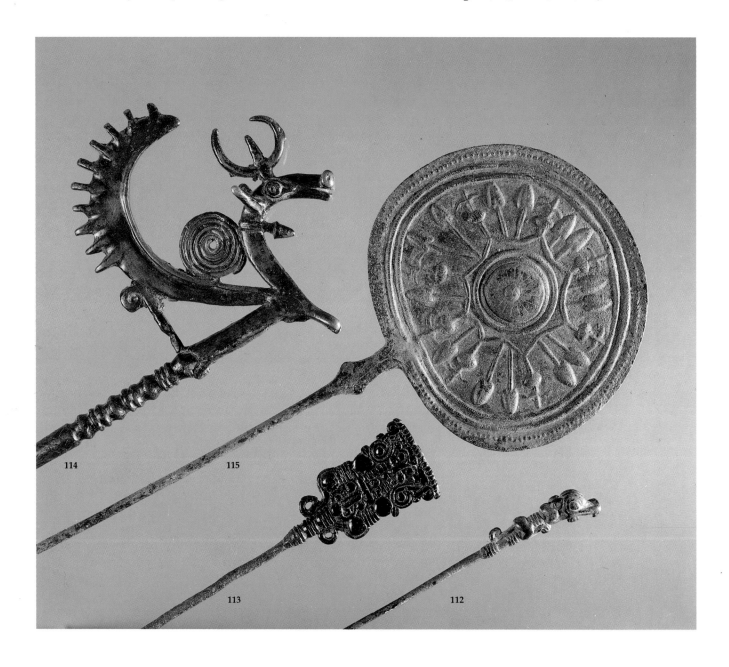

114   115

113   112

54

116 Silver hoard from Tepe Nūsh-i Jān, Iran, buried *c.* 600 BC. This group of spiral pendants, rings and scraps was found, with much more material of a similar nature, concealed beneath a floor. It demonstrates what must have been the usual fate of ancient jewellery, being cut up or melted down to serve as currency when it fell out of fashion or its owners needed to realise their capital. This economic function of jewellery was particularly important before the invention of coinage. The spiral pattern on the pendants in the hoard is comparable with a type also found in the royal graves of Ur (**11, 12, 26**). W (largest pendant) 4cm

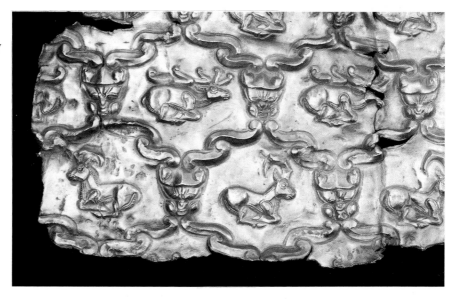

117 Detail from a fragment of a belt said to be from Ziwiye, in the Kurdistan region of modern Iran (*c.* 8th–7th century BC), made from sheet gold, embossed and chased with a pattern of lions' masks linked by looped tendrils which enclose figures of stags and goats. H (of fragment) 8.5cm

period and a vast geographical area, from Europe to the borders of China. A finger-ring from the Oxus Treasure, dating from about the fifth to the fourth centuries BC, shows how successfully this stylistic approach could be adapted to the manufacture of small-scale jewellery.   146

Other items from this treasure also follow the traditions of Mesopotamia and Elam. A gold bracelet from Iran of about the seventh century, with duck-head terminals, is of a type which can be seen on ninth-century Assyrian sculptures and which is still represented in the Oxus Treasure in the magnificent gold armlets with their griffin terminals.   118 139

JER

118 Gold bracelet from Iran (*c.* 7th century BC). The bracelet is hollow, with the 'terminal' section, in the form of two ducks back to back, made separately from the main hoop. D 9.67cm

119 Part of an Assyrian carved slab from the palace of Ashurnasirpal II (883–859 BC) at Nimrud (northern Iraq). The carving shows Ashurnasirpal himself wearing court dress, with the distinctive type of hat worn only by kings. His jewellery includes earrings, a bead necklace, bracelets, and armlets on his upper arms. The armlets, with their terminals ending in rams' heads, are a type frequently portrayed on sculptures and comparable with the gold bracelet of the 7th century BC from Iran (**118**). This type can also be seen later in the 5th and 4th century in the Oxus Treasure (**139**, **147–50**). The bracelets with central rosette ornaments are also often depicted; this type of bracelet later appears among Phoenician jewellery from the 8th century BC onwards.

CHAPTER FIVE

Phoenician, Greek Etruscan and Persian Lands

850–325 BC

Phoenician

On the eastern Mediterranean, along the coasts of Lebanon and Syria, lay the cities of the Phoenicians, who were both traders and colonists. By the eighth century Phoenician colonies were establishing themselves in the west of the Mediterranean, and the arts and crafts of the ancient Middle East were being introduced into southern Spain and elsewhere. Often it is hard to distinguish between the products of the Phoenicians and those of the European natives who learned from them, but jewellery from graves at the colony of Tharros, in Sardinia, seems to be authentic Phoenician work. For instance, one bracelet is of a type for which parallels have been found in Syria, Cyprus, Malta, Tunisia, and Spain.

Much Phoenician jewellery is extremely intricate, with sumptuous effects achieved, in the Tell el-'Ajjul tradition, at relatively small expense. Colourful glass necklaces were also popular. A distinctive

121

LEFT

Above **120** A Phoenician bracelet (*c.* 7th–6th century BC). The centre-piece, set in a gold mount, is an ivory button-like roundel, with a rosette carved on one side and a fictitious Egyptian cartouche on the other. The spacer-beads on the strap, each consisting of four gold beads soldered together, recall those on the Ur head-dress (**28**). The bracelet is fastened by inserting a pin through the hinges at the back. L 10cm

Below **121** Part of a gold bracelet from a Phoenician grave at Tharros, Sardinia (*c.* 7th–6th century BC). Its oblong gold plaques are attached to one another by hinges swivelling on silver pins. Separate pieces of gold, decorated by embossed and granulated floral motifs, are soldered onto the plaques. Comparable bracelets have been found as far apart as Syria, Cyprus, Malta, Tunisia and Spain. L 13.2cm

122 A detail from a necklace of glass beads and gold pendants from a Phoenician grave at Tharros, Sardinia (*c.* 7th–6th century BC). The central pendant is a flat plaque with embossed decoration showing uraeus-cobras on either side of a bottle-shaped motif; this is probably a divine symbol. H (central pendant) 2.2cm

characteristic of the Phoenician style is the use of motifs derived from Egypt. Many of these had originally had an amuletic value, and presumably retained it for the Phoenicians, but the patterns have sometimes been misunderstood or transformed into shapes and combinations which would have been unacceptable in Egypt itself.

From the eighth century BC Phoenicia came to be dominated by the Assyrians from further east, in Mesopotamia. Under the Assyrian Empire bracelets with central rosette ornaments, much like the modern wristwatch in effect, became common and can be seen on many sculptures. JER

The Orientalising Period of Greek Jewellery

In the Greek world some two centuries of great poverty were to follow the collapse of Mycenaean power about 1100 BC. Artistic creation was at a low ebb, and luxury articles were rare indeed. About 900 BC, however, contacts with Western Asia, especially with the civilised cities of Phoenicia, were resumed. The jewellery in this age of Greek revival, which lasted until shortly after 600 BC, was again plentiful and of the highest quality.

From 900 to 700 BC we see the production of superb goldwork at certain important centres such as Knossos in Crete, Corinth, and Athens. Jewellery was also extremely plentiful, though not produced to such a high standard, at a centre in Euboea whose modern name is Lefkandi. It is probable that immigrant goldsmiths from Phoenicia, which was famed at this date for its craftsmen, settled at these places, set up workshops, and taught the secrets of their trade to local apprentices. Much of this jewellery rather puzzlingly recalls that of the Mycenaean period, some five centuries earlier, in certain motifs and certain technical processes. We know that there can scarcely have been continuity of tradition in Greek lands, and the

Above **123–4** Gold earrings and a pair of gold fibulæ (Greek, 8th century BC). The earrings (**123**, top) are decorated with fine granulation. The centres of the discs and the curved 'stalks' which spring from the backs of the discs were originally inlaid.

The fibulæ (**124**, bottom) are decorated with engraving on the catch-plates; on one side is a deer and on the other a swastika. L (**124**) 6cm

Right **125** A gold rosette ornament (Greek, 7th century BC). The rosette's six petals are decorated alternately with a female head and a rosette; in the centre is a lion's head in high relief. A runner on the back of the rosette indicates that it was used as a diadem ornament. D 4.3cm

125

127

only possible explanation is that Mycenaean fashions had found their way to the coasts of the Levant, where they were kept alive by the Phoenicians through the Dark Ages of 1100–900 BC, to be re-introduced to the Greek world when it was once more in a position to enjoy the luxuries of life. A collection formed by the seventh Earl of Elgin in the early 1800s, probably from excavations in Athens, is the British Museum's principal source for the ninth and eighth centuries BC.

In the seventh and early sixth centuries BC the best jewellery came from the Islands and Asia Minor, which were becoming richer as Athens was becoming poorer. Among the most important sources are the cemeteries of Camirus in Rhodes, excavated in the 1860s, and the Temple of Artemis at Ephesus, excavated in 1904–5.

Closely related to the Rhodian tradition is an exquisite class of rosettes made for attachment to diadems of cloth or leather. Most surviving examples have been found on the island of Melos, where they were doubtlessly made. They are decorated with human and animal heads, and with insects and flowers.

The jewellery from Ephesus, made in the late seventh and early sixth century BC, was excavated on the site of the Temple of Artemis (the Roman Diana). It was evidently dedicated to Artemis by the faithful at a sanctuary on the same site as the later Temple, which was counted as one of the Wonders of the World. Although deposited as votive offerings to the goddess, these articles are so substantial that we may conclude that they were made in the first place to be worn. The style has much in common with contemporary Rhodian jewellery, but the Oriental element is stronger in view of the Asiatic connections of the Ephesian Artemis, and certain later motifs are included in the repertoire. RH

Far left **126** A gold plaque from a pectoral ornament, from Camirus, Rhodes (7th century BC). The plaque shows a winged goddess with a pair of lions in relief, all richly embellished with granulation. At the top of the plaque are two hawks and a flower modelled in the round. H 5.2cm

Left **127** A gold brooch in the form of a hawk, from the Temple of Artemis at Ephesus (*c.* 600 BC). H 3.1cm

Right Etruscan gold fibulæ (7th century BC). **128** is a bolt-fibula found in the Campagna (the lowland area around Rome). It is composed of four curved tubes which have female heads as finials. The fibula is made in two halves. On one side a pin protrudes from each of the two outer tubes; to fasten the fibula these pins are inserted into the two corresponding hollow tubes on the other half. The outer pairs of tubes are connected by four plates, each decorated with four crouching sphinxes modelled in the round.

129, a serpentine fibula from Vulci or perhaps Cerveteri (north-west of Rome), is covered with designs in superfine granulation and figures of lions, lions' heads, horses' heads and sphinxes modelled in the round, all of which are also richly granulated. The pin is inserted into a sheath, which has eight pairs of lions and terminates in a pair of lions' heads. The bow (see detail, *below right*) is decorated with a complicated arrangement of horses' and lions' heads. Above the lions' heads are four sphinxes. Three pairs of lions clamber up the section from the point where the sheath and bow are joined. L (**129**) 18.6cm

Etruscan

The origin of the Etruscans has been much debated but, according to present thinking, they were largely native Italians domiciled in central Italy, the modern Tuscany, who had developed their natural resources so skilfully that they became extremely wealthy. In return for their mineral and agricultural products they were able to import luxuries from Greece and Phoenicia. The period of their greatest power covers the seventh and sixth centuries BC. The decline began shortly after the beginning of the fifth century BC, and continued till

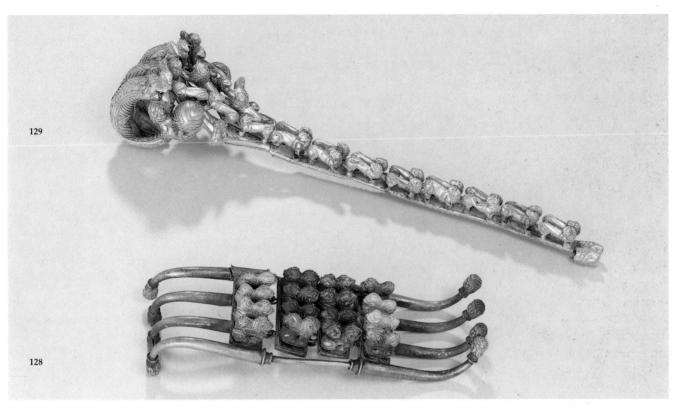

129

128

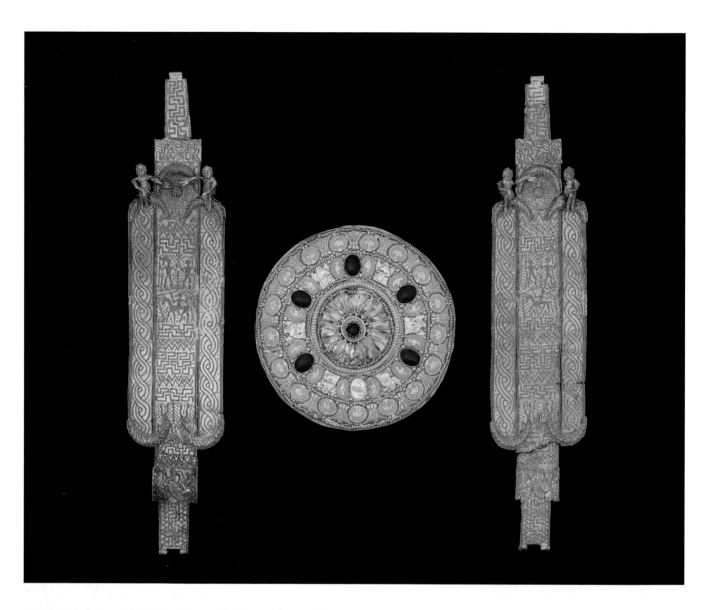

Top left **130–1** Gold Etruscan jewellery. The pair of bracelets (**130**) are from Tarquinii (7th century BC). They are decorated on the front in suprfine granulation with abstract patterns and animal and human figures; the backs have embossed patterns and figures.

131 (centre) is an ear-stud (6th century BC), richly decorated with filigree, granulation and inlay. It has a projection in the back for insertion in the ear-lobe. D (**131**) 6.8cm

Bottom left **132** A silver and parcel-gilt Etruscan comb-fibula (7th century BC). The central element is a richly decorated tube with a wire running down each side. The two comb-like elements were originally sewn onto opposing corners of a cloak and hooked over the side wires of the central element to fasten the cloak on the shoulder. The Etruscan terracotta figure (**133**, *bottom far left*) shows how these fibulæ were worn. L 12.4cm

Top right **134** A gold Etruscan strap-necklace from the Tuscan Maremma (6th century BC). The necklace is hung with the heads of a river-god, sirens, flowers, buds and scarabs. L 27.6cm

Bottom right **135** A gold Etruscan myrtle wreath (*c.* 4th century BC). It is composed of two curved tubes flattened into strips and hinged in the centre, with the stems of the leaves and berries inserted into the tubes at regular intervals. The ends of the wreath are pierced for fastening. L (inner curve) 27.9cm

the middle of the third, when the Etruscan cities were absorbed by the growing power of Rome.

Etruscan jewellery is best considered in two phases: Early Etruscan (seventh–fifth centuries BC) and Late Etruscan (400–250 BC). After 250 BC there was still plenty of jewellery being made in Etruria but it was now in the universal Hellenistic Greek style, which the Romans had learned from the Greek cities in southern Italy, and which they passed on to the Etruscans. Wreaths, earrings, necklaces, bracelets and finger-rings of gold were worn in profusion by well-to-do Etruscan ladies at all periods.

Early Etruscan jewellery is characterised by its abundance, its

technical perfection and its variety. The technical knowledge reached the Etruscans from the same Phoenician sources that supplied the Greeks, but the Etruscans made different and more extensive use of it. Granulation was the decorative process *par excellence*, and its possibilities were developed to a far higher degree than in Greece. The grains were not merely disposed in simple patterns; whole scenes were portrayed in silhouettes of granulation, or, by a reversed process, the figures were in relief and the background granulated; alternatively the whole surface was covered with 'gold dust'. All these techniques were probably first used by Phoenician goldsmiths but the evidence is so far lacking. Filigree was at first used sparingly, but on occasion was applied in openwork patterns without a background, an extremely difficult process.

Towards the end of the seventh century Greek influence first made itself felt, not so much in the forms of the jewellery as in new decorative motifs and technical innovations, such as an increased use of filigree and the introduction of inlay and enamelling. These changes should probably be explained by the arrival of immigrant East Greek goldsmiths, who may well have been forced to leave their homes in Asia Minor by invasion and persecution. The Etruscans loved colour, and their necklaces of delicately granulated gold beads frequently included glass and faience beads of Phoenician origin, to give a rich polychrome effect.

136 A gold necklace from the Greek city of Tarentum, southern Italy (4th century BC). The filigree-decorated necklace is composed of interlocking rosettes and other ornaments, from which hang flower-buds and female heads. L 30.6cm

Late Etruscan jewellery (about 400–250 BC) is very different in form and execution, consisting as it does of large convex surfaces of sheet gold. Decoration is meagre: filigree and granulation were occasionally used, but in general the goldsmith restricted himself to embossed patterns of the simplest kind. The repertoire was as limited as the style: flimsy wreaths for burial with the dead, earrings, necklaces, bracelets and finger-rings. The explanation of this sad state of affairs is surely to be found in the political and economic decline of Etruria, which set in soon after 500 BC. After this poverty-stricken art the adoption of Hellenistic fashions comes as a pleasant surprise.   RH

The Archaic and Classical Periods of Greek Jewellery

In Greece, between about 575 and 475 BC, jewellery was very rare, but after the Persian Wars of 490 and 480–479 BC it became more plentiful. The Archaic period, between shortly after 600 and 475 BC, is represented principally in Greek colonies in southern Italy, Sicily and the Crimea (there are virtually no examples of such jewellery in the British Museum). The cause of this uneven distribution is not clear, but a temporary shortage of gold in Greece proper, for reasons which are obscure, may have been an important factor. The jewellery of what is usually known as the Classical period, from about 475 to 330 BC, follows closely in style and technique from what little we know of the previous period. The workmanship is fine, but perhaps rather less fine than in the seventh century. Filigree was used in decorative patterns, and enamel was becoming more popular. Granulation was rarely used; inlay of stone or glass even more rarely. Towards the end of the period, however, we first find engraved

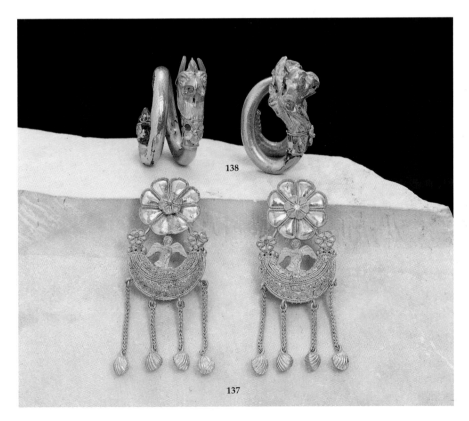

138

137

Earrings of the 5th century BC. The pair of spiral, gold-plated bronze earrings ending in griffins' heads (**138**) are from Amathus (Cyprus). They are decorated with blue and green enamel. This type of earring is a Greek Cypriot speciality.

The gold filigree-decorated earrings (**137**) are from Eretria, Euboea (Greece). They have green enamelled rosettes and eight tiny pendants in the form of cockle-shells. On top of the crescent sits a siren. H (**137**) 6cm

stones in the bezels of finger-rings. In general the sculptural forms of the gold were left to speak for themselves, diversified only by the processes mentioned above.

The forms were very varied. Naturalistic wreaths developed in the fifth century and flourished in the fourth. They were worn by both sexes at parties and religious ceremonies, and by the dead. Diadems continued in many varieties. Earrings proliferated; human figures, some of great elaboration, which were to be typical of the Hellenistic period, made their first appearance as adjuncts to earrings about the middle of the fourth century. Beads and pendants of types already familiar are found in this period, altered to suit the taste of the new age. Elaborate necklaces were made, with interlocking beads; and acorns, birds and human heads were popular as pendants. Bracelets took the form of spirals or penannular hoops with elaborate finials. Finger-rings are found in several varieties: some engraved as signets, some set with seal-stones, some purely decorative in purpose.

In general, the comparative scarcity of Classical jewellery is compensated for by its very high quality. And when, in the Hellenistic period, gold again became plentiful, the craftsmen had a more than adequate reservoir of expertise on which to draw.   RH

Persian Lands

The Assyrian Empire was succeeded by the end of the seventh century BC by the Neo-Babylonian, and then by the Persian Empire of the Achaemenids, based in modern Iran. The jewellery of the Persian lands, though influenced from the West in some respects, tends to be technically simpler but, because of the lavish use of gold, more imposing in its general effect. A hoard of gold treasure, discovered somewhere on the Oxus River in Central Asia about 1877, illustrates the opulent taste in jewellery at the Persian court. The Greek historians commented several times on the remarkable quantities of gold worn, in various forms, by the Persian kings and their high officials and bodyguards; they refer, not only to bracelets and torcs, but also to applied ornaments that were sewn on to clothes.

The Oxus Treasure has an obscure history. It was carried by merchants to India, where most of it was eventually bought by a British official. The cosmopolitan nature of the Oxus Treasure jewellery, and indeed of other objects from the Oxus Treasure, has caused considerable confusion among scholars attempting to assess its date and origin. It is not clear whether it came from a single hoard; even if it did, it may incorporate the contents of a temple treasury that had accumulated over two or more centuries. It is possible that much of the jewellery was hidden about 330 BC, when the Greek army of Alexander the Great was advancing into Central Asia, and that it represents offerings deposited during the period of the Persian Empire.

Many items in the Oxus Treasure show the influence of traditions inherited by the Persians from Mesopotamia and Elam. Thus bracelets ending in fine animal-heads are familiar on Assyrian sculptures of the ninth century BC, and there are many comparable pieces in

139 One of a pair of gold armlets from the Oxus Treasure (c. 5th–4th century BC). The hoop is almost solid metal at the back, but becomes tubular towards the ends, which are fashioned in the shape of winged griffins. The hollows chased into the horns, face and body of the monsters were originally inlaid, as were the applied gold cloisons on the wings and upper parts. The pair to this bracelet is also in the British Museum, on loan from the Victoria and Albert Museum (London). H 12.4cm

the Treasure. The earlier gold bracelet from Iran is more elaborate and imaginative. The gold armlets from the Oxus Treasure have terminals in the form of a distinctively Persian development of the griffin; this variety has horns, high ears, the body and forelegs of a lion, and the wings, head and hindlegs of an eagle. These magnificent but impractical armlets may have been designed for use on ceremonial occasions.

A piece that may have been buried about the same time as the Oxus Treasure is part of a pearl necklace from the old Persian capital of Pasargadae; pearls seem to have been valued as jewellery from a very early date, but few examples have survived. JER

140–3 Four gold dress ornaments from the Oxus Treasure with embossed decoration: **140** (bottom right) shows a sphinx whose wing terminates in a griffin's head; **141** (bottom left) has the head of the Egyptian god Bes and **143** (top right) a lion's head. **142** (top left) is in the shape of a bird's head with a curved beak, emerging from a serpentine body. Gold wire has been soldered across the **143** for attachment and on **142** there are also loops for attachment at the back. D (**140**) 5cm

151 Part of a necklace of gold and pearl beads, with one gold bell-shaped pendant, from Pasargadæ (Iran). These beads, dating from the Persian Empire (c. 4th century BC) came from a large hoard of jewellery which was probably hidden about 330 BC, when Alexander's Greeks were advancing through Iran. Pearls, presumably from the Persian Gulf, appear to have been fashionable from a much earlier date, but few have survived. D (largest pearl) 0.5cm

144–50 A selection of the major items of gold jewellery from the Oxus Treasure (*c.* 5th–4th century BC).

144 (top left) is a torc; its present arrangement, twisted into three rings, may be a modern alteration; it should probably be a single ring, worn around the neck. The terminals are in the form of goats' heads.

145 (centre top) is an elaborately embossed and chased ornament, representing a stylised griffin. The griffin is still identifiable, but its tail ends in a leaf, while its legs, which are bent without regard for anatomy, end in hooves rather than claws. It was originally inlaid. Two pins, presumably for attachment, extend horizontally from the back. The function of this unique object is unclear, but it may have been designed to fasten a turban.

The finger-ring (**146**, centre front) was originally inlaid; it represents in openwork a highly stylised and distorted lion.

The remaining four pieces are bracelets; three are evidently Persian in inspiration, though possibly locally made; their animal-head terminals are in the form of lions (**147**), rams (**148**), and ducks (**149**). **148** has turquoise inlay in the applied cloisons. The fourth bracelet (**150**) shows the adaptation of a Persian motif to the requirements of nomadic art; the bracelet is cast and chased to represent two stylised griffins, their tails interlocked at the back of the hoop while their heads form the ends. D (**144**) 8.6cm

CHAPTER SIX

China
Celtic Europe
Mexico and Peru

600 BC–AD 600

China

Personal ornaments were made in China as early as the Neolithic period (*c.* 5000 BC), and perhaps even before. Small pendants of bone, pierced for threading on a cord, have been found at several sites, including the early Neolithic settlement of Panpocun near Xi'an in Shaanxi province. Later Neolithic cultures established in south-east China from about 3000 BC employed finely polished jade pendants and beads for personal adornment. Thus a Chinese pre-occupation with polished precious stones was established early and has continued without interruption until the present day.

Jade is the name given to two minerals, nephrite and jadeite. Sources of nephrite near Lake Baikal to the north of Mongolia and at Khotan in the Tarim basin to the north of Tibet are well defined. It is not known, however, whether the Chinese obtained jade from these distant sources in the Neolithic or Early Historic periods. Whatever its source, jade was widely used for ornaments throughout the periods of domination of the great dynasties of the Shang (*c.* 1700–1050 BC) and Zhou (*c.* 1050–221 BC). As many of these jade ornaments seem to have had some purpose other than the simply decorative they are illustrated in Chapter 16. Bone hairpins, how-

152 A silver belt-plaque in the shape of a crouching pony, from the Ordos region of China (3rd–2nd century BC). The stylised ears, mane and hooves are cast as sunken droplets. On the underside of the hollow plaque is an impression of a coarse textile. A hook above the mouth is part of the belt fastening. The art of the nomadic peoples of the Ordos area, which lies north of the Great Wall and borders Mongolia, reflects their concern with horses and hunting, and shows important relationships with the work of peoples living further to the west.
L 13.5cm

154

153

155

Three Chinese belt-hooks. The jade piece (**153**) dates to the Eastern Zhou or Han period (3rd–1st century BC). The hook is a simplified dragon's head; there is a rectangular stud on the lower side for attachment. Burial has altered the dark green, grey-flecked jade in places to white.

The bronze belt-hook (**154**) dates from the Han dynasty (3rd–1st century BC). Each of the two sections inlaid with turquoise represents a fish between two confronted birds. A small dragon's head forms the hook.

Also of the Han dynasty (2nd–1st century BC) is the gilt-bronze belt-hook (**155**) with an inlay of white jade in the shape of a coiled dragon. Another dragon's head forms the hook, and a round stud lies behind the oval body.

L (**154**) 24.5cm

ever, excavated in large numbers from the capital of the Shang dynasty at Anyang, were clearly decorative. Such hair ornaments were to remain an essential component of Chinese jewellery down to the twentieth century.

Personal ornaments of gold, silver or gilt-bronze appeared rather later. These bright precious metals seem to have become popular with the Chinese following their contact with nomadic peoples living on their northern and western borders. These peoples fashioned personal and harness ornaments in the shape of animals. A belt-buckle, third to second century BC, of silver cast in the shape of a crouching pony or mule was made by the peoples living in the Ordos area, a desert region within the northern loop of the Yellow River. Such Far Eastern animal-shaped buckles or harness ornaments are the equivalent of the golden ornaments made by the Scythians or more easterly groups of nomads living in south Siberia, some of whose fine gold plaques were owned by Peter the Great and are now in the Hermitage Museum in Leningrad.

The Chinese seem to have adopted the belt-hook from the nomads to fasten belts from which swords were suspended, a weapon that they likewise borrowed from their war-like neighbours. Occasionally made of gold or silver, these belt-fastenings were often finely cast in bronze and embellished with gilding and with inlays of semi-precious stones. While the interest in most forms of cast bronze declined at the end of the Zhou period, much attention was paid to varied decorative effects in these belt ornaments.

In later centuries belt-hooks were replaced by buckles, also borrowed from China's nomadic neighbours. From the second or third centuries AD belts decorated with plaques of gilt bronzes or of precious stones were essential items of male dress and will be more fully illustrated in later chapters. JMR

Celtic Europe

Throughout Celtic or pre-Roman Iron Age Europe there is a measure of uniformity in jewellery, and grave finds show that most corpses had been fully dressed and ornamented. The most universal piece of Celtic jewellery is the brooch, a functional cloak-fastener worn on one or both shoulders and found from Ireland to Turkey. It operates as a safety-pin, with the pin secured in a catch-plate at the foot of the brooch; a bow links the foot and the spring. Brooches were made in gold, silver and iron, but most

158

157

156

Left A group of brooches from the Iron Age cemetery at Hallstatt (Upper Austria). **156** is of cast bronze and dates from the Late Hallstatt period (6th century BC). On top of the bow are set a pair of horns and a pair of wheels – the wheels were made separately and riveted on. This brooch is of the 'perambulator' variety of a type in fashion in northern Italy, whence it was probably exported to Hallstatt.

157 is a silver brooch of a North Italic type (Early Iron Age, *c.* 6th century BC). The foot turns back in a stylised ram's head, with horns added in the filigree technique.

158, a bronze brooch modelled as a dog barking at or about to bite an unconcerned duck, is one of a small group of *Tierfibeln*, brooches with animals modelled in the round, known from 5th-century BC contexts in Central Europe. This badly corroded example is unusual in depicting a scene rather than a single animal. L (**156**) 5.9cm

commonly in bronze. They were usually cast in one piece, one end being worked and drawn into the spring and pin. The bow and foot provided obvious fields for decoration and even inlay ornament; precious coral from the Mediterranean was a popular form of inlay from the fifth to the third centuries BC and red glass was also used.

Changes in shape and decoration of brooches give a guide to Iron Age chronology, with the development of the foot providing a particularly useful typological sequence. In the sixth and fifth centuries BC the catch-plate often ended in an upright decorative finial (on a bronze brooch from Hallstatt in Upper Austria the finial is modelled as a duck). From the fifth to the third century this foot was turned back towards the bow; then, in the third and second centuries, it was clasped to the bow by a collar. Eventually, in the first century BC, it came to be cast in one piece with the bow. The names of two important sites are used to label the main divisions of Iron Age chronology in Europe: Hallstatt (from a huge cemetery in

Above right This group of brooches serves to illustrate the complexity of the vast range of types in use during the La Tène period. The silver brooch (**159**), one of a pair dating from the 5th–4th centuries BC, is of a variety developed from the 6th century in northern Italy and disseminated to the Alpine regions and further north, where local varieties were developed from the 5th century BC. The pin curves down at the point and has a barely perceptible constriction on its upper side 6.5cm from the point, apparently to hinder the brooch from falling out should it accidentally open when in use.

160, a bronze Early La Tène brooch (*c.* 400 BC), is a fine specimen of one of

158

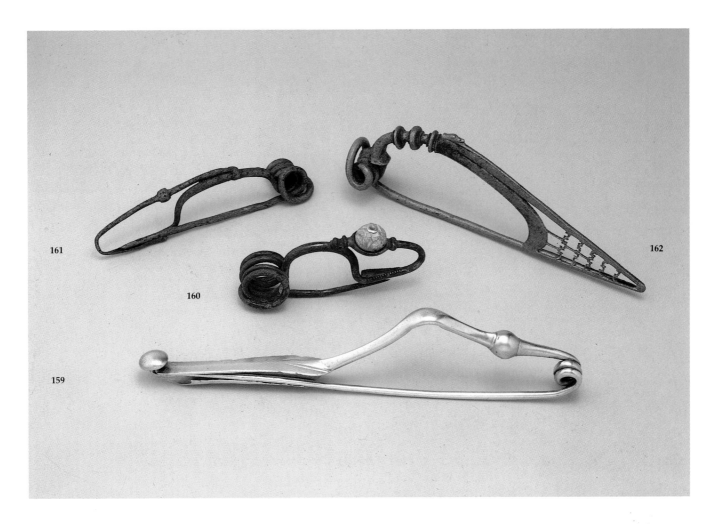

the most widespread types of La Tène brooches, found as far apart as Britain and Austria. It is decorated by a bone stud attached by a gold rivet to a setting on the foot; there is chased ribbing on the catchplate.

161 is of wrought iron; it comes from the type-site of La Tène itself and dates to the Middle La Tène period (3rd and 2nd century BC). It was made in a single piece, with the end of the foot bent round to clasp the bow.

162, of bronze (mid-1st century BC), is a particularly ornate and rare type of Late La Tène brooch normally found along the southern fringes of the Alps in south Switzerland, north Italy and west Slovenia. Details of the decoration include a duck's head at the crest of the bow. L (**159**) 16.8cm

Upper Austria) and La Tène (from a site on the shores of Lake Neuchâtel in Switzerland).

Finger-rings and toe-rings were rarely worn, although, exceptionally, finger-rings were elaborately fashioned in gold. Far more common are bracelets. These are usually quite simple and employ a variety of fastening devices: the most common is a simple opening on one side. Most are made of bronze, but bracelets in other materials are known: a gold bracelet was found with the Snettisham Treasure (see below), and a hoard of silver objects from Córdoba in Spain included two fine bracelets with animal- or snake-head terminals. A related type is the 'massive armlet', which is only found in Scotland. These armlets, usually found in pairs, are cast in bronze using the *cire-perdue* (lost-wax) technique and are often decorated with enamel or glass ornament on the terminals.

Occasionally it is possible to trace changes in fashion, and variations from one area to another. Thus in Champagne (north-east France) in the fifth and fourth centuries BC it was customary for women to wear a pair of bracelets, one on each arm, whereas in the third and second centuries a single bracelet was more usual. In Switzerland throughout this period pairs of bracelets were worn as well as pairs of anklets. But such information is available only from inhumation burials, and only then when the skeleton was fully dressed as in life. Burial rites changed over the course of time and

Top left **163** A detail from the silver Gundestrup cauldron, found in a bog in Jutland and dating from the early Iron Age. The cauldron is embossed inside and out with figures of gods and goddesses, fantastic animals, and a sacrificial scene. Torcs are worn by all of the goddesses and some of the gods. This detail, from the inside of the cauldron, shows an antler-horned god wearing a torc round his neck and holding another in his hand.

Bottom left **164** Cast-bronze torc of the Early La Tène period (*c.* 4th century BC) from a grave at Courtisols (dép. Marne, France). The three circular collars on either side of the terminals are ornamented with sinuous grooves. D (max) 14.9cm

Below **165** Detail of another Early La Tène cast-bronze torc, also from Courtisols (dép. Marne, France). On the hoop on either side of the buffer terminals is a pair of highly stylised human faces framed by fleshy s-scrolls in relief. D (terminals) 3.3cm

from place to place, and in some areas at some times they have left no trace, while elsewhere cremation was in vogue.

One distinctive item of Iron Age jewellery is the metal torc, or neck-ring, which is found in graves and hoards and is also mentioned in Classical literature. It can range from a simple undecorated iron ring to an elaborate gold version made of multiple twisted strands with magnificently decorated cast terminals, such as the Snettisham Great Torc. Most torcs were made of bronze, and by and large they seem to have been a female ornament. But in some areas bead necklaces of glass and amber were preferred, and many female graves have produced

174

166 Cast-bronze torc (*c.* 4th century BC) from Pleurs (dép. Marne, France) . A type of torc worn by high-ranking women in Champagne in the Early La Tène period. The hoop is made in two pieces; a detachable segment can be removed by forcing open the torc. This section is held in place by a mortise-and-tenon joint at each end (see detail, *right*). D 19.2cm

neither beads nor torcs. According to Classical writers, Celtic warriors wore torcs in battle, but it is rare for a warrior's grave to include one.

Britain, and especially East Anglia, has seen the discovery of a number of spectacular gold torcs, but they have never been found in burials. One of the most impressive finds comes from a field at Snettisham in Norfolk, where between 1948 and 1990 eleven separate hoards of gold and electrum objects were found, including the remains of at least 150 torcs. It may be that all the hoards were deposited at the same time, and represent the stock of a metalworker dispersed and buried for safe-keeping. Some of the gold torcs may have been intended for the gods, but one at least seems to have been worn by a queen – Boudicca, Queen of the Iceni (in Norfolk) wore 'a large golden necklace', according to Dio Cassius.   IS

Above **167** Silver Early La Tène finger-ring (*c*. 3rd century BC), excavated at an Iron Age settlement on Park Brow, near Worthing, Sussex (England). Since this type of ring – an oval hoop bent to a U-shape – is found predominantly in Switzerland, this specimen, the only known one from Britain, was probably imported from there. Objects of silver were very rare in Britain before the 1st century BC. D 1.8cm

Left Two brooches of the Iberian Iron Age. **168**, of bronze (*c*. 3rd century BC), is a variety of brooch characteristic of the Iron Age Duero culture. The territory of this culture coincided more or less with the basin of the River Duero in north-western Spain and northern Portugal. The bow and foot are cast in one piece. The decoration on the foot and its terminal was executed with a ring-punch. The ends of the six-coil spring are covered by hollowed biconical terminals, which are held to the spring by a rivet; this also secures the spring to a loop at the head of the bow.

169 is silver and parcel-gilt (2nd–1st century BC). Its foot is turnèd back and the terminal, shaped like the head and neck of a horse, is soldered to the bow; two further horses are clamped on top of the foot. A metal rod projecting from the head of the bow secures the arms, which are also adorned with horse-head terminals; the rod is ornamented with beasties. This is a rare type,

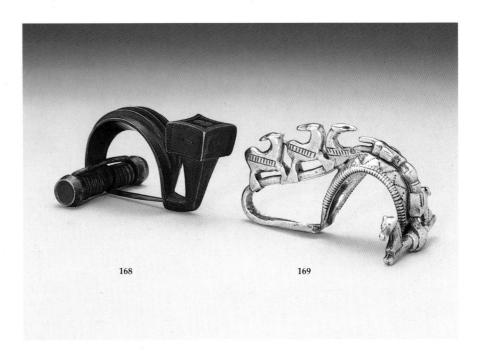

168   169

though parallels to it have been found in hoards of silver from southern and eastern Spain. L (**169**) 6.7cm

Right **170** Jewellery from a hoard of silver objects (*c*. 100 BC), found at Córdoba (Spain) in 1915. This is one of many silver hoards – comprising jewellery, coinage, ingots, and vessels – buried in Iberia during the 3rd–1st centuries BC. The torc has biconical mouldings on the hoop and biconical terminals, and chased decoration.

One of the bracelets is a plain hoop with very worn snake-head terminals. The second is a broad hoop with

animal-head terminals, simply modelled, largely by chasing alone. Four ridges decorate the outside of the hoop, the inner two obliquely nicked with a tracer.

The coiled armlet consists of two silver rods swelling in thickness towards the centre, twisted together with two twisted wires. Most of the wire is now missing. When found, this piece had two perforated coins, each linked by a length of chain to one of the loop-terminals. This item may originally have been a neck-ring and only later coiled up. w (torc) 16.2cm

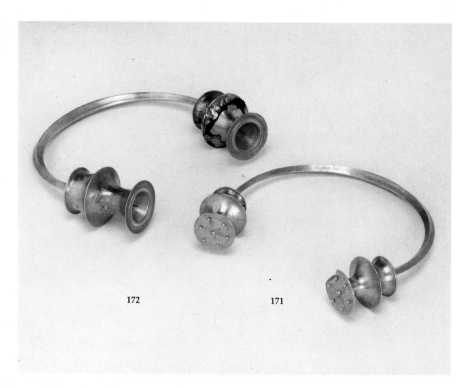

172   171

Left Two gold torcs from Iberia (2nd–1st century BC). Their similar hollow terminals of sheet gold are slotted onto diamond-sectioned rods. The terminals of **171** are stamped with a design of a six-petalled rosette; the terminals of **172** have a conical indentation, with a spike rising from the base of each. Torcs of this type belong to the Galician Castro Culture of north-western Iberia, which probably developed in the mid-1st millennium BC and lasted until the Roman Conquest in the 1st century BC. The Celts are generally considered to have arrived in Iberia from France early in the 1st millennium BC.
W (172) 15.5cm

Top right **174** The Snettisham Great Torc: a Late Iron Age torc (1st century BC), found on Ken Hill, Snettisham, Norfolk (England), in 1950. The hoop is composed of eight strands of electrum twisted together, each strand being made up of eight twisted wires. The hollow ring-terminals are soldered to the hoops. The relief decoration on the terminals would have been cast with the terminals themselves, but details have been added by chasing. This piece was found with a gold bracelet and part of another torc; a small coin was found in the torc. D 19.5cm

Bottom right Two North British Iron Age armlets (1st–2nd century AD). Each is one of a pair found in Scotland. They were cast complete as hoops with relief ornament. The open terminals of both pairs are decorated with roundels inlaid with red and yellow champlevé enamel. The bronze armlets (**175**) were found at Castle Newe, Strathdon, Aberdeenshire; they retain only one of the panels, decorated with a chequer pattern. The brass armlets, found at Pitkelloney Farm, near Drummond Castle, Perthshire (**176**) still have all four roundels: on one armlet the two panels have a cruciform design; on the other armlet a four-lobed rosette. D (**175**, max.) 14.6cm

Above **173** A detail of a terminal of one of the Ipswich torcs (2nd–1st century BC). Six Late Iron Age gold-alloy torcs were found in two hoards at Ipswich, Suffolk (England). This example is one of five found together in 1968, each wrought from two faceted rods twisted together. The cast-on loop-terminals are decorated with ornament in relief, with some chased or engraved detailing. Although the sixth torc was found separately in 1970, all may have been buried as one hoard.

175

176

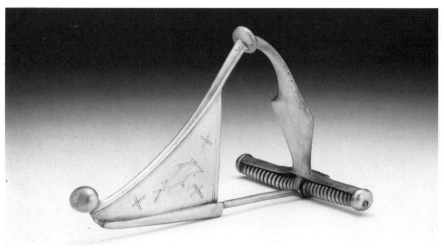

Left **178** A Pannonian silver brooch from Székesfehérvár (Hungary), of the 1st century AD. On the front of the arched bow, just below the collar, are pair of chased 'eyes'. The catch-plate is ornamented on both faces in pointillé technique – one side has a fish, possibly a dolphin, and the other a snake. The long spring has 15 coils on each side, and is protected by domed caps. This extremely rare type of brooch is closely matched in only one other find: a 1st-century AD hoard containing a silver armlet and 17 silver brooches of this type from Okorág. As both Okorág and Székesfehérvár lie in the eastern part of the Roman province of Pannonia, it is likely that these brooches were made in the same workshop in eastern Pannonia. L 12.7cm

Mexico and Peru

From the civilisations of the Andes region to the Aztec, Mixtec and Maya of South and Central Mexico, bodily adornments echo the profound metaphysical notions of these peoples. Not only does the spirituality of the ornamentation reveal itself in many of the elements of the designs, but it also pervades the material of which the objects are manufactured and at least partly determines the technique of their production.

Objects used for personal adornment date back to well before the birth of Christ but the materials used differ considerably between South and Middle America. The Olmec (200 BC–AD 300), the earliest

Left **177** An electrum torc from the Snettisham Treasure (1st century BC). This torc, found alone in 1950, is made of two round bars twisted together. The ends of the bars are coiled into circular loop-terminals, and a coiled, tapered strip of electrum is threaded through one of these. D 21.2cm

high civilisation of Mexico, occupied a territory which corresponds to the south of the present-day state of Veracruz and Tabasco. The ceremonial centres of La Venta, Tres Zapotes and San Lorenzo are the first examples of monumental architecture which influenced the styles of subsequent cultures. Similarly, their intellectual achievements in the use of a calendrical system and hieroglyphic script prefigure later preoccupation found throughout all Mesoamerican cultures. The Olmec lapidaries were exceptionally skilled in the working of jadeite, nephrite and serpentine. Caches of highly polished celts are found, as well as large ceremonial axes, masks, pendants, ear-flares and so-called stilettos of jade associated with the ritual letting of blood. In both small carvings and monumental sculptures an anthropomorphic jaguar is a persistent theme, while highly stylised reptilian monsters and birds occur to a lesser degree. Such representations suggest a religious significance and may depict deities related to the earth, rain and fertility.

Unlike Middle America, the adjacent cultures in the Andean region had developed techniques to work gold and silver into representations of deities not dissimilar from those of the Olmec; Chavin (1200–300 BC) ornamentation incorporates the feline motif, sometimes hiding behind an eagle mask, sometimes framed by serpents.

A certain continuity between this earlier period and the later cultural development of the associated regions can be identified. The Mochica of the North Coastal region of Peru (*c.* AD 300–800) inherited much of the intellectual acumen and technological skills of the Chavin period. The Mochica built large ceremonial centres, the best known of which is at Moche itself, where two vast pyramids –

179 An Olmec jade pendant from Mexico (1000–100 BC). It is carved in high relief in the form of a human head; the nasal septum is pierced. Two glyphs are incised on the panel to the left of the head, and traces of four more can just be seen, two on either side at the extreme edges of the broken panel. These may not be contemporary with the original carving. The rounded depressions which appear below the saw cuts representing the eyes are secondary workings and thus alter the original character of the face. H 10.5cm

the Huaca del Sol, probably consecrated as a temple, and the Huaca de la Luna, the possible residence of a ruler or priest – rise up out of the now arid valley. Most of our knowledge of Mochica society is derived from the pottery vessels found in cemeteries together with Mochica artifacts worked in gold, silver, copper, bone and shell. Metalworking techniques were varied, but the Mochica possessed an elaborate knowledge and technical mastery of hammering and embossing, hammering around moulds, stretching and shaping with repeated annealing, soldering, sheathing and inlaying, plating and the casting of both solid and hollow objects. Hollow casting was achieved by the *cire-perdue* (or lost-wax) method.

In the earliest time metallurgy was less developed on the south coast of Peru than elsewhere and metal casting was unknown until the end of the Nazca period. The Nazca (200 BC–AD 600) are best known for their elaborately decorated polychrome pottery. As in other regions of Peru, the decoration of ceramics, textiles and metal ornaments made use of a common repertoire of motifs, the chief of which are so-called cat-demons, stylised birds, fish, as well as animal designs, human figures and severed human heads. Most of the personal ornaments found in graves are made from hammered and cut gold. They include masks and mouth-masks which covered only the bottom half of the face.   AS

180 A mosaic pendant of the Nazca people, Peru (200 BC–AD 600). It consists of half of a bivalve shell of the *Spondylus* family decorated in mosaic with an anthropomorphic figure wearing a pectoral and a head-dress. The face is carved in bone; the mouth and eyes are of pearl shell. The rest of the mosaic consists of different coloured shells, malachite and black stones, fastened with a wax-like substance. Two perforations near the hinge are threaded with a spun string of cotton for suspension. W 12.5cm

Gold jewellery of the Nazca people, Peru (200 BC–AD 600). The bracelet (**181**), made from a sheet of hammered and cut gold, has repoussé decoration in the form of geometrical shapes and feline motifs. There is a perforation at each side of the bracelet.

The semicircular nose ornament, or 'mouth-mask' (**182**), is also cut out of hammered gold, and is further decorated with repoussé motifs.

Photographed with the jewellery is a Nazca polychrome pottery vessel (**183**), depicting a mythological animal wearing a mouth-mask from the same period. w (**182**) 13.5cm

184 A mosaic ear ornament of the Mochica, Peru (AD 300–800). It consists of a hollow wooden plug and matrix, decorated with a mosaic of pearl shell and different coloured stones. The mosaic, which is secured with a resin-like substance, is in the form of a human figure wearing an elaborate head-dress. D 10.5cm

Illustrated with the ornament is a vessel in the form of a seated human figure wearing ear-flares and a gold nose ornament (**185**). His elaborate head-dress is decorated with the head of a monkey.

CHAPTER SEVEN

The Mediterranean, Parthia, India, Egypt Roman Britain and Byzantium

325 BC–AD 600

Hellenistic

The so-called Hellenistic Age lasted from about 325 BC until the inauguration of the Roman Empire in 27 BC. The conquests of Alexander the Great between 333 and 322 BC completely transformed the Greek world. Vast new territories of the former Persian Empire were Hellenised by settlements of Greeks, and Greece in return was exposed to influences from the newly conquered territories of Egypt and Western Asia.

As far as jewellery is concerned, the most important factor is the far greater quantity of surviving material, thanks to the greater availability of gold. For the first time since the Bronze Age, gold was plentiful in Greece, partly because of the intensive mining operations in Thrace initiated by Philip II, but mostly from the dissemination of the captured Persian treasures. The general appearance of the jewellery was at first much as before, but by the early second century BC new forms took their place beside the old, and the system of decoration soon radically changed. Then, for about two centuries, there was little further change.

The principal innovations took place in three areas: new decorative motifs, new forms of jewellery, and new systems of decoration. The beginning of the period saw the introduction of the so-called Heracles-knot (the reef knot), which retained its popularity as an ornament for jewellery into Roman times. It may be presumed to have come from Egypt, where its history as an amulet goes back to the beginning of the second millennium BC (see **16**). The crescent was another foreign import, introduced from Western Asia, where it had a high antiquity and whence it had already reached Greece in the eighth and seventh centuries BC. In its homeland it was sacred to the moon-god. It is found in Hellenistic necklaces as a pendant; although its purpose was doubtless primarily decorative, it must have had a certain amuletic value. Of purely Greek motifs, figures of Eros (the god of Love) and Nike (the goddess of Victory) are among the most popular, as in all Hellenistic art.

Among the new forms came, about 325 BC, the animal- or human-headed hoop-earrings from the repertoire of Achaemenid Persian

189

206

186–8 A group of Hellenistic Greek gold jewellery. **186** (top) is a diadem (only a detail is shown here), dating to the 3rd century BC; it was found on the island of Melos. It is made up of three twisted gold bands, the middle one of which is decorated with rosettes. The reef-knot in the centre is richly enamelled and has a large cabochon garnet.

187 (centre) is the central part of a diadem (2nd century BC). The reef-knot is inlaid with garnets, and the flanking squares of goldwork are decorated with enamel and filigree.

The necklace (**188**, bottom) is from Taormina, Sicily (2nd century BC); its crescent-shaped pendant is decorated with filigree and inlaid with garnets.
L (**187**) 8.6cm

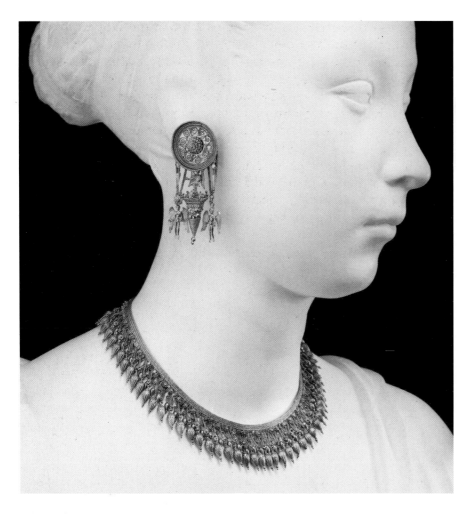

189–90 Hellenistic Greek jewellery. The earring (**189**) is one of a pair found at Kyme, on the east coast of modern Turkey (4th–3rd century BC). It is richly decorated with filigree. On the pendant, an inverted pyramid, sits a figure of Victory, and two other Victories hang by chains from the earring's disc.

The necklace (**190**) is from the island Melos (3rd century BC). The necklace strap has pendants in the shape of miniature gold jars (or flower-buds), each hanging from five chains; where the chains cross are small enamelled discs. H (**189**) 6.5cm

jewellery and these also remained popular in certain regions till the Roman period. Diadems, frequently with a Heracles-knot as a centre-piece, are first found about 300 BC and lasted for about two centuries (see **186** and **187**). Bracelets in the same general style were also made, doubtless to accompany the diadems.

New types of necklaces are also found, of which chains with animal-head finials and straps with pendants of buds or spearheads are the most important. Such necklaces are mentioned in temple inventories from Delos of the early third century BC. Beads not threaded but linked together are, however, more typical of the second and first centuries BC.

The most important technical innovation, which transformed the appearance of Greek jewellery, is the polychromy provided by the inlay of stones and coloured glass. Of the stones, chalcedonies, cornelians and above all garnets (from India) were in use from 325 BC onwards. In the second and first centuries BC we also find emeralds and amethysts from Egypt and small seed-pearls from the Red Sea. RH

Roman

In the early history of Rome jewellery was one of those luxuries under official disapproval, and consequently surviving examples are very scarce. However, with the inauguration of the Empire in 27 BC and the annexation by Rome of most of the Hellenistic world, the old austerity was quickly put aside. In artistic matters Rome was always deeply in the debt of Greece, and the jewellery of the early Empire was, in many respects, simply a continuation of Hellenistic. Gradually, however, certain other influences – Late Etruscan and Western Asiatic in particular – made themselves felt, and by the end of this period much Roman jewellery was an anticipation of the Byzantine style which was to follow (see pp. 97–100).

Jewellery at the beginning of this period was essentially of gold. Towards the end of the period, however, an increasing emphasis was placed on precious and semi-precious stones for their own sake, and less pains were taken over the working of the gold in which they were set. Now for the first time the very hardest stones were

A group of Roman jewellery. **191** is from Rome (1st century AD). The necklace chain is set with garnets; the butterfly-shaped pendant has an oval garnet for its head, a circular sapphire for its body and two white stones for its wings.

The second necklace (**192**) is of the 2nd century AD, its gold links with their cut-out patterns alternate with emerald crystals. L 41.6

193 is a hair ornament from Tunis, North Africa (3rd century AD). It is inlaid with emeralds and has pearls around its border; the pendants are pearls and a sapphire. H (**193**) 10.7cm

193

192

191

194 A portrait, painted in encaustic on a wooden panel, of a young woman, from Hawara, Egypt (2nd century AD). Despite the painting's Egyptian origin, the woman is depicted wearing types of jewellery common throughout the Roman world. Her gold earrings are each set with three beads; a black stone between two pearls. Of her two necklaces, one is of green and red gemstones; the other is of gold and has a pendant set with a green stone. Her hair is arranged in the elaborate style typical of this period and is held in place with a gold pin. This painting is one of a series of realistic portraits of men, women and children found with mummies of the Roman period in Egypt.

195 A gold bracelet in the form of a coiled snake (Roman, 1st century AD). D (external) 8.2cm

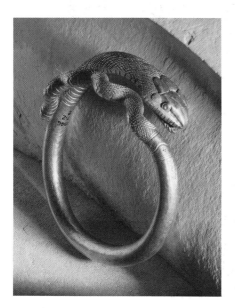

used; diamonds occasionally, although uncut; sapphires; and above all emeralds from the newly discovered Egyptian mines in the Red Sea hills, which were used in the natural hexagonal prisms in which these stones are found.

One form of goldworking was, however, popular towards the end of this period, and that is a kind of metal-fretwork, called by the Romans *opus interrasile*, in which patterns are cut out of sheet gold with a chisel. The ensuing lace-like effect is something new in ancient jewellery, and brings out the quality of the gold. This process was to be further developed by Byzantine jewellery. Inlaying was still practised. Coloured stones and glass were cemented to the gold background, usually surrounded by gold cloisons. Enamel was rarely used, except in the Celtic areas, and a related form of decoration, niello, made its first appearance.

The chief centres of production were probably Alexandria and Antioch, and also Rome itself, whither many craftsmen had migrated from the Greek East. We have evidence that goldsmiths and silver-smiths were now organised in guilds like medieval craftsmen. Their workmanship, though skilled, falls short of the high standards maintained by the Hellenistic goldsmiths.

It is difficult to give a date for the end of the Roman period (although a reasonable date would be AD 313, the year of the Edict of Milan, the official recognition of Christianity by the Emperor Constantine), and in any case such a distinction would be artificial, for Late Antique and Byzantine jewellery developed without a break from the Late Roman tradition.   RH

Parthia

The eastern part of Alexander the Great's empire eventually came to be loosely controlled, in principle, by the Parthian dynasty of northern Iran, which lasted from about 250 BC to AD 230. In some respects, however, the Parthian Empire was still part of the Hellenistic world, and its jewellery reflects the existence of strong contacts between east and west. There are a few pieces in the British Museum, but the appearance of this jewellery may best be judged, perhaps, from the portrait busts showing the women of rich trading families resident in the caravan city of Palmyra in the Syrian desert (see **196**).

Meanwhile, on the borders of the Parthian and Roman empires, the region of Georgia had its own distinctive culture. Among the finds are bronze belt-clasps, showing stylised animals; these may

196 A portrait bust of a woman, from a tomb at Palmyra, a largely autonomous oasis city on the border of the Roman province of Syria. The principal families of Palmyra were greatly enriched by the city's flourishing trade between the Roman Empire in the west and the Parthian and Sasanian empires in the east. The stone portraits which the leading Palmyrene families placed in their tombs amply illustrate their wealth: the ladies are richly bedecked with chains, necklaces, earrings, hair ornaments, diadems and finger-rings.

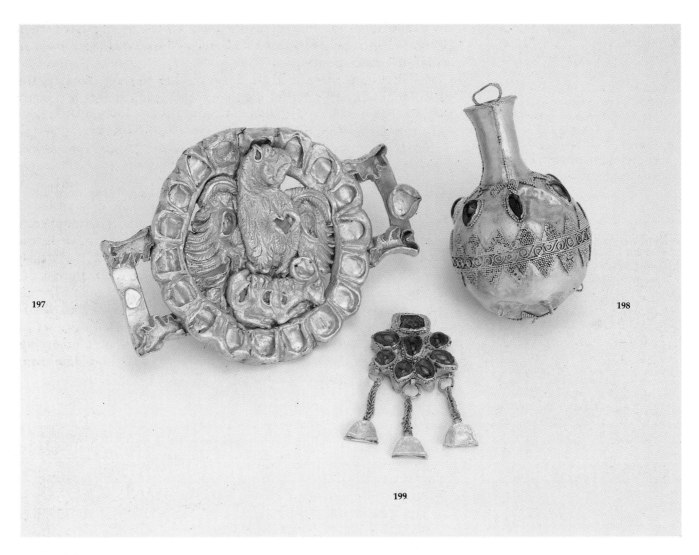

197

198

199

Left **200** A cast-bronze belt-clasp from Georgia (*c.* 200 BC–AD 250). The stylised openwork decoration represents a horse with a bull above its back, a bird between its legs and another dog-like animal in front, with a spiral infill. A hook is attached on the reverse, in front of the horse, and a loop behind. Bronze belt-clasps of this distinctive kind have only been found in Georgia. W 13.8cm

Top Parthian gold jewellery. The buckle (**197**), from the Nihavand area in Iran (*c.* 1st century BC–1st century AD) is embossed and chased to show an eagle gripping a young goat. The inlay, mostly now lost, is of turquoise and another stone. Buckles of this kind may have been used for fastening belts or cloaks, though they may have come from horse harness. This is one of a pair found in a hoard which may have belonged to a principal noble family of Parthia, the Karens; its pair is in the Metropolitan Museum of Art, New York.

198 and **199** are earring pendants, both inlaid with garnets (**199** also has inlay of another material). The vase-shaped pendant (**198**) has seven loops, which would have been hung with extra pendants, probably representing bells and pomegranates. H (**198**) 6.67cm

imitate plaques of thin gold or silver which would have been decorated with twisted wire and filigree and nailed at the corners to wood or leather backings.

The Parthians were succeeded by another Persian dynasty, the Sasanians, who lasted until the coming of Islam. There are many magnificent works of art, in gold and silver, from the Sasanian Empire (AD 224–642), but its jewellery is poorly represented in the British Museum; a signet-ring of agate, however, is from this period.

JER

India

Jewellery has long played an important role in the Indian subcontinent. Evidence for personal adornment appears early, as on terracotta figurines of the Mother-goddess in Pakistan of the fourth millennium BC. In the north-west the great Harappan culture complex of the Indus Valley (2300–1700 BC) has yielded quantities of jewellery, including beads of precious metals, faience and semi-precious stones. In southern India spectacular jewellery occurs in graves of the later first millennium BC. The finds accompanying burials in the Nilgiri Hills, to the south of Mysore, may date from the same or a slightly later period.

Above (**201**) and *right* (**202**) Gold ornaments excavated from burials in the Nilgiri Hills, southern India (100 BC–AD 300). The burials also included other gold pendants, pearled circular beads, earrings, a ribbed bead, a crushed circlet, chains and floral ornaments, silver finger-rings and etched cornelian beads. D (**200**) 2.2cm; W (**201**) 2.5cm

Below right **203** Gold flowers with centres of sapphire, strung on modern wire with gold conch shells. These pieces, possibly dating to the early centuries AD, were excavated in 1881 from in front of the throne in the Temple of the Enlightenment (Mahabodhi), Bodh Gaya, Bihar (India); they were found in a ball of clay containing other gold ornaments, coins, silver objects and a quantity of precious stones. D (flowers) 2cm

The flourishing urban centre of Taxila, once a great city of Gandhara but apparently insignificant by the seventh century, was enriched by trade and foreign influences around the start of the Christian era. The site has yielded magnificent and well-preserved gold jewellery, notably necklaces, ear-pendants and finger-rings, characterised by a mastery of granulation and inlay. Stones used for inlay were variously cut and engraved and etched beads occur abundantly here and elsewhere. Some of the Taxila finds have affinities with the Iranian world and through it with the traditions of the Asian steppes. As Indian funerary custom turned almost universally to cremation, jewellery deposited in Buddhist shrines of the early centuries of the Christian era becomes an important source of information. An eight-sided talisman box found in a *stupa* is clearly of the kind worn by Buddhist deities familiar from sculpture. *Stupas* were solid domed structures often with a relic chamber in which personal remains were enshrined, along with articles of jewellery, in boxes of precious metals made by techniques in which the jeweller's art is fully exercised.

Inevitably much precious jewellery has not survived, but sculpture of deities, regally adorned, tells much about the Indian use of adornment. As Hindu and Buddhist sculpture developed the jewellery represented on it shows the greatest diversity and profusion; indeed, figures can sometimes appear overloaded and adornment can predominate over dress. WZ

Egypt

After the end of the New Kingdom Egypt underwent a troubled period, often termed the Third Intermediate Period, until order was restored throughout the country by Egyptianised Nubians who

204 A gold flying falcon, modelled in the round, with coloured glass inlaid in cloisons (Saite – Ptolemaic periods, *c.* 600–100 BC). Details of the head, eyes and beak are moulded and chased on the underside. The glass inlay was probably blue, green and red in colour, but is much decayed. The body must have been moulded over a core and wings and legs added separately. Each of the cloisons is separately made. This very fine piece of workmanship was presumably worn as a pectoral, although no suspension loops have survived. Wing span 14.8cm

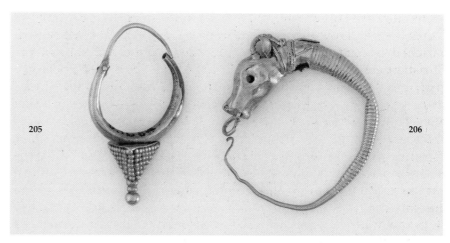

207 A gold diadem ornament from Egypt in the Roman period (1st–3rd centuries AD). Each of the eight rays or petals is separately made and soldered to a central circular base around a boss. A ring for attachment is soldered in the centre at the back. D 3.4cm

Above Two gold earrings of the Egyptian Ptolemaic period (*c.* 300–100 BC), each one of a pair. Both the pyramid-shaped pendant of 205 and the gazelle- or antelope-head terminals of 206 are forms used in Hellenistic earrings throughout the eastern Mediterranean, and are not Egyptian in origin. The body of 205 is of sheet gold; the earring is closed by inserting the swivelling wire into the open end of the crescent.

The hoop of 206 is made from gold wire twisted to form a tapering coil, the end of which hooks into the ring in the mouth of the animal. The head is hollow; the twisted wire horns were soldered on separately. D (206, hoop, external) 2.6cm

Right 208–9 Two Egyptian gold bangles of the Ptolemaic or Roman periods (*c.* 100 BC–AD 300). 208 (top), one of a pair, is made of gold wire twisted around a central wire (possibly bronze). The snake's head terminals appear to be hollow cast and were slipped over the ends of the wires.

209 (bottom) is made from two pieces of thin sheet gold twisted together; two long pieces of wire are soldered at the ends and twisted together in a complicated fashion. D (209, external) 8.3cm

ruled as the Twenty-fifth Dynasty (*c.* 747–656 BC). Apart from the splendid bracelets, collars, pectorals and finger-rings found in the royal burials at Tanis, which really belong in form and inspiration to the late New Kingdom, hardly any jewellery except that of the poorest kind from provincial cemeteries has survived. Information can only be gleaned from contemporary sculpture, relief and painting which show jewellery being worn.

To judge from pictorial evidence the succeeding Twenty-sixth Dynasty marked a return to the style and taste of earlier times; unfortunately few pieces of jewellery can be dated definitely to this period. Only signet-rings bearing the names of known personages can be said to be indisputably Saite. However, an elaborately inlaid gold pectoral in the form of a falcon may date from this period.

The glass industry revived under the Ptolemies and provided the material for multicoloured beads, amulets and bangles which the Egyptians continued to wear throughout the Graeco-Roman Period. The wearing of earrings had largely died out by the Saite Period, but during the Ptolemaic Period it returned with forms frequently found throughout the Hellenistic world: pyramid-shaped pendants such as those found on earrings of the Hellenistic period throughout the eastern Mediterranean area, and earrings with animal-head terminals are widely spread in the eastern Mediterranean world during the fourth to first centuries BC. Those with antelope- or gazelle-heads are apparently not Egyptian in origin and date more precisely to the fourth and early third centuries BC. Although cloisonné work remains excellent, the emphasis is on unadorned gold; gold bracelets and bangles made from quite untraditional strip-twisted wire and gold diadem ornaments of Greek origin are often indistinguishable from Hellenistic or Roman work.   CA

Roman Britain

The technical and artistic standard of craftsmanship in gold and other metals was exceptionally high in Celtic society, and this native tradition made a major contribution to Romano-British jewellery. The Iron Age inhabitants of Britain were already strongly influenced by the Romanised culture of the Continent well before the invasion of AD 43, and after the Conquest the trickle of imported Roman goods became a flood. Finger-rings, chain necklaces and earrings had hardly existed in pre-Roman Britian, and when they did become common the types tended to be purely Classical ones which could be matched in any Roman province. Fibulae (safety-pin brooches), on the other hand, had existed in Britain for centuries, and while some varieties are distinctively Roman, others are British developments. A complex fusion of Celtic and Classical traits is characteristic of the whole culture of Roman Britain, and the jewellery is no exception.

The range of materials used included precious metals, base metals (copper alloys and iron), bone, jet, glass and gems. The use of silver for jewellery, rare in the Iron Age, became fairly frequent. Although many of the finer gold and silver items would have been imported, both metals were mined in Britain and were exploited by the

210–13 A group of Romano-British pins. 210 is of silver (1st–2nd century AD); its head represents a hand holding a pomegranate. This pin was found in the bed of the River Walbrook in the City of London.

211, a bone hair-pin, has its head modelled as a bust of a woman with an elaborate hairstyle fashionable in the later 1st century AD. This pin was probably made in a workshop in Roman London (*Londinium*).

212 is another silver pin (2nd–4th century AD); it was excavated in the City of London. The design of the head, Venus adjusting her sandal, is common in the Roman world, but its crude execution suggests that it is provincial work.

Another bone pin, 213 (2nd century AD), is decorated with a figure of Fortuna holding a cornucopia and a steering oar. L (212) 12.8cm

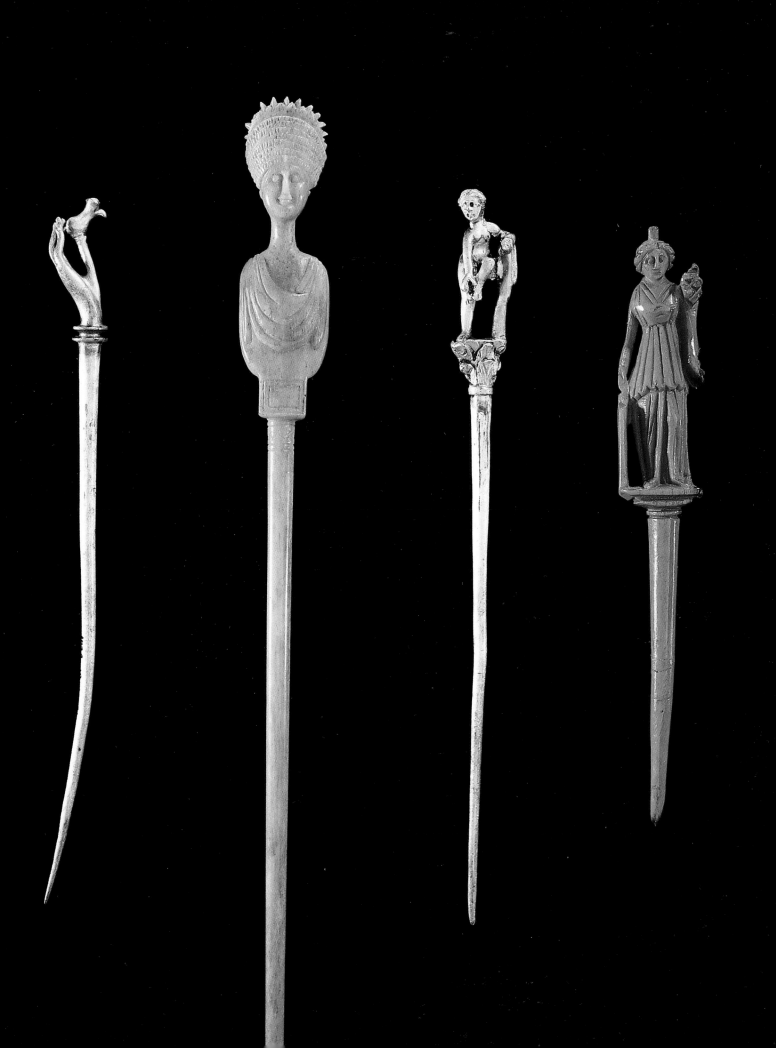

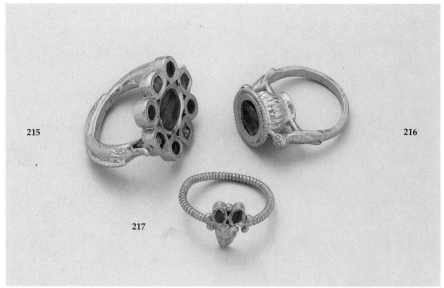

Above Three gold rings from a hoard of jewellery and silver spoons of the late 4th or early 5th century AD found at Thetford, Norfolk (England). **215** has a large bezel set with an amethyst surrounded by alternating garnets and emeralds. The shoulders are in the form of stylised dolphins.

The shoulders of **216** are in the form of woodpeckers, supporting a bezel shaped as a miniature vase which contains a green glass setting.

217 has a hoop of beaded wire; the bezel incorporates a mask of Pan or Faunus set with two garnets.

The motifs have religious significance in the pagan context of the Thetford Treasure. D (**215**, hoop, internal) 2cm

Above **214** A cast-bronze Romano-British brooch (late 1st–early 2nd century AD) with blue and white champlevé enamel. This is a type of brooch ('dragonesque') found principally in northern England and southern Scotland. Its style of ornamentation, in the Late Iron Age tradition, was developed in southern Britain in the decades preceding the Claudian invasion (AD 43), but persisted almost unchanged for decorating small objects, principally jewellery, well into the 2nd century. L 6.2cm

219 A gold crossbow brooch from the Moray Firth, Scotland (4th century AD). The brooch incorporates a screw mechanism for fastening the pin. The pointed end of the pin was inserted into a socket at the foot of the brooch; the pin-head slotted into a perforation at the back of the brooch's head. One of the three onion-shaped terminals screws into position to hold the pin in place. This is a fine example of the widespread late Roman 'crossbow' type of brooch and is richly ornamented, with an openwork running scroll on the arms, friezes of triangles inlaid with niello on the bow and foot and applied motifs on the foot. L 7.9cm

Left **218** Six gold bracelets from a hoard of Roman treasure found at Hoxne, Suffolk (England) in 1992. The treasure, one of the richest from Roman Britain, was buried early in the 5th century AD at a time when Roman rule in the province was breaking down. It comprises almost 15,000 gold and silver coins and around 200 other gold and silver objects. The twenty-nine pieces of gold jewellery include nineteen bracelets – an unprecedented number. Several are matching sets, like the pair at lower left with repoussé hunting scenes. Four are very finely made in intricate pierced work. The large ornate example is an armlet, which would have been worn on the upper arm. D (external) of largest bracelet 10.3cm

Romans shortly after the Conquest; the local manufacture of some fine-quality jewellery is a virtual certainty. The use of precious and semi-precious stones was an ancient Graeco-Roman tradition new to Britain, but enamelling on bronze was a Celtic speciality, and is often found on Romano-British ornaments, where it may display Celtic rather than Roman design traits (dragonesque brooch). The large quantities of bronze brooches and of bronze and iron finger-rings which were in use would have been made principally in Britain, as was much of the non-metallic jewellery. Bone and jet ornaments are sometimes elaborate enough to be classified as miniature sculpture.

In the latest phase of the province, at the end of the fourth century, we see the development of the universal late Antique tendency towards greater elaboration, rich surface ornament, and brilliant colour, but the presence of some stylistic details which are as yet unparalleled elsewhere emphasises the likelihood that a separate Romano-British tradition was still active. This is epitomised in the magnificent rings from the Thetford Treasure; though the place of manufacture of the Thetford jewellery is impossible to establish in the present state of knowledge, a good case can be made for a British origin.   CJ

Late Antique and Early Byzantine Jewellery

There was no break in continuity between the jewellery of the Roman period and that of the fourth and fifth centuries AD. Much the same repertoire of techniques and motifs was used, and it was not until the late fifth or early sixth century AD – the Early Byzantine

211

period – that this jewellery assumed an explicitly Christian character. Late Antique jewellers were not, however, mere slavish imitators. On the contrary, innovations in decoration and new technical methods were introduced: these included new styles in polychrome jewellery, where the gem predominates over the goldwork in decorative importance, and the widespread use of niello – a black sulphide, usually acanthite – to give contrast to bright precious metal. The adoption of Christianity as the state religion of the Roman Empire by Constantine the Great (AD 306–37) eventually led to the emergence of new forms of jewellery with new iconography and the consequent development of expertise in figural representation.

The most innovative and characteristic technique in Late Antique and Early Byzantine jewellery was perhaps that of *opus interrasile* ('pierced work'), which reached a high point in the fourth century AD, only to go on to a further peak around AD 600. In the late Antique examples the gold sheet was either pierced with a round awl and then chased or carved on the face only, or it was cut through with tiny chisels; in the later Early Byzantine examples the piercing

220 Late Antique jewellery from the Carthage Treasure (*c.* AD 400), found on the Hill of St Louis, Carthage (Tunisia), in association with silver dishes and spoons, some with Christian symbols, belonging to the prominent Cresconius family. The jewellery comprises a necklace and earrings of emerald crystals, sapphires and pearls, a gold loop-in-loop necklace with lion-head terminals, a gold ring with a pearl in a claw setting, a plasma intaglio with a bust of Heracles, a nicolo intaglio with a figure of Fortuna and a retrograde Latin inscription meaning, roughly, 'Safe voyage', and an onyx cameo with a bust of Minerva. The possession of this cameo and these intaglios by a family with at least one Christian bishop in it and with Christian symbols on some of its silver is an indication of the persistence of the outward and visible signs of paganism long after the formal adoption of Christianity as the official religion of the Roman Empire. H (earrings) 5.7cm

Right **221** A late Antique (4th century AD) gold necklace-pendant incorporating a double-*solidus* of AD 321. Between the coin and each of the pendant's angles is a bust in full relief, probably cast by the lost-wax technique; between the busts and on the suspension loop the decoration is in *opus interrasile* (pierced work). The lower left-hand bust is that of Atys; the other busts, which have yet to be identified, are therefore probably also of mythological figures. An almost identical pendant is in the Dumbarton Oaks Collection in Washington, DC, and there are round versions in the Louvre and at Dumbarton Oaks. D (max) 9.25cm

Below **222** A Byzantine necklace and earrings from Egypt (*c.* AD 600). Thought to have been found with the body-chain (**223**), the necklace and earrings are of gold with emerald crystals, sapphires and pearls (compare **220**). L (earrings) 12.4cm

Left **223** A Byzantine gold body-chain from Egypt (*c.* AD 600). The ornament comprises four chains made of *opus interrasile* discs of two alternating patterns, connecting two large discs worn at the front and back. The 2nd-century AD terracotta figure from El-Faiyum in Egypt (**224**, *above*) illustrates how the body-chain was worn.
L (as worn, approx.) 68cm

was done on a much larger scale, sometimes in conjunction with embossing.

The main centres of jewellery production during the fourth and fifth centuries AD were probably still the great cities of Rome, Alexandria and Antioch. The status of Constantinople was probably subsidiary at this time, but by the sixth century AD its position was paramount. This was an age of enormous wealth: the emperor Anastasius, for instance, left 320,000 pounds of gold in the imperial treasury when he died in AD 518.

The prestige which Constantinopolitan jewellers enjoyed in the sixth and seventh centuries AD can be gauged both from the quantities of high-class jewellery found outside the borders of the Empire (just such a seventh-century AD necklace has recently been found in a royal grave in China) and from the fact that their styles and techniques were copied by barbarian jewellers.   CE

CHAPTER EIGHT

Europe, China, Korea and Japan

AD 300–1000

Germanic Jewellery: The Continent and Anglo-Saxon England

Increasing numbers of Germanic mercenaries employed in Roman imperial service, and the gradual collapse of the Empire's defences, followed by massive invasions and settlement by Germanic tribes from the fourth century, led to a spread of Germanic fashions throughout Western Europe. As in contemporary jewellery of the eastern Roman Empire and Early Byzantium, much of the Germanic jewellery of the late fourth to seventh centuries draws its technical and decorative repertoire from Late Roman styles. Germanic metalwork owes much of its strong visual impact to an exuberant exploration of light and colour contrasts. The use of gold and silver, cast in high relief and as sheet decorated in repoussé, was frequently extravagant. Surface work might be enhanced by stamping or punching, for example, or by filigree and granulation; effects might be further heightened by inlays of black niello or coloured glass and precious stones. Copper alloy was often gilded or tinned to imitate the richness of gold and silver. The geometric patterns and sinuous animal shapes with their variegated surfaces must have glittered in flickering torch- or fire-light.

The power and prestige of the owner was conspicuous not only in the sheer weight and splendour of metal and other exotic raw materials, but also in the skill and virtuosity of the jeweller at his command. The regalia found in the royal ship-burial at Sutton Hoo mark the heights achieved by such craftsmen and the wealth of their royal patrons.

242, 243

A dominant technique of decoration is inlay with garnet, a semi-precious stone, some of which was probably imported from as far away as India or Afghanistan at this period. It had a long history of use, but it was cosmopolitan craftsmen serving the tastes of the Goths, a Germanic tribe which had occupied parts of southern Russia from the third century, who increasingly exploited its properties. The westward migration of the Goths from the late fourth century was to spread the fashion throughout Western and Northern Europe. When split into thin sheets and backed with gold foil (often hatched or patterned to reflect light through the gem) this otherwise dark stone became blood red. Sometimes it was sparingly used as a simple collared disc or circular cabochon to emphasise the eye of an animal or bird of prey. At its most spectacular, garnet inlay

230

Left **225** A Byzantine gold, amethyst and pearl necklace-pendant (early 7th century AD). The pendant, which is embossed, pierced and chased, is thought to have been found with other fragments of necklaces, bracelets and a ring. H 5.55cm

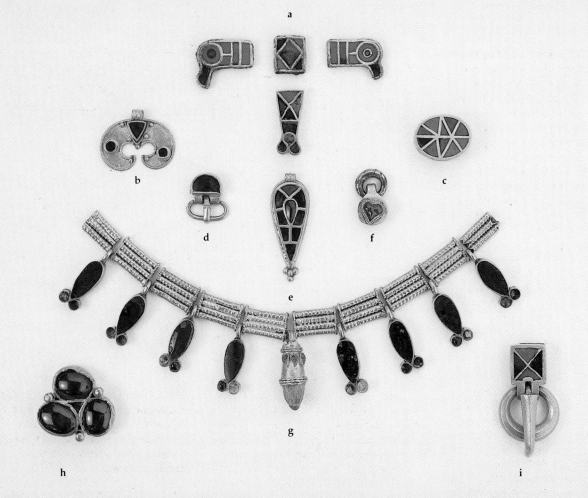

a

b

c

d

e

f

g

h

i

Top left **226** A group of gold Migration-period jewellery inlaid with garnet, probably all from the Krym area of the Ukraine, USSR (4th and 5th centuries AD). In their simplest form garnet pebbles might be perforated as beads or pendants. Split and ground to present one regular convex face, they formed relief cabochon settings (**h**). These might be combined with flat-cut garnets (**e**). The heart-shaped cabochon (**f**) has its surface ground to form lobes. When split into sheets the garnet could be wheel-cut to geometric shapes of varying complexity, to be set in cloison cells; such sheets might be further embellished, as in the bird's eye of **a**, where a ring has been ground out and filled with gold. L (**g**) 16.5cm

Bottom left **227–30** A group of Anglo-Saxon jewellery. The 5th-century AD silver-gilt quoit brooch from Sarre, Kent (**227**, left) is the most splendid surviving example of a type found in graves of the earliest Anglo-Saxon settlers, but which was probably made in native Romano-British workshops. The elegant engraved animal ornament derives from late Roman motifs.

The repoussé gold pendant (**228**, top) is from a woman's grave in the Anglo-Saxon cemetery at Buckland, Dover, Kent, and is early 7th century. The characteristically Germanic animal ornament also ultimately derives from late Roman art.

The gold and garnet-inlaid pendant cross (**229**, right) was found at Wilton, Norfolk. It is set with a Byzantine gold *solidus* of Heraclius I and Heraclius Constantine (AD 615–32). The precision and style of the garnet inlay links the cross to the workshop which made the Sutton Hoo jewellery (**242**, **243**).

The gold pendant set with a triskele of cloisonné birds' heads on a base with filigree decoration (**230**, bottom) comes from a rich Anglo-Saxon cemetery at Faversham, Kent. The hatched gold foil beneath the garnets adds depth and brilliance to the inlay. D (**227**) 7.8cm

Above **231** Silver-gilt square-headed brooch from a 6th-century AD Anglo-Saxon woman's grave at Chessel Down, Isle of Wight. The surface of the brooch is densely covered with Style I animal ornament; the borders are decorated with niello. Brooches of this type derive from Scandinavian prototypes and are widespread in eastern and south-eastern England; they would have been worn singly on a cloak or outer garment. L 13.8cm

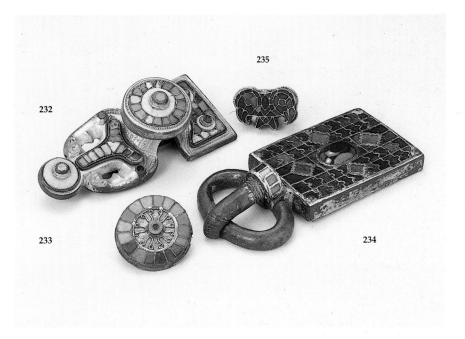

Above A group of garnet-inlaid Germanic jewellery (6th century AD). Individual forms of such jewellery were evidently more fashionable in some areas than others. The gilt-bronze disc-on-bow brooch (**232**) is frequently found on the Island of Gotland (Sweden), while the sheet-silver disc brooch (**233**) is from the Amiens region of France. The gilt-bronze belt-buckle (**234**) and gold bird-headed brooch (**235**) are both associated with the Ostrogoths; there are similar examples from the Rhineland and Italy. L (**234**) 9.8cm

Far left **236** A sheet-gold disc pendant (bracteate), of Scandinavian type, enriched with filigree and granulation (6th century AD). The central motif, executed in repoussé, is a horse galloping left, surmounted by a profiled anthropomorphic head with an elaborate coiffure, and (above right) a hovering bird. The inspiration for this form of jewellery lies ultimately in late Roman coin or medallion types; some of these had entered Scandinavia as loot or the wages of mercenary troops, and their motifs were heavily adapted to reflect Germanic mythology. D 3.6cm

Left **237** A sheet-gold Vendel-period disc pendant (bracteate), of a type found almost exclusively on Gotland, Sweden (8th century AD). A broad stamped border surrounds the central stamped and repoussé roundel. It contains a stylised anthropomorphic bust with an elaborate head-dress or coiffure, beneath which radiate three profiled animal heads that originally constituted the decoration of a neck-ring or collar. Above is an animal mask in filigree and granulation surrounded by a thick mane of filigree scrolls. D 5.6cm

238 An early Slav cast-silver bow brooch (late 6th–early 7th century AD). One of a pair found in a hoard at Martynovka in the Ukraine, USSR, with Byzantine silver vessels and a cut-up fragment of another. The anthropomorphic figure at the top of the head-plate presides over two pairs of projecting profiled animals and an animal mask at the end of the foot-plate. Other incised decoration depicts foliage and ears of grain. The whole may be associated with a fertility cult. L 13.1cm

239 Three early Avar gold earrings, from Hungary or from the Ukraine, USSR (late 6th–early 7th century AD). The form and technique of these earrings reflect general late Antique and Byzantine styles. The largest is a type sometimes found in 'princely' burials with other rich accessories. The gold from which they are made probably originated in Byzantine *solidi* looted or extorted by the Avars who several times mortally threatened the Empire in the Balkans. L (max.) 5.8cm

240 An Anglo-Saxon gold buckle, decorated with cloisonné garnet and glass inlays and filigree wire (*c.* AD 600). The central field of the buckle-plate contains a sinuous animal interlacing with its own body, executed in filigree wire on a repoussé base. It is an early example of Style II animal ornament.

Decorated belt-buckles were worn by high-ranking men in the 6th and early 7th centuries AD. This splendid example comes from a richly equipped princely grave at Taplow, Buckinghamshire. L 9.9cm

241 A Lombardic cast-silver radiate-head brooch, parcel-gilt and decorated with niello, probably from Toscana (Tuscany), northern Italy (late 6th – early 7th century AD). The exuberant profusion of Style II bird-of-prey and animal ornament is striking; masks and profiled heads project from around the edges and at the ends, and interlaced snake-like bodies fill the main fields at the head and foot. Geometric decoration fills other available space on the borders and down the bow in a *horror vacui* characteristic of Germanic jewellers. L 16.5cm

Left Jewellery from the Anglo-Saxon royal ship-burial at Sutton Hoo, Suffolk (early 7th century AD).

Top **242** A pair of gold shoulder-clasps, each formed of two separate hinges secured by a pin. The undersides of the clasps have loops for attachment to fabric or leather. The upper surface is elaborately inlaid with cloisonné garnet and millefiori glass, interspersed with complex motifs in filigree.

The supreme skill of the court jeweller is exemplified by the paired boar images at the end of the clasps, and in the elaborate scheme of the central panels, which are thought to have inspired the so-called carpet pages in the earliest Anglo-Saxon illuminated manuscripts. L (max.) 12.7cm

Bottom **243** Gold and garnet-inlaid mounts from a sword harness, made in the same workshop as **242**. The sheer technical virtuosity of the cloisonné inlay has rarely been equalled; it includes stones cut to minute size, in irregular shapes, fitted to curved surfaces and even set on moving parts. The superb quality of these fittings proclaims the exalted status of their owner. The drawing (**244**, *below*) is a reconstruction of how the sword harness might have been worn. L (buckle) 7.3cm

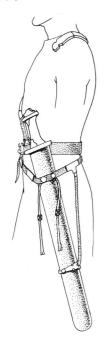

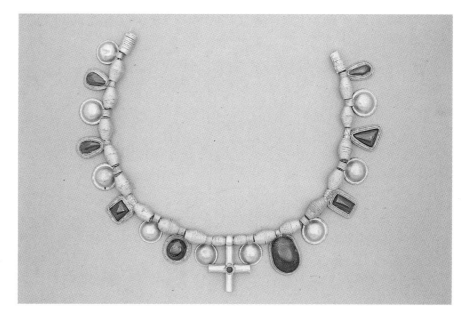

Above **245** A gold and garnet necklace from an Anglo-Saxon woman's grave at Desborough, Northamptonshire (7th century AD). Its cabochon garnet pendants, gold wire biconical and cylindrical beads, pendant *bullæ* and central cross reflect Mediterranean fashions of jewellery which began to appear in England early in the 7th century. The necklace, like many other items of 7th-century Anglo-Saxon jewellery, proclaims its owner's Christianity. L 25.4cm

covered the whole surface of a piece of jewellery, contained in a carpet-like arrangement of cellwork (cloisonné).

The first Germanic settlers arriving in what became England in the fifth century came primarily from north-western Germany and Denmark, where ornamental traditions had already been adopted from the repertoire of the workshops of the late Empire. These included geometric motifs, running scrolls and, most notably, zoomorphic ornament derived from the naturalistic dolphin and sea-beast motifs found on military belt fittings. Animal ornament, in one form or another, was to develop as a dominant element in Anglo-Saxon, Continental and Viking art for the next five hundred years. Its earliest phase, known as Style I, occurs especially in Scandinavia and England. It is characterised by highly analytical animal forms whose abbreviated components are often reduced to barely legible dismembered fragments. Behind this seemingly anarchic surface, however, there lurks a discreet delight in regular formulae and in visual games. For example, apparently chaotic decoration may turn out on inspection to be symmetrical, or a pair of disjointed animals set back-to-back may also be read as a frontal human mask. The love of dense textures, of intricate patterns and riddling images which runs through Anglo-Saxon poetry finds its visual counterpart in these ambiguous and complex images. From the late sixth century Style I gradually gives way to more elegant and legible ornament, the so-called Style II, in which the interlacing of animal bodies in regular patterns becomes the principal theme. This widespread style occurs with local variations from Scandinavia to Lombard Italy, and from the middle Danube to England.

242

231

240

241

Just as the Eastern Roman Empire had influenced large parts of Europe beyond its frontiers, so its successor Byzantium and its fluctuating Mediterranean empire deeply influenced the Germanic kingdoms and other groups on its borders, such as Avars and Slavs. Its gold and silver, spread in diplomacy and war, provided raw materials, giving rise to episodes of heightened brilliance in native jewellery. Its luxuries were traded over long distances, reaching even Anglo-Saxon England, particularly the south-east, from across the Channel. Throughout Western Europe Christianity had gradually spread, and from Rome itself the Augustinian mission to England in AD 597 led to an intensification of further contacts with the Mediterranean world. In Anglo-Saxon female dress, for instance, the traditional paired brooches and swags of beads gave way to the Mediterranean taste for pins and pendants, some carrying explicitly Christian motifs. DK/LW

Late Anglo-Saxon and Viking Jewellery

We know a great deal about the forms and evolution of earlier Germanic jewellery because it was customary to bury the dead with their personal possessions, including jewellery. Under the growing influence of the Church, however, this practice was eventually abandoned in much of Western Europe. Thus, from the early eighth century onwards, evidence for Anglo-Saxon jewellery is much diminished. The stray finds and rich hoards that survive show that the jeweller's craft flourished. By contrast, in pagan Scandinavia,

247 An Anglo-Saxon silver disc brooch, known after its former owner as the 'Fuller' Brooch. It is decorated with niello in a design representing the Five Senses. Sight, most precious of all, occupies the central field, surrounded by the personifications of Taste, Touch, Smell and Hearing. The outer border is decorated with birds, beasts, men and flowers, perhaps as a celebration of the variety of Creation. Large disc brooches became fashionable in the 9th century (see **249**), but this piece is a unique survival in its iconographic sophistication. This, and certain stylistic traits, suggest that the brooch is a product of the artistic and intellectual climate of renewal associated with the reign of Alfred the Great (AD 871–99). Its history is unknown before the end of the last century, but its superb condition suggests that it may never have been buried, but simply passed on from generation to generation. D 11.4cm

Left **246** The 'Castellani' Brooch, said to have been found at Canosa, Puglia (Italy), and named after its former owner. The brooch consists of a sheet-gold casing over a calcite core, with a silver back-plate; the central medallion of cloisonné enamel , originally a flesh colour and shades of blue, yellow and red, against a blue background, depicts a woman flanked by cypress branches, wearing earrings and a brooch comparable to the present example. The outer ring of geometric enamelling, originally red, blue and green, is bordered by two rows of gold loops holding pearls (one row of pearls is lost).

Because of the lack of firmly attributable pieces, the brooch's date and place of origin are uncertain, although an Italian workshop seems to be the most likely. It may have been made in the 7th century under strong Byzantine influence for the Germanic Lombards; or it may be a 7th- to 8th-century provincial Byzantine piece; it could be as late as the 9th century and relate to northern Italian work. These problems notwithstanding, the significance of this outstanding piece lies in the richness and highly inventive repertoire of techniques developed where Western European and Byzantine influences merged.
D 6cm

Right **248** A Viking-period silver thistle brooch, found near Penrith, Cumbria (England), so-called from its distinctive terminals. This is one of the most extravagant examples of a penannular brooch type which was worn by 10th-century Viking settlers in Ireland. Such brooches were worn with the pins pointed diagonally up over the shoulder or sometimes with the pin bent back to avoid risk of self-damage. Nevertheless, the huge size of examples like this make them barely practical as functional dress fasteners; their primary purpose was as portable and visible wealth. L 51.5cm

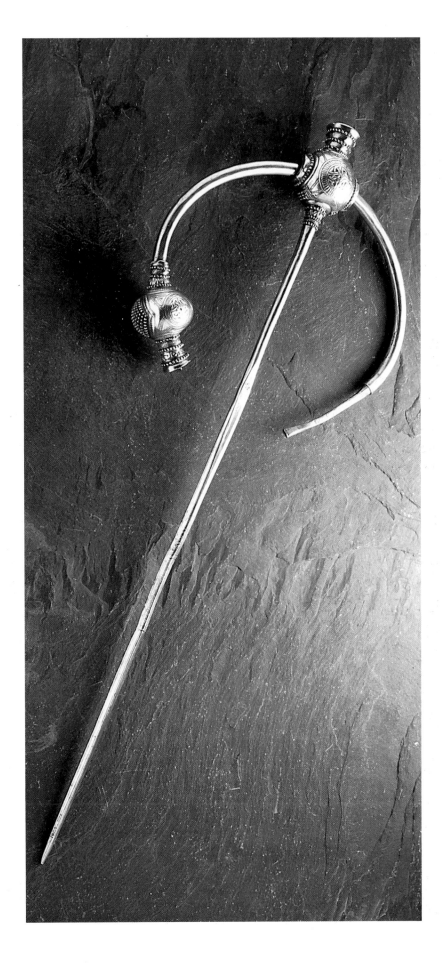

Above **250** A silver neck-ring from a hoard of AD 1025–6 found at Halton Moor, Lancashire (England) containing 860 coins, gold discs and a Carolingian bowl. Neck- and arm-rings of twisted wires were worn widely in the Viking world and functioned partly as portable bullion. D 18cm

Left **249** A hoard of six Anglo-Saxon silver disc brooches found in the churchyard at Pentney, Norfolk, in 1977. All are of silver except the smallest, which has a gilt-bronze base under an openwork silver facing. There are two singletons and two non-identical pairs with elaborate openwork ornament; one of the pairs and the largest brooch are inlaid with niello. The smallest brooch shows signs of wear; it is of the later 8th century AD. The others, all made in the first half of the 9th century, are lavishly decorated in the 'Trewhiddle' style. They are in mint condition and probably come from one workshop. D (largest) 10.2cm

Above **251** A Viking cast-silver disc brooch, perhaps from Gotland, Sweden (10th century AD). The elaborate symbolism of this piece has never been adequately explained. Each of the two opposed human figures around the edge grasps a rope around his neck; his legs are thrown over arms bent at the elbow, which must draw it even tighter. Two animals peer over the edges of the brooch at four animals in the round who are backward biting onto their own tails. From the high central openwork boss, eight animal heads project all round on long necks. D 7.8cm

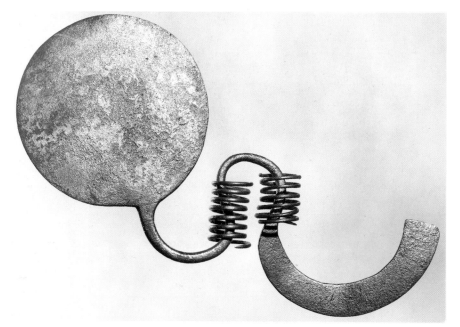

252 A Celtic copper-alloy 'latchet' found in the River Shannon at Athlone, Ireland (7th century AD). These uniquely Irish objects, some elaborately enamelled, were probably used as some kind of dress fastening, for instance, by slotting a belt or braid through its undulations. The two wire spirals on this example presumably served to attach it more securely to the fabric; similar spirals occur on some penannular brooches. L 17.5cm

there is a wealth of objects from graves as well as hoards which document an unbroken jewellery tradition, especially in animal ornament. During the ninth and tenth centuries Viking trade and raiding brought exotic luxuries, among which were masses of silver, from the Muslim Near East to Northern Europe, even to the British Isles, where parts were settled by Scandinavian immigrants.

In both Britain and Scandinavia, however, major changes can be observed, most notably the striking shift from the use of gold to the medium of silver. The increased scarcity of gold led to it being used mainly for finger-rings or for gilding and inlay. Anglo-Saxon and Viking metalwork in the ninth and tenth centuries is distinguished by the increasing size of the richest brooches, whose function is clearly to display wealth and status, as much as to embellish or merely fasten a garment. While some jewellery such as neck- and armrings is simple unadorned bullion, the love of animal ornament and of densely decorated surfaces also continued unabated, gaining new scope and meaning from Christian iconography. Recent finds, such as the splendid ninth-century hoard of silver disc brooches from Pentney (Norfolk, England) have considerably extended our knowledge and appreciation of the jewellery of this fertile later Anglo-Saxon and Viking period. DK/LW

249

Celtic Jewellery

The indigenous Celtic population beyond the areas of Anglo-Saxon settlement, particularly in Scotland and Ireland, continued to make and develop their own forms of jewellery. Techniques, forms and even the materials employed are very different from those of their Anglo-Saxon and, later, Viking neighbours. Some aspects, such as enamelling, inlaid millefiori glass and the distinctive curvilinear decoration, owe something to the traditions of the antique world; this legacy the Celtic craftsmen share in some measure with their Anglo-Saxon counterparts. During the eighth century the flowing

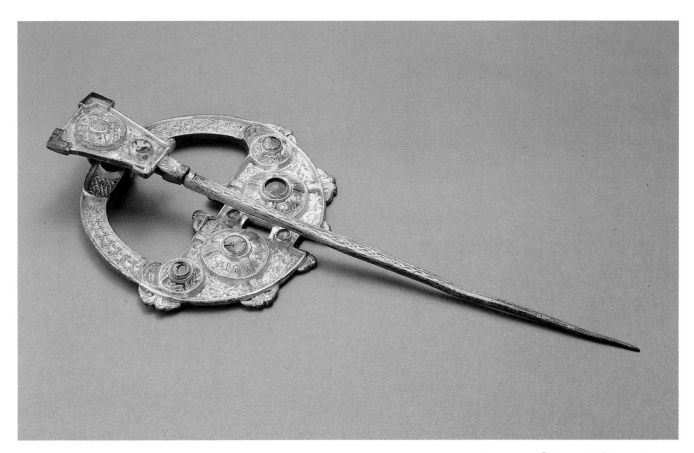

Above **253** The 'Londesborough'
Brooch, a silver-gilt penannular brooch
of Irish type (8th century AD). The entire
front is densely covered with chip-
carved and engraved patterns, and set
with inlays of amber and blue glass.
The back also has glass inlays, and inset
foils with curvilinear motifs. The use of
animal ornament, interlace and glass
inlay shows the influence of
contemporary Anglo-Saxon metalwork,
brilliantly exploited and transformed
by Irish craftsmen. L 24.2cm

Right **254** A Celtic copper-alloy
penannular brooch from Co. Cavan,
Ireland (7th century AD?). It is decorated
with red enamel and millefiori roundels
set in bronze cells. The hoop and back
of the brooch have lightly incised
decoration. The penannular brooch was
the dominant type in Ireland
throughout the early Christian and
Viking periods, evolving from simple
early forms to ones with lavishly
decorated terminals. L 12.7cm

abstract peltas, spirals and trumpet-shaped scrolls begin to be extended and combined with motifs taken from other sources – interlace from the Mediterranean world, animal ornament from the Anglo-Saxons. Around this time, too, gilding enters the Celtic repertoire, and glass and amber inlays begin to appear; the result is some of the most intricate and accomplished jewellery of the entire early medieval period. New influences were absorbed from the Viking settlers of Ireland – abundant silver and Scandinavian forms of animal ornament – but the native forms of jewellery persist, and the style of decoration remains distinctively Celtic.   LW

We know very little of the organisational conditions under which any of this splendid jewellery was made, though archaeological evidence indicates that fine metalworking was carried out on or near high-status sites. As one would expect, kings and princes must have had craftsmen working close at hand to the court. But at a less exalted level of production, we do not know to what extent the craftsmen were itinerant or based in permanent workshops, until, with the gradual development of urban trade and commerce, we see the establishment of organised workshops. It remains, however, abundantly clear that these craftsmen, working under obscure and no doubt primitive conditions were capable of producing some of the most splendid and sophisticated jewellery of early medieval Europe.   DK/LW

China

Chinese jewellery comprises a large range of hair ornaments for women, and belts and pendants for men. In later periods some rings were also made. However, the necklaces and brooches that dominate medieval Western jewellery were rare and at many periods unknown.

Perhaps the properties of the hair of Far Eastern women stimulated the development of elaborate hair ornaments. The hair of Far Easterners is straight because it is round in cross-sections; it is also heavy and usually dark in colour showing up the bright gleaming pins and combs in gold and silver. Poetry throughout many centuries sings of the beauty of women in terms of their hair. Thus it is that in Chinese jewellery hairpins and combs play a very significant part. Gold seems to have become the material preferred for these ornaments in the late Han dynasty and during the Western and Eastern Jin dynasties of the third to fourth century AD. That is not to say that gold had not been used in small quantities at a much earlier date. Excavated examples of earlier appliqué designs and beads are known, but it is only in the Han period that personal ornaments were made in any significant quantities in gold. Early hairpins, usually of plain gold in a U-shaped form, have a solidity which by the Tang dynasty (AD 618–906) had been changed into a delicate fantasy. The vogue for elaborate hair-styles in this period is recorded in painting. In a Buddhist painting of the tenth century, the lady, a donor, wears pins and a comb reminiscent of 258 and 259.

256 A drawing of a necklace from the tomb of Li Jingxun, the granddaughter of the eldest sister of the Sui-dynasty Emperor Yangdi; she died at the age of nine and was buried in AD 608. The necklace is of gold, set with pearls, lapis lazuli, agate and crystal; the fastening includes a seal stone. In character the necklace is Central Asian.

255

255 A detail of the donor figure in a Chinese Buddhist banner painting from Dunhuang (late 9th century AD). From her attire, the lady is a noblewoman or a princess; she wears a comb (see **259**) and other hair ornaments.

The Tang dynasty hairpins illustrated here are decorated in a florid style that seems to reflect some contact with Central Asia and perhaps even Iran. From at least the sixth century elaborate hair ornaments and decorated plaques were made in which sheets of gold or a framework of pins, as here, were embellished with filigree, granulation and inlay of precious stones or pearls. These techniques were used on a necklace found in the tomb of Li Jingxun, a nine-year-old princess of the Sui dynasty, whose tomb near Xi'an was constructed in AD 608. Before this time necklaces were rarely worn in China and the fashion must have been introduced from the West. Details of the construction are also Central Asian in flavour, reflecting distantly Western Classical features, including the central stone surrounded with pearls and a small seal used as part of the fastening. Each of the beads, made as openwork balls covered in granulation, was set with pearls.

258

256

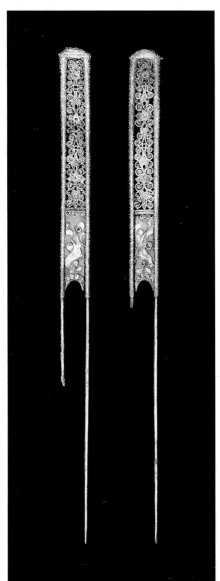

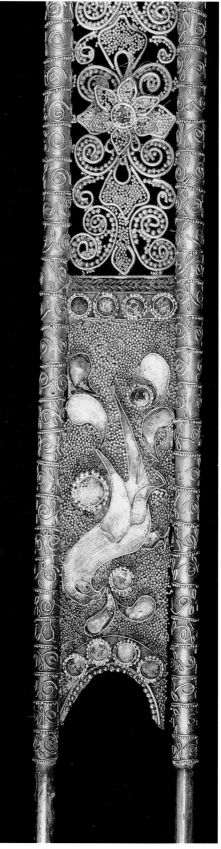

Above **257** Five Chinese gold beads (3rd–5th century AD). Each bead is suspended from a double loop of twisted wire, and decorated with granulation and twisted wire. L 2.2cm

Left and *right* **258** A pair of Chinese hairpins of the Tang dynasty (7th–8th century AD). The pins are constructed from silver-gilt prongs, with a broader, flattened section at the top. Gold foil is wrapped around the upper part and enhanced with wirework and granulation. The space between the prongs is filled with a rich decoration of applied wirework scrolls and flowers, further embellished with granulation and including settings which would originally have been inlaid with precious stones. The lower part has a sheet of gold, with further settings for semi-precious stones; the motif of a bird among flowers, set against a background of granulation, would also have been inlaid. The reverse has a simple scroll design.

Similar to this quite exceptional work is the head from a pin in the Metropolitan Museum of Art, New York. Plain Tang-dynasty pins have been excavated at a number of sites in China, but examples of this technical complexity are very rare. L 17cm

259 A late Tang- or Liao-dynasty silver comb (10th century AD). The gilded upper section is worked with raised decoration enhanced with chasing, against a ring-punched background. This comb was intended to be worn in the hair (see 255). The decoration derives from Tang-dynasty bird and flower motifs. W 18.2cm

The technique of granulation mentioned in connection with this small group of highly decorated jewellery seems to have been shared with Central or Western Asia. Granulated ornaments were worked from the Han dynasty (220 BC–AD 220), and were very popular in the succeeding centuries in north China. These northern regions were in close contact with Korea where granulation was also widely practised. In the Far East the technique seems to have continued in use into the Song dynasty (AD 960–1279).

Another important technical point is the early preoccupation with casting that gradually gave way to work in thin sheet metal. The

260 Two Chinese gilt-bronze belt fittings of the Song period (10th–11th century AD), decorated with figures against a background of clouds. The fittings are hollow and pierced with a horizontal slit through which a subsidiary strap would have been threaded. A belt with fittings of the same type was found in the tomb of Fuma Zeng, Prince of Wei, buried in AD 959 at Dayingzi, near Chifeng in Inner Mongolia. 4.8×4.5cm

Right **261** The central plaque from the Tang-dynasty agate set. It is larger than the other eight plaques and may have covered the belt-fastening. The low-relief carving shows a dancer and musicians. H 9.8cm

259   silver Tang- or Liao-dynasty comb is an example of the use of thin sheets of precious material.

What hair ornaments were for women, belts seem to have been for men. Early examples have already been encountered in the form of belt-hooks. As mentioned in Chapter 6, belt-hooks were replaced by buckle fastenings in bronze, with openwork designs of animals filling the various rectangular ornaments with which the belts were embellished. Belt-clasps have been found in north China in tombs of the third and fourth centuries AD and very similar examples, presumably imported from the mainland, have come to light at Nara in Japan.

Such early decorated clasps are the ancestors of the belt set, fully established by the Tang period and represented here by an agate set. A large plaque covered a belt-fastening and the rest of the leather or cloth belt was decorated with approximately square plaques. Such belt ornaments might be made of metal or jade, or just occasionally agate, as here. Several later belt-plaques are illustrated in Chapters 11 and 13. These belts were important articles of dress and were used to indicate rank and position. JMR

Korea and Japan

In the periods of the Three Kingdoms (37 BC–AD 668) and Unified Silla (AD 668–918), elaborate and striking jewellery was in use among the Korean royal families and the members of the ruling élite. Several famous gold crowns have been excavated from royal tombs: the tall gold constructions are hung with small comma-shaped pendants, often known by their Japanese name *magatama*. Other items included necklaces and belts, sometimes decorated with granulation. The belts resemble those worn by Siberian peoples and can also be compared with the belts that were introduced to China. In later periods Korean jewellery was less striking and shared some features with China.

The relationship between Japan and the rest of the Far East was more unusual. Indeed, later developments on the mainland had a minimal influence on Japan, where from the historical period onwards (mid-seventh century) jewellery scarcely existed at all. Rings, necklaces, bracelets, earrings and the like had no place in traditional dress, and the only adornments approaching jewellery were the lacquered combs and pins and artificial flowers worn in the hair by young women.

In earlier periods there had been a tradition of rather elementary earrings and *magatama* pendants made from stone, pottery or shell.

Centre left **261** A set of pale-grey agate Chinese belt-plaques (Tang dynasty, 7th-8th century AD). The eight smaller plaques are carved in low relief with seated musicians playing various instruments. The backs are pierced for attachment to a leather belt. A number of such sets, mainly in jade, have been excavated from tombs of the Imperial family or high officials, dating from the Tang to the Ming periods. A set in jade, also carved with musicians but in a style which is evidently later, has been excavated from a Song-dynasty tomb (AD 960–1279) in Jiangxi province. Small plaques 5.2×5.2cm

Right **262–3** Korean earrings of the 5th–6th century AD. The single earring (**262**, centre) is decorated with granulation. The pair of earrings (**263**) consist of openwork roundels hung with small leaf-shaped pendants, with another large leaf-shaped pendant below.

Although these earrings are typically Korean, they were clearly part of a goldworking tradition shared with north-east China. Granulation may have been learned from the Chinese; the small suspended pendants on (**263**) are typical not only of Korea, but also of the north-east area of China. L (**263**) 6.2cm

This began about 1000 BC and eventually developed in the early Great Tombs period (third to fifth centuries AD) into a very high level of stone carving, probably as a result of the diffusion of Chinese jade-working skills through Northern China and Korea. Apart from the polished stone bracelets, beads and *magatama* of this period, some fairly skilful copies were done of the contemporary Korean gilt-bronze jewellery in the fifth to seventh centuries.

Japanese stone and glass jewellery from the Great Tombs period (3rd–5th century AD).

Top Beads such as these examples have been found in large numbers in the Great Tombs. They were probably thought to have a magical significance, in the sense that the number of beads was apparently important, as though they had the force of a repetitive charm, for example. The cylindrical beads (264) are carved from a dark-green hardstone. The round beads (265) are of blue glass. Although many glass beads have been found in the Great Tombs, it is not known whether the glass was made in Japan or imported. L (264) 2–2.4cm

Bottom The bracelets are of a type thought to reproduce the style of metal bracelets worn during a person's lifetime. The stone bracelets must have had a ritual or spiritual significance as they are usually found carefully arranged around the coffin in a tomb.

The comma-shaped beads (268, 269), or *magatama*, are known in Japan as early as the late Jōmon period (c. 1000 BC). Then they almost disappeared until the period of the Great Tombs, when they appear again in profusion, perhaps because of their wide popularity in Korea at the same time. D (266) 4.5cm

The Great Tombs period is named after the many barrows with rich collections of grave-goods, left by the emperors and nobles of a state established by a war-like people from Korea, who had conquered most of southern Japan in the mid-3rd century AD.

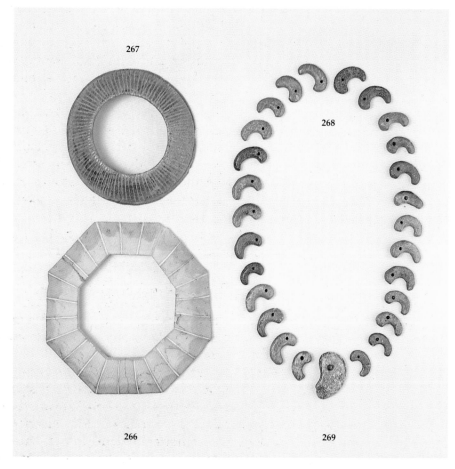

CHAPTER NINE

Mayan Central America

AD 600–1000

The techniques of metalworking diffused rather slowly from South America through the isthmus to be incorporated into the Maya, Mixtec and Aztec worlds. However, only in these latter two do metals play an important role in the manufacture of ornaments. Apart from a few circular gold relief panels and pendants found in the *cenote* or 'Sacred Well' at Chichen Itza, few metals are known from the Maya area. People speaking Mayan languages still live today within the area where their ancestors developed the pre-eminent civilisation of pre-Columbian Mesoamerica.

Remains of great Maya ceremonial centres, constructed between about AD 300 and 900, are found throughout parts of southern Mexico, the Yucatan peninsula, Guatemala, Belize and the western fringes of Honduras and El Salvador. Even in a ruined state their magnificence attests the skill of the Mayan architects, masons and sculptors of the Classic period.

After that time the civilisation declined, although even at the dawn of the Conquest the Spaniards found a pattern of life which still closely followed the forms of the civilisation in its heyday. Small scattered settlements of farmers cultivated the maize, beans, squash and other staples which supported the priestly rulers and the specialist craftsmen and merchants living in or near the great centres. This pattern was general in Mesoamerica, but the Maya ceremonial centres of the Classic period, with their great temple pyramids, ball-game courts, plazas, palace structures and monumental sculptures, are certainly the most impressive of their kind.

Although other Mesoamerican peoples also had a knowledge of calendrics, the Mayan mathematicians and astronomers evolved calendrical and hieroglyphic writing systems which surpassed all others in the New World. The priest–kings so often represented in Maya sculpture were the custodians of this knowledge, the interpreters of the law, curators of the monumental inscriptions and the painted books. They presided over the rituals and ceremonies necessary to satisfy the demands of the complex pantheon of gods with the deity Itzam Na at its head. The rulers are shown wearing elaborate regalia and jewellery, sometimes so prolific that it all but obscures the human form.

From such representations and others on painted pottery, in stucco work and in a few mural paintings and wood-carvings which survive, we have considerable evidence of Maya craftsmanship to add to the tangible evidence uncovered by archaeology. Apart from the sometimes richly carved jades which decorate head-dresses, ear ornaments, lip-plugs, nose-pins, necklaces, bracelets, and anklets,

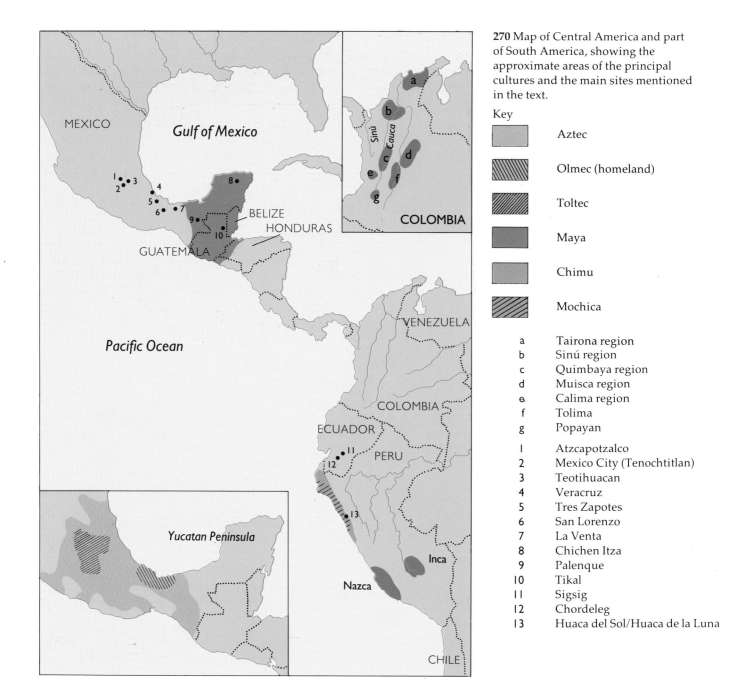

270 Map of Central America and part of South America, showing the approximate areas of the principal cultures and the main sites mentioned in the text.

Key

	Aztec
	Olmec (homeland)
	Toltec
	Maya
	Chimu
	Mochica

a	Tairona region
b	Sinú region
c	Quimbaya region
d	Muisca region
e	Calima region
f	Tolima
g	Popayan
1	Atzcapotzalco
2	Mexico City (Tenochtitlan)
3	Teotihuacan
4	Veracruz
5	Tres Zapotes
6	San Lorenzo
7	La Venta
8	Chichen Itza
9	Palenque
10	Tikal
11	Sigsig
12	Chordeleg
13	Huaca del Sol/Huaca de la Luna

many of which have survived, we know that the Maya made wide use of other more perishable materials including feathers, flowers, elaborately woven or embroidered textiles, animal skins and shells. Tattooing and body painting and the filing and inlaying of teeth were other forms of adornment. We also know that artificially deformed skulls and artificially crossed eyes were considered marks of aristocratic beauty as well as a profile with a straight line from forehead to the end of the nose, sometimes produced by the use of an artificial bridge of jade or other material.

Metalworking techniques were not well developed and apart from copper bells and a few other items, many of which were probably imported from outside the Maya area, gold and other metal ornaments are rarely found. In the early post-Classic period (AD 1000–1300) the Toltec from Central Mexico began to move into the area of Yucatan, eventually taking control and establishing a Toltec–Maya kingdom. In the early thirteenth century the Itza, possibly from Campeche Mexico, were the next to dominate this area and finally by the middle of the sixteenth century the Spanish had effectively gained control.   AS

Below and *right* **272–4** Maya jade jewellery from Pomona, Belize (AD 600–800). The ornaments include a bead necklace (**271**), two ear-flares with scalloped rims (**272**), a small earplug with triangular-shaped perforations (**273**), and three long tubular beads (**274**).

Jade, highly valued by the Maya, was often buried with the dead. The number of jade pieces in a person's tomb was an indication of his importance or wealth. The composite jade ear-flares were either worn through the distended lobe of the ear or, if very large and heavy, were probably attached to a head-dress. D (**272**) approx. 4.5cm

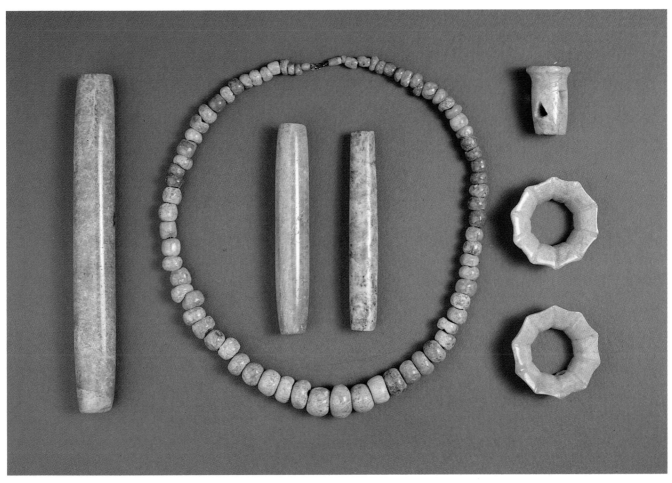

Right **277** A Maya jade ornament, carved in the form of a human head (AD 600–800). The back is hollowed and three sets of double perforations are drilled for attaching the head, which no doubt formed part of a larger ornament. H 6.8cm

Left **275** A Maya pectoral made of half of a bivalve shell (*Spondylus* family), from Pomona, Belize (AD 600–800). The shell is carved with two kneeling human figures (possibly ball players) facing each other, wearing elaborate costumes, head-dresses and necklaces. On the upper part of the shell is another carving, representing two opposing figures, one crouching, one kneeling. Some depressions which form part of the carving, particularly those at ear, waist and wrist level of the two large figures, were possibly intended for inlay of other materials. L (max) 15.3cm

Below **276** Four Maya jade figurine pendants from Pomona, Belize (AD 600–1000). H (largest) 4.8cm

Right **278** A Maya jade pendant (AD 600–800), probably part of a pectoral ornament, head-dress or waist ornament. It is said to have been found at Teotihuacan (Mexico), which is outside the Maya area, although other Maya trade items have been found there. The pendant is carved in bas-relief with two figures. The larger, seated figure has a speech scroll issuing from his mouth, and wears elaborate regalia including a jewelled head-dress, an ear-flare and pendant, a pectoral ornament and a belt with a jade mask at the centre. w 14cm

Right **279–82** Four Maya jade pendants (AD 600–800) with low-relief carvings of human figures. Each is drilled transversely for suspension.

279 (top right) is carved with a face said to represent the Maya maize god. Three small pairs of tubular drillings at the base indicate that some further ornamentation was attached.

The seated figure shown on (**280**, bottom right) wears a tubular jade bead suspended by a cord around the neck. The long transverse tubular drilling of this piece represents a considerable technical feat.

281 (top left) is from Tikal (Guatemala) and has the carved head and torso of a human figure. The seated figure on **282** (bottom left) wears ear ornaments, necklaces and armlets. Despite the irregular shapes of both these pendants, they are complete, the carvings fitting into the contours of the stone. H (**282**) 9.5cm

283 A Maya pendant made of a shell of the *Spondylus* family (AD 600–800). The incised decoration is in the form of a hieroglyph. Two holes have been drilled for suspension on one side; the other holes appear to be natural. L (max) 10cm

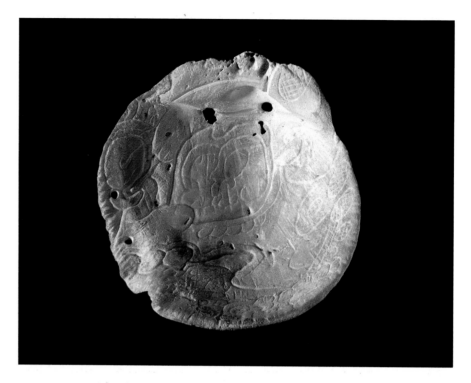

284 A Maya jade nose-pin, with spiral decoration in relief (AD 600–800). Pins of this type were worn through the perforated nasal septum. L 9.8cm

Two polished obsidian lip-plugs (**285**, **286**) and a gold pendant (**287**). Lip-plugs, or 'labrets', were worn through a perforation in the lower lip, with the wider, flattened end against the teeth and gums. Although common in Mexico, they are less typical of the Maya area and may have been imported by the Mexicans, who infiltrated the area about AD 900–1000.

The gold pendant, said to have been found at Palenque (Mexico), by Frederick de Waldeck, may be the upper part of a bell. It is in the form of a human head, with ear ornaments, an artificial nose bridge and a necklace with a central pendant. It is an extremely rare example of fine *cire-perdue* casting from the Maya area. Cast-bronze bells are quite common in the later periods of Maya culture, but probably most were imported from Central America. H (**287**) 4.5cm

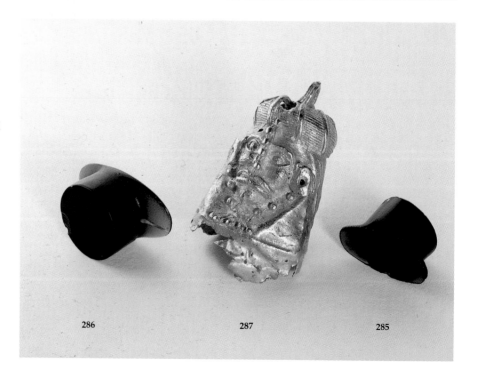

286   287   285

CHAPTER TEN

Central and South America

AD 500–1500

Metal ornaments were manufactured not only from gold, silver, tin, copper, lead, and even platinum, but also from alloys of two or more of these. Certain metals and their alloys were associated with specific deities and were appropriate in their use only to certain social classes within these stratified societies. The Inca associated gold with the solar deity Inti, and its use was restricted by the near monopoly held over it by the Imperial ruler. Its widespread use in trade and commerce was not permitted, it was reserved for distribution by the Inca ruler himself and worn as insignia by nobles who had fought valiantly in battle or distinguished themselves in the service of their ruler. The wives of such nobles were permitted to wear golden ear-flares to distinguish their rank, a custom that can be traced back to pre-Inca times. There existed a symbolic association

288 A detail from the Codex Zouche Nuttall (*c.* 1500), showing three warriors mounted on canoes. The three figures are wearing ceremonial regalia. The elaborate head-dresses show the high craftsmanship attained in featherwork and the use of animal skins for masks. All have facial paintings and two of the figures wear nose ornaments.

between the solar deity, the Inca ruler and the highest echelons of the stratified society in which prestations of the noble metal gold acted to articulate supernatural power with the temporal authority of the Inca ruler.

In a similar though less clear way, copper was the material for which ornaments destined for the lower strata within this society were fashioned. As one would expect, the sources of metals affiliated to distinct deities were themselves sacrosanct. According to Father Cabol's *Historia del Nuevo Mundo*, hills and mines in which gold-bearing ores occurred were venerated as sacred shrines, *huaca*, at which ceremonies and ritual injunctions had to be performed to persuade the earth to yield the precious metal.

In Ecuador most pre-Columbian jewellery comes from the country's north coastal areas, although goldworking centres have also been located in the south Ecuadorian highlands at Sigsig and Chordeleg. The Ecuadorians used the technique of casting, but they also made extensive use of sheet metal, which was cut and embossed in high and low relief.

In Colombia a number of regional and cultural variations have been distinguished. The earliest goldworkings are associated with San Augustin and dated *c.* 500 to 150 BC, but the finest goldwork from the central Cauca valley in south-west Colombia occurs at least 650 years later. Here the population lived in small settlements under the authority of localised chiefs. These local polities were less developed or sophisticated than in other areas. The Muisca region further to the east had a more complex social organisation while

289–90 Two pairs of ear ornaments from Peru (AD 1000–1500). The top pair (**289**), from the Chimu, consists of hammered gold-copper alloy plugs. The repoussé design of stylised birds is outlined by incision and surrounded by chased and repoussé dotted decoration. The remains of a cotton wrapping are still present around the ornaments, and this was probably used as packing in order to secure the plugs in the ear-lobes.

The lower pair (**290**) consists of rings cut from hammered sheet gold and filled with lattice designs of wires soldered together at intervals. A silver alloy plug is soldered into position onto the back of each. D (**289**) 4.2cm

Left **291** A breast ornament from Coastal Ecuador (AD 500–1500) of thin hammered gold. It is in the form of a mask in high relief; the border is decorated with stylised animals, faces and geometrical designs. The nostrils are perforated and there are two holes on each side of the head for attachment. D 10.3cm

Below **292** A nose ornament from Calima, Colombia (AD 500–1500), cut from sheet gold. The whole design is of a stylised human face, the nose being emphasised by repoussé work. The ornament was worn through a perforation in the nasal septum. Because of the thinness of the gold and of the attachments, which are suspended from wires, the whole piece would have trembled when worn. L (total) 38.8cm

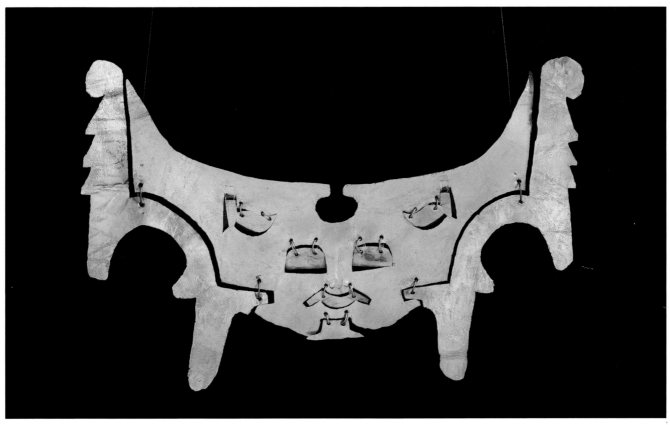

Below **293** A pendant from Calima, Colombia (AD 500–1500) of surface-enriched, gold-copper alloy. It is cast in the form of a standing warrior wearing a face mask, and carrying a club or sceptre and what appears to be a shield. H 7.5cm

towards the north, especially in the Tairona region, there is evidence of a more urban-oriented settlement with stone architecture.

The Spanish chronicles have described the golden crowns, diadems, ear-flares, bracelets, anklets, necklaces, and ornaments fastened to the septum of the nose, which were found in Colombia, Panama and Venezuela. The rank of noble women in some Colombian tribes was expressed by gold plates worn over their chests, while Cueva women of Panama used straps of gold to support their breasts. Hammered sheet gold was preferred in south Colombia. As in Peru and Ecuador the technique of *cire-perdue* casting reached refinement in many areas of Colombia, but perhaps the most striking examples were those from the Quimbaya region, such as the mask shown here and lime bottles in the shape of human figures.

A later development by the craftsmen of the Sinú valley was the perfection of the technique of filigree casting, which is particularly

Below **294–5** A nose ornament and pendant, probably from the Quimbaya region, Colombia (AD 500–1500). The nose ornament (**294**, left) is formed from a thick drawn gold wire bent into a spiral, with hammered flat discs attached to each end.

The pendant (**295**, right) is cast by the *cire-perdue* technique from surface-enriched, gold-copper alloy. It is in the form of a stylised bird; the outspread wings and tail were probably further worked by hammering. The bird wears two pairs of plumes, spiral ear

ornaments and a nose ornament of the same type as **294** (see detail, *below right*). H (**295**) 9cm

Right **296** A gold mask from the Quimbaya region of Colombia (AD 500–1500). It is cast as a human face wearing a nose ornament; pieces of gold metal hang from the ears and forehead. H 12cm

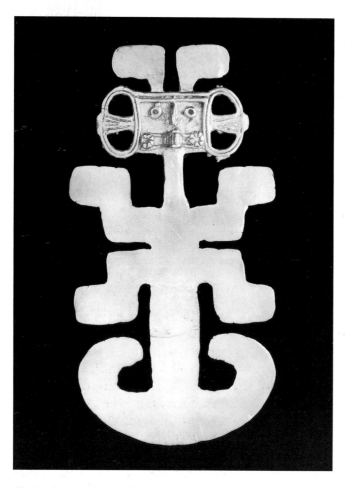

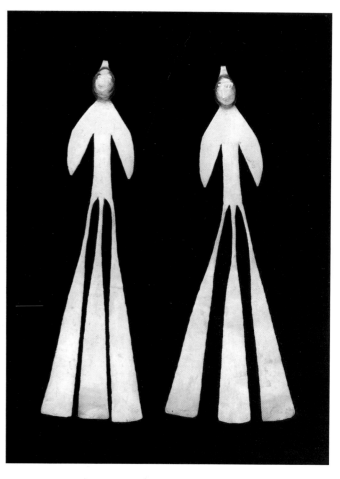

302 effective in the delicate crescent-shaped earrings. Much of Colombian ornamental work, and particularly that from the Quimbaya region, was made of an alloy of gold and copper known as *tumbaga*. A technique of depletion gilding was used in connection with the working of this material. By pouring acid over the alloy the copper was eaten away, concentrating the gold on the surface and producing a warm yellow colouration.

This technology had interesting implications which help illuminate another facet of this people's conceptualisation of the world. What appears to be of most importance is not the metal from which the ornament is made but the golden colour which gives it specific symbolic connotations. The use made of this process suggests an attitude where the external appearance of an object has to reflect the essential nature of the material from which it was manufactured. The surface must reflect the true nature of the material as a whole. In one sense the process makes manifest the most important quality of the material which would otherwise be hidden. It reveals a secret of the presence of gold and in so doing invites the beholder to acknowledge its relationship to the Inca nobles appointed by the Inca himself, and this last and greatest of the lords as descendant of the sun-god. The mystery of statehood and religion is revealed through the processes by which the sacred gold is made visible from an apparently base metal.

The Mesoamerican artisans, like their South American counter-

Above left **297** A gold pendant (AD 500–1500) in the form of a stylised figure with an axe-shaped base. It was cast by the *cire-perdue* technique, stretched by hammering and polished. Such pendants, in the shape of flat ceremonial knives and decorated with stylised figures, are characteristic of the Tolima region of Colombia, from where this example comes. H 13.5cm

Above right **298** A pair of ear ornaments from Antioquia, Colombia (AD 500–1500). The hammered gold ornaments are cut in the form of birds with their heads raised in relief; the eyes are defined by repoussé work (see detail, *below*). L 21cm

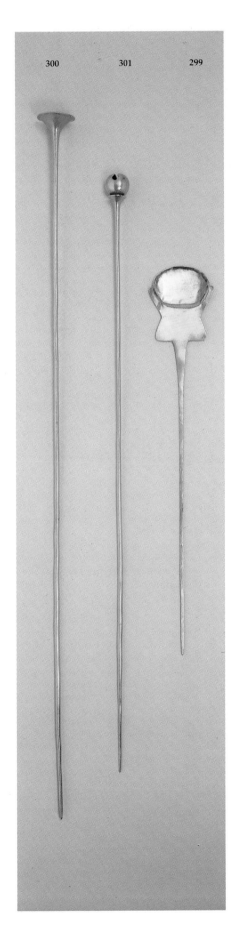

parts, and metalworkers were organised into fraternities. They inhabited particular areas in the community and were placed under the patronage of a special deity. The Aztec goldsmiths, *teocuitlahuaque*, were concentrated in Azcapotzalco on the shore of Lake Texcoco and placed under the patronage of Xipe Totec, the deity of spring and earthly renewal. Early post-Conquest chroniclers and connoisseurs have borne witness to the technical excellence of the Aztec metalworkers, and have recorded the Aztec manufacture of articulated pieces and bimetallic ornaments from gold and silver. Unfortunately few of these have survived.

As with the Maya, it was not gold that was given most value but jade; the word *chalchihuitl* not only designated the stone but alluded to everything precious. In Aztec cosmology jade symbolised sky and water, and small balls of the stone were placed in the mouth of the dead as a means of denoting their eternal life to come. In contrast, gold (*teocuitlatl*) was 'the excrement of the gods'. It was with lofty disdain that the Aztec saw the Spanish passion for this metal. Jewellery manufactured from gold includes nose ornaments and serpent-and-eagle labrets worn through perforations in the lower lip of Aztec rulers, whereas jade was used in necklaces, bracelets and in the manufacture of ceremonial masks. In addition to these materials the plumage of exotic birds was fashioned into decorative crest designs emblazoned on shields and magnificent head-dresses worn by rulers and nobles as insignia of their rank.

Exceptional among Mesoamerican cultures are the gold ornaments manufactured by the Mixtec craftsmen, considerably more of which have survived to the present day because they were buried alongside their owners after death. The Mixtec civilisation flourished in

Left Three gold pins (AD 500–1500). **299** is from Andean South America; its head is formed by hammering, cutting and repoussé.

300, with its trumpet-shaped head, and **301**, with a bell-shaped head, are from Calima, Colombia, and are cast by the *cire-perdue* technique. L (**299**) 54cm

Below **302** One of a pair of openwork earrings cast in gold-copper alloy from Sinú (AD 500–1500). This piece is typical of the work of the Sinú region of Colombia, where the art of openwork casting and the use of false filigree had been perfected. W 9.5cm

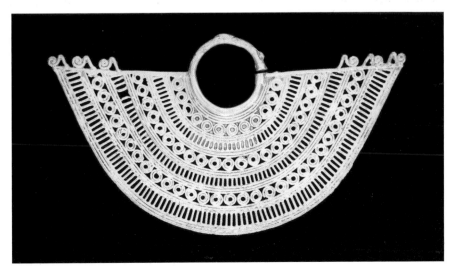

late post-Classic times (1300–1400 AD) in south central Mexico along the valleys of Oaxaca. Using the techniques probably derived from the South American metalworking traditions, the Mixtec cast pectorals, pendants and rings which depict not only the gods of their pantheon but also the arrangement of the heavens and the order of world levels, all of which are of fundamental importance in understanding their religion and symbolism.

AS

A group of Mixtec cast-gold jewellery (AD 1000–1500). The two pendants, **303** and **304**, are from Tehuantepec (Mexico). **303** has a human face wearing articulated earrings, which are hung with four chains which end in bells.

304 is in the form of a human figure, carrying a club, a shield and arrows, and wearing moveable ear ornaments and a small mask suspended from his lip-plug.

The finger-ring (**305**), cast by the *cire-perdue* technique, has a feline head flanked by serpent heads and geometrical designs. Although finger-rings are not common in pre-Columbian America, the Mixtec did produce some very fine ones, including some with attached pendants. Many of the designs are examples of false filigree, such as the one shown here.
L (**303**) 13.5cm

CHAPTER ELEVEN

Europe, Islam, China Korea and Java

AD 1000–1500

Later Byzantine Jewellery

The most notable development in Byzantine jewellery after the end of Iconoclasm (AD 730–87, AD 813–43), during which images were banned, was the introduction of gold cloisonné enamel, already highly developed in Western Europe. Enamel is glass, heated to the point at which it melts and bonds with metal with which it is in contact. In the cloisonné technique the design was laid out in tiny strips of gold (cloisons, 'partitions'), soldered or welded to the gold base-plate. Coloured glass (usually from mosaic *tesserae*) was then introduced as a powder, and the whole plaque fired in a kiln. The glass was topped up and refired as necessary until the composite surface of gold and glass could be ground smooth and polished.

The technique was soon a speciality of Byzantine jewellers, particularly in the representation of saints; the tenth century AD saw the development of *Senkschmelz*, a variation in which the figure or motif is silhouetted against metal instead of having a fully enamelled background (*Vollschmelz*).

504

503

DB

306 A gold filigree openwork brooch, decorated with granulation and set with pearls. The central cloisonné-enamelled roundel shows a crowned bust. Although this brooch was found in England, at Dowgate Hill, London, its closest parallels seem to lie in German workshops of the late 10th and 11th centuries AD. Certain features of the metalwork, the pearl settings and the delicate enamelling are all characteristic of German goldwork at this time. The crowned figure suggests a king, but any closer identification of this simplified image is impossible. D 3.5cm

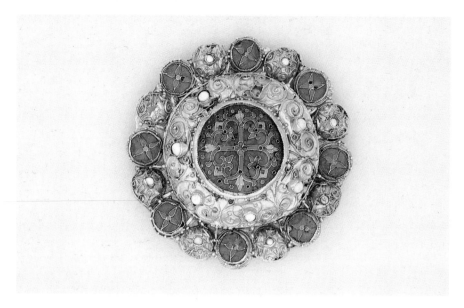

Left **307** The 'Townley' Brooch, made in Ottonian Germany (first quarter of the 11th century AD). Incorporated as its centre-piece is an enamel disc made in Trier in the late 980s or early 990s. The round brooch is of gold, with filigree, pearls and cloisonné enamel; the loops around the centre-piece once held a string of pearls. D 5.9cm

Right **309** A group of Kiev Russian silver jewellery, some decorated with niello (12th–13th century AD). The material is part of a hoard discovered in 1906 in the Street of the Three Saints, Kiev (Ukraine, USSR), and may be associated with others of similar composition from the city, buried perhaps under threat of the Tartar invasions of the 1230s. Nielloed motifs of interlaced griffins and geometric patterns occur on the head-dress pendants, known as *kolts* (**a**–**c**), while the silver beads on other such pendants (**d**–**h**) are heavily enriched with filigree and granulation. The finger-rings (**i**–**k**) have decoration in niello, and two are incised with a *tamga*, or noble family symbol. The terminals of the twisted rod armlet (**l**) have foliate decoration in niello. D (**l**) 6.7cm

Middle left **308** A sheet-gold head-dress pendant (*kolt*) of Kiev Russian type (12th century AD). On each face of the hollow pendant the overall shape of the decorative motif is cut out and filled with polychrome enamels in cloisons. Around the edge are supports for a string of pearls (now missing). This is one of a series of such pendants which display a rich and innovative iconographic repertoire, drawing on both Slav paganism and Byzantine-inspired Christianity. L 4.1cm

Bottom left **309m** A silver hinged bracelet from the 12th to 13th-century hoard found at Kiev (*right*). It is richly decorated with motifs including birds, fish, a fabulous creature and elaborate foliate forms on a ground which was originally nielloed (the pecked surface now visible was for keying the niello). The decorative motifs on this and other comparable bracelets have a deep pagan significance. Such jewellery is a regular part of rich female costume in the cities of Kiev Russia. H 5.3cm

The Influence of Byzantine Jewellery

Byzantine influence had long spread widely beyond the frontiers of the empire. This can be seen, for example, in the art of the Carolingian and Ottonian court schools in Western Europe (Charlemagne was crowned Emperor in the West in AD 800; the Emperor Otto I married the Byzantine princess Theophano in 972). Similarly, in Russia diplomacy and religious ties linked the court of Kiev with Byzantium from the late ninth century, and imperial fashions inspired techniques and richness in the 'courtly' jewellers of Kiev and allied cities. The twelfth-century gold head-dress ornament, in its shape, iconography and technique of cloisonné enamel, is typical of such a workshop. The silver work with skilful niello inlay is representative of twelfth- and early thirteenth-century jewellery current in a number of cities within Russia.　　　　　　　　　　　　　　　　　　DK

308
309

Medieval Jewellery

Representations of medieval jewellery show that it was usually worn on clothing and that its effect was achieved by the use of silver, gold and stones against the varied silks, cloths and brocades of medieval costume. There is no evidence for earrings in Northern Europe and it is only in the later Middle Ages, with the adoption of more closely tailored dresses often with low necklines that necklaces began to be worn there. Unlike Byzantine jewellery, the effect of medieval jewellery was obtained not so much by the use of enamelling as setting stones in gold or silver or by inscriptions.

The ring brooch, one of the most common types of medieval jewel, was used to fasten the dress at the neck. This is amusingly illustrated by the gold brooch from Writtle (Essex, England). The inscription itself is one way of decorating such ring brooches. Another is the use of stones, sometimes set in high collets or, like the one of Hungarian origin, alternately set with monsters. In the fourteenth century the shape of the ring brooch was varied by the increasing choice of shapes such as lozenges or hearts. The heart-shaped brooch was particularly favoured as a gift between lovers.

323

328c

The development in the fourteenth century of more three-dimensional jewellery may be illustrated by the Holy Thorn Reliquary. Set between two fragments of rock-crystal it is in the form of leaves with enamelled scenes of a King and Queen adoring the Virgin, the Presentation in the Temple, the Flight into Egypt, the Deposition and the Crucifixion. Shaped like a small illuminated Book of Hours, and even including as the central panel a manuscript illumination of the Nativity and the Annunciation to the Shepherds, it provides an unusual example of the effect of illuminated manuscripts on the design of jewellery. It is a courtly jewel whose translucent enamel gives a vivid and colourful effect.

509

The Dunstable Swan Jewel, probably pinned to the hat or dress, uses enamel in quite a different way. The shape of the swan is delicately sculpted in gold with the feathers covered in opaque white enamel. It may be compared to the jewels of the white hart worn by Richard II and the angels attendant on the Virgin Mary who welcomes him on the painting known as the Wilton Diptych now in

Right **310** The Dunstable Swan Jewel. The swan is modelled in gold covered with white enamel on the head, body, wings and legs; there are traces of black enamel on the legs and feet. At the back are the original pin and catch. This is a fine example of the use of opaque white enamel *en ronde bosse* over gold, a rich technique used in Paris at the beginning of the 15th century for large reliquaries, and also probably used in England. A rubbing of the monumental brass of Joan Perient (**311**, *far right*) shows how the Swan badge might have been worn. Joan Perient, buried at Digswell, Hertfordshire (England), was chief lady-in-waiting to Joan of Navarre, wife of Henry IV.
H (**310**) 3.2cm

Below right English medieval finger-rings. The gold ring from Wittersham, Kent (**312**), of *c.* 1200, is set with a sapphire. This is an extremely fine example of the stirrup-shaped type of ring, which was in use in England by the middle of the 12th century.

The six silver rings were found at Lark Hill near Worcester in 1854, together with coins of Henry II; the hoard was probably deposited *c.* 1180. Three of the rings have rectangular bezels, set with a crystal (**313**), an amethyst (**314**), and a yellow paste (**315**). The bezel of **316** is decorated with niello; that of **318** is in the form of clasped hands. D (**312**) 3.7cm

Below **319** A gold 13th-century ring brooch from Writtle, Essex (England). On the two sides is an inscription reading: IEO : SUI : FERMAIL : PUR : GAP : DER : SEIN : + KE : NU : SVILEIN : NIMETTE : MEIN, which may be translated; 'I am a brooch to guard the breast that no rascal may put his hand thereon'. D 2cm

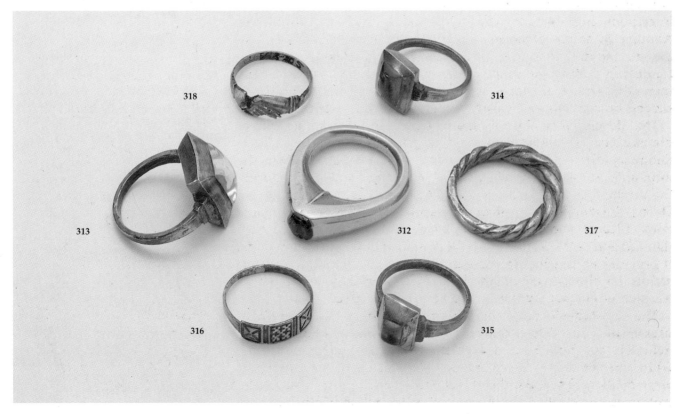

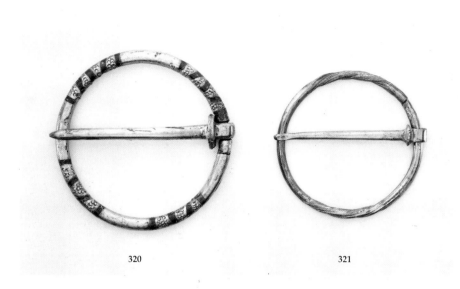

320 321

Left Two 13th-century silver ring brooches from Coventry, Warwickshire (England). The decoration on the larger brooch consists of punched ornament and inlaid bands of niello. These brooches were found with a coin hoard deposited in the last decade of the 13th century, and probably date from the second half of that century. Many simple silver ring brooches have been found in hoards in northern England and Scotland deposited at the end of the 13th and the beginning of the 14th century. D (**320**) 4.6cm

the National Gallery. The jewel provides an indication of the love of display in courtly circles at the beginning of the fifteenth century. The swan was used as a livery badge by the Lancastrian kings, particularly of the Prince of Wales. The use of the badge by Henry of Lancaster, later Henry IV, derived from his marriage to Mary de Bohun. The de Bohun family were particularly attached to the badge since they considered themselves descended from the Swan Knight of medieval romance. In this way medieval romance had an influence on medieval jewellery.

Medieval jewellery and rings were often exchanged between lovers. Some pieces bear inscriptions or posies indicating the thought behind the gift. Such posies were rarely the invention of the purchaser but were usually chosen from a repetitive stock of phrases such as *Vous avez mon coeur* (you have my heart), *Sans de partier* (without any division) or *A ma vie de coeur entier* (you have my whole heart for my life). A hoard from Fishpool (Nottinghamshire, England) deposited in the 1460s, provides some good examples of love jewellery with the inscriptions in black letters set amidst enamelled flowers and foliage.

328

Much more study is needed on the differences in the jewellery worn in different parts of Europe in the Middle Ages. There is a very clear contrast between the decorative gold jewellery of the Fishpool hoard, with its enamelled inscriptions and flowers, and the cruder silver jewellery of the Chalcis hoard (from the castle of Chalcis on the island of Euboea, Greece) with its greater preponderance of belt fittings and its use of niello and filigree enamel.

326–7

Brooches, rings, pendants, hat badges or ornaments and decorative belt-clasps were worn by both men and women. From the fourteenth century sumptuary laws were passed limiting the wearing of gold jewellery to the wealthier or more noble sections of society. It is not clear how far they achieved this aim, although they do provide clear evidence of the desire to maintain a social hierarchy in terms of ornamental display.   JC

OPPOSITE

Top left **322** A gold 13th-century ring brooch, set alternately with rubies and sapphires *en cabochon*. This attractive brooch, of French or English origin, was a lover's gift. On the reverse is engraved: IO SUI ICI EN LIU DAMI : AMO: – meaning 'I am here in place of the friend I love'. D 3.8cm

Top right **323** A gold 14th-century ring brooch. The four raised openwork bosses, which alternate with sapphires and emeralds, are in the form of monsters. The eight projections are set with sapphires and pearls. The close similarities between this piece and jewellery found in Hungary (in the Hungarian National Museum, Budapest) suggests that it was probably made in Hungary. D 5.6cm

Bottom left **324** A gold lozenge-shaped brooch set with spinels and sapphires, of north-west European origin (14th or 15th century AD). At the end of the pin are three small pearls, and there was originally a pearl at each of the points of the lozenge. L 4cm

Bottom right **325** A gold 15th-century brooch, said to have been found in the River Meuse. It is in the form of a pelican in her piety standing on a scroll; on her breast is a ruby, and on the scroll a pointed diamond, a smaller bird and the letters YMTH (their significance is unknown). L 3.8cm

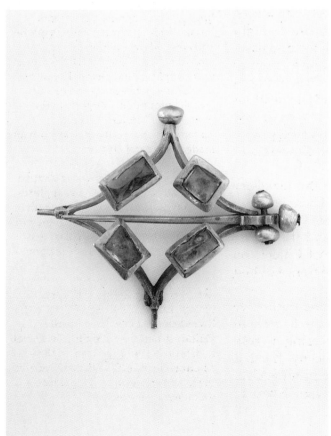

Left **326** The Chalcis Treasure: a selection from the silver rings and personal ornaments (possibly Venetian, 15th century AD) found in the 19th century at the castle of Chalcis, Euboea (Greece). The group includes silver-gilt belt fittings and terminals, a medallion, a chain and two belt-plaques. The buckle and belt-terminals are decorated with openwork tracery. Filigree work is found on the medallion and the belt-plaques. On the medallion the bird is reserved against a background for translucent enamel. The plaques have brown and opaque green enamel, divided by filigree. This technique is thought to have originated in or near Venice in the second half of the 14th century, and is best known from Hungary in the 15th century.

Top right **327** A silver buckle from the Chalcis Treasure, showing a man's helmeted head in profile modelled like a cameo. Although the use of open tracery and grotesque animals on jewellery in the Treasure recalls northern European Gothic decorative motifs, the cameo-like head on this piece is more classical in derivation. L 98cm

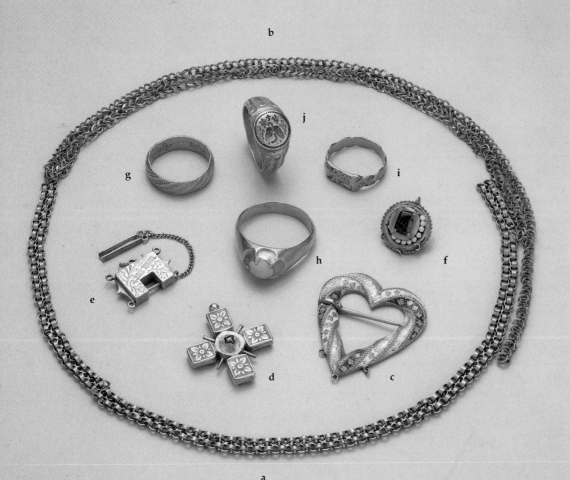

Left **328** The Fishpool Hoard of gold jewellery. The hoard, which included 1,237 gold coins, consists of two chains, a heart-shaped brooch, a pendant cross, a padlock, a gemset roundel, and four finger-rings. The coins indicate that the hoard was buried early in 1464. The richness of the hoard suggests that its owner would have been either a very rich merchant or a prominent member of one of the opposing factions in the Wars of the roses: one of the rings (**j**) is a signet engraved with an unidentified heraldic device.

The jewellery is elaborately decorated with black letter inscriptions, engraved flowers and foliage and enamelling. The heart-shaped brooch (**c**), with opaque blue and white enamel on the front, has an inscription on the back: *Je suy vostre sans de partier* (I am yours without any division). The cross, with engraved flowers on the arms, is set with a ruby on the front and four amethysts on the back (**d**). The roundel (**f**) has a central sapphire surrounded by white enamel beads on stalks. It has been suggested that it may have been imported from the Continent or possibly made in England by craftsmen working in a Continental style. Ring **g** is inscribed on the inside with an inscription meaning, 'raise your heart'; **h** is set with a turquoise and **i** has the figure of a saint engraved on the bezel.

Right **328e** The gold padlock from the Fishpool Hoard, inscribed on one side *de tout* and on the other *mon cuer*, amidst foliage and leaves. D 1.5cm

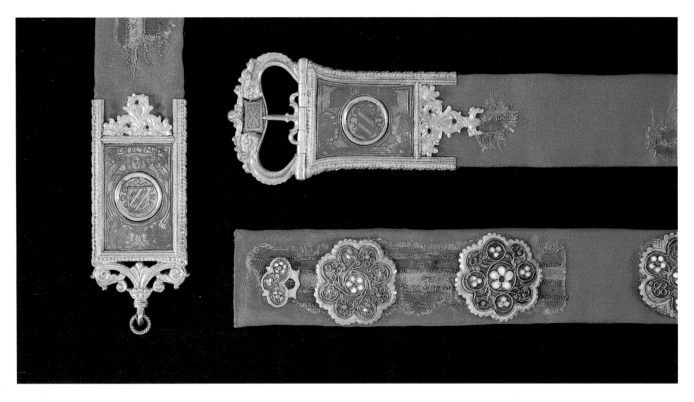

Above **329** Silver-gilt belt fittings from a Venetian velvet belt (15th century AD), including a buckle, plaques and a belt-end. The velvet has been remounted and the exact original position of the fittings is uncertain. The buckle and belt-end are fine examples of Italian niello work. Filigree enamel is used on the belt-mounts, and is very close to that found in the Chalcis Treasure. On the buckle, between a male and a female bust, is a shield of arms, probably those of the Malatesta of Rimini; the facing busts suggest that this was a betrothal gift. The belt-end also has a medallion with a shield of arms set into each side, but their significance is unclear. L (buckle) 9.8cm

Left Three silver Venetian pendants, each inset with a niello roundel (15th century AD). They show, on one side, busts of a youth and girl in profile (**330**) and female busts (**331, 332**). On the other side of **330** is the sacred monogram, IHS, while **331** and **332** have interlaced patterns. The presence of profile faces on these three medallions suggests that they are secular rather than religious and that, because the profiles are facing, these were betrothal medallions. D (**331**) 2.3cm

331

330

332

Islam

Our knowledge of the development of Islamic jewellery is hampered by the lack of a tradition in Islamic society of burying goods with the dead. As a result very little jewellery has survived (precious metal was melted down and precious stones restrung or remounted on a more fashionable setting by later generations), and that which has survived is usually without provenance or date. Pictorial representations are of little assistance; they are rare before the fifteenth century and are anyway inadequate as a record of what was actually worn.

During the first few centuries of Islam, craftsmen continued in the Roman, Byzantine and Sasanian traditions; in form, technique and decoration, Islamic jewellery is virtually indistinguishable from that

333–4 Plaques from two sets of silver and parcel-gilt belt-trappings found at Nihavand, West Persia (11th–12th century AD). These two contemporary sets of trappings show an interesting contrast in style: one (top) is decorated in a repoussé technique with a bevelled design, enhanced with niello (**333**); the other (bottom) uses niello to create a scrolling palmette design (**334**). The pointed plaques have a pair of studs on the reverse for attaching to a leather belt. The circular and square plaques are backed by another piece of metal and would have been threaded onto the belt to cover the place where the pendant straps were joined to it. The pointed plaque with the ring attached would have sheathed the end of one of the pendant straps, enabling a sword or dagger to be hung from the belt. L (**333**, rectangular plaque) 5.3cm

of earlier cultures. It is not until the eleventh century, and the growing popularity of Arabic epigraphic decoration, that jewellery can be positively identified as Islamic.

A buried hoard, discovered at Nihavand in Western Persia, provides us with a rare and fascinating insight into the treasured possessions of Abu Shuja Inju Takin, an officer of the Turkish military élite in Persia. The hoard consists of a gold wine bowl, and silver belt fittings, weapon fittings, beads and an amulet-case. The hoard demonstrates the popularity of gilt and nielloed silver in medieval Persia; although the quantity of silver must reflect the financial situation of its owner rather than a preference for silver over gold. The finest of the silver objects are the belt fittings. The belt was of great importance in Turkish and Islamic society; it was an integral part of male costume, often presented to him by the ruler, and symbolising his status at court. One of the belts has a bevelled design, which, in a society where Turks were dominant, may be a conscious reference to the ethnic origins of its owner. Another style of belt, featuring a massive buckle and two pierced rectanguler plaques, was fashionable in the lands west of Persia between the thirteenth and fifteenth centuries.

A large proportion of the gold jewellery which has survived from this period is decorated with filigree and granulation. Much of it was produced in Cairo, although the wide spread of find-spots of jewellery of this type, suggests that it was produced in several other centres too. Cairo was also the source of a group of cloisonné enamels, some of them decorated with Arabic inscriptions, inspired by contemporary Byzantine enamels.   RW

Above **335** An 11th-century gold pendant from Fatimid Egypt. Filigree ornament and granulation surround an enamelled design of confronted birds. The hoops around the rim would have held a string of seed-pearls or beads. w 2.1cm

Below **336** A pair of 12th-century gold earrings from Syria, decorated with filigree and granulation. Hoops placed around the rim would have secured a string of seed-pearls or beads. This type of earring recurs throughout the medieval Near East, in Byzantine, Persian and Arab cultures. w 2.6cm

337–8 Two gold filigree finger-rings from Egypt, Syria or Persia (11th–12th century AD). The rings are enhanced by granulation, and each has a rectangular bezel with concave sides curving outwards to the shoulders. The face of each bezel is decorated with an Arabic inscription in Kufic script, one of which may read *Uthman*. H (**337**, left) 3cm

China and Korea

The main types of Chinese jewellery established by the Tang period, hair ornaments and belts, continued in use throughout the Song (AD 960–1279) and Yuan periods (AD 1280–1368). Hair ornaments were increasingly elaborated, with heavy pins and complicated pendants. A few exotic large pins have been found in excavations. 378, 379

Techniques of openwork and granulation continued in use and were if anything advanced; similar developments took place in the decoration of thin sheet metal. The belt-plaque decorated with fruit is finely and skilfully executed. By comparison with the tenth-century comb the technique of chasing combined with relief is used to much more striking effect and is utterly appropriate to the decorative theme. The control of this technique laid the foundation for the elaborate work of the Ming dynasty in the fifteenth and sixteenth centuries. 344
259

To the north of China lay the region dominated successively by the Liao (AD 907–1125) and the Jin (AD 1115–1234) – the reign titles assumed by the Khitan and Jurchen tribes – who adopted many customs of their neighbours. Both peoples appreciated luxurious personal ornaments, and ample examples of the crowns favoured by the Liao and the pins and necklaces popular with the Jin have been found in their tombs.

The Koreans further east had their own distinctive tastes in jewellery. Small cast plaques are peculiarly Korean, although the themes of birds, animals and flowers were shared with their Chinese neighbours. Likewise some Korean hairpins are idiosyncratic. Short, rather heavy pins with rounded knobs incised with scrolls are unlike the larger, more elaborate pins fashionable in China. JMR 339

345

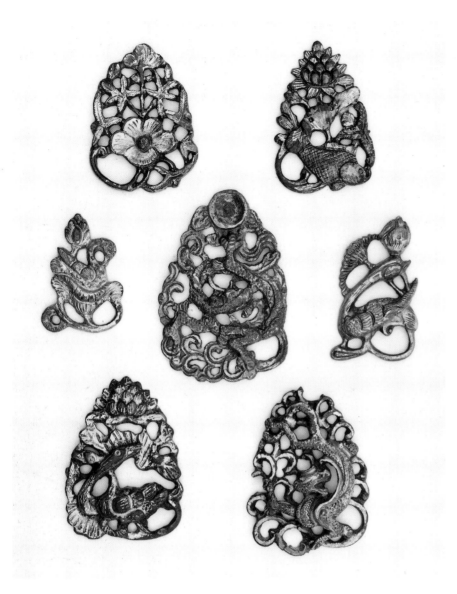

Left **339** A group of seven Korean plaques (11th–13th century AD), cast in silver and gilded; the openwork decoration is of dragons, birds, fish or flowers. H 2.4–4cm

Bottom left **340** A pair of Chinese gold armlets of the Yuan dynasty (13th–14th century AD). Armlets were certainly used at an earlier date in China and have been found in tombs of the 5th and 6th centuries. However, this pair belong to a tradition of rather longer armlets which was established in the Song dynasty. L (approx.) 19cm

Below Three gold Javanese finger-rings of the Majapahit period (*c.* 1293–1520), or perhaps later. **341** is set with a cabochon crystal; its hollow shanks have pearled ribs at the shoulders. **342** and **343** have chased decoration in high relief, and **343** has a plain gold bud as its bezel, surrounded by chased foliage and lotus leaves. D (**343**) 3.5cm

The Majapahit Empire was one of the greatest of the pre-Islamic states of Indonesia. Based on far-flung trading connections, this Hindu–Buddhist state, with its capital at Majapahit in eastern Java, wielded considerable political and military power in the Indonesian archipelago during its heyday in the second half of the 14th century.

341

343

342

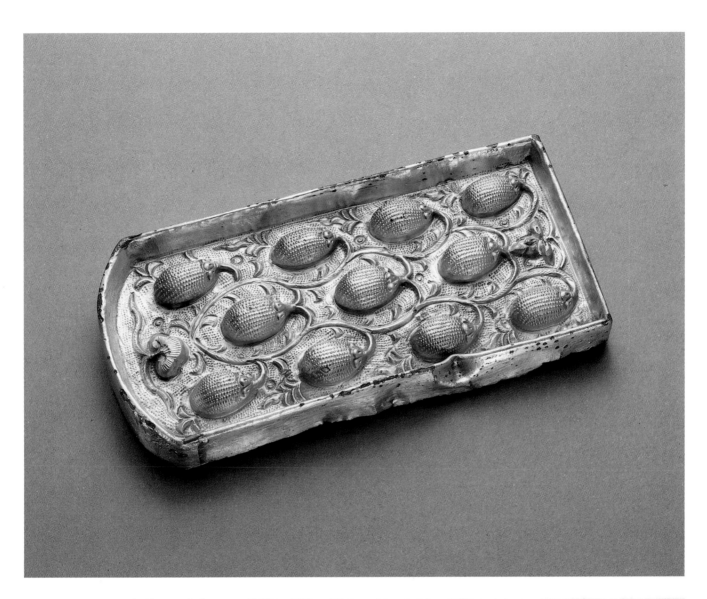

Above **344** A silver-gilt Chinese belt-plaque of the Yuan dynasty (13th–14th century AD). The decoration of fruit on a climbing plant is worked in relief against a stippled background. This is the buckle plaque from a set (the others would have been approximately square), which would probably have been attached to a leather belt. L 11.6cm

Right **345** Three silver Korean hairpins of the Koryo period (13th–14th century AD). The silver prongs have solid gilded heads, each with a small knob (missing on one of the pins) at the centre of a ring of radiating incised lines and a scroll border. This is a very unusual form of pin, contrasting with the more usual, slender types. The scroll design can be paralleled in other types of metalwork and on other materials of this date. L 6.1cm, 5.4cm

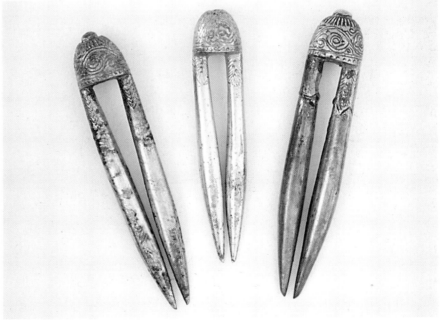

CHAPTER TWELVE

Europe

AD 1500–1700

For a brief period, lasting little longer than the second half of the fifteenth century, Renaissance Italy seemed to have experienced a period of harmony between body, dress and ornament. The extreme artificiality of the fashions of the French and Burgundian courts of the first half of the century, which had been much copied throughout Europe, gave way in Italy to a simplicity and a natural grace that, no doubt, was directly connected with the discovery of human beauty in the nude, even perhaps with the recognition of man as an individual whose natural dignity springs from his qualities and merits, not from his origins and inheritance. From mid-fifteenth-century Florence these concepts and ideas flowed through the courts of Ferrara, Mantua and Urbino to the great cities of Italy and found expression in a hundred different ways. Judging by the Italian portraits of the period, jewellery was being worn with discrimination more in order to enhance the beauty of the female body and less as a symbol of rank.

Despite the official forbidding of 'a display of the neck and shoulders', the neckline steadily fell during the last decades of the fifteenth century until the full *décolletage* became universal, and, with it, the return to the jewelled necklace and choker (or gorgeret), which had been such favourite items of jewellery in Classical antiquity but which had virtually disappeared during the Middle

346 A gold enamelled hat-jewel. The repoussé scene depicting the Conversion of St Paul is set with diamonds and rubies. The hat-jewel, which is probably Italian or possibly Spanish (mid-16th century AD), has an inscription on the back in Italian, recording that it was set in the cap of the Marchese Camillo Capizucchi, the distinguished Roman military commander, by Don John of Austria (1547–78), half-brother of Philip II of Spain and the victor at the Battle of Lepanto against the Turks in 1571. D 4.8cm

347 Two designs by Hans Holbein the Younger (1497–1543). They are apparently alternative versions for the same girdle prayer-book, presumably to offer the patron a choice. It is thought that they were made for Sir Thomas Wyatt and his wife Jane around the time of their marriage in 1537, since both of these pen and ink drawings incorporate the three initials, T W I. Certainly, Wyatt's portrait was drawn by Holbein, and Thomas and Jane were prominent figures at Henry VIII's court. Wyatt is now better remembered as a poet and the student of Renaissance literature, who introduced the sonnet from Italy into England. The two designs have been preserved in the British Museum since 1753.

Ages. Conversely, the ubiquitous medieval brooch fell completely out of fashion.

There was, however, little accurate knowledge of Greek and Roman jewellery and so in no sense could the new Renaissance jewellery be described as a rebirth of the Classical tradition, except in cameo carving – though, of course, many cameos were never intended for jewellery but for the cabinets of connoisseurs and collectors. The Renaissance jewellers and goldsmiths took their designs and decorative motifs from the general repertoire of Renaissance ornament, a new vocabulary built up by the artists of the Quattrocento. Though the forms and techniques were not Classical in origin, the jewellery of the Renaissance was visually quite distinct from the Gothic.

The hair, hitherto hidden beneath wimples and coifs or those steeple head-dresses, was now revealed and either entwined with strings of pearls or aigrettes of precious stones. Earrings, especially hung with pearls, came back into fashion, for the hair was often gathered up to reveal the beauty of the neck; unfortunately, few seem to have survived in their early Renaissance settings.

The bracelet also reappears for the first time in Europe since Classical antiquity and ladies of rank took to wearing pomanders and tiny prayer-books, hanging from the waist on a long chain reaching almost to the floor. Indeed, Henry VIII's great court painter, Hans Holbein, produced at least two alternative designs for one of his English patrons, notably for Thomas Wyatt soon after his marriage in 1537, although it is doubtful if either met with approval and was ever executed. A remarkably similar little girdle prayer-book with

352

Above A group of Tudor jewellery, with enamelled scenes embossed in relief. The girdle prayer-book (**348**) is datable to *c.* 1540 because of the form of the English inscriptions on both the front cover, with the scene of the Brazen Serpent (Numbers xxi, 8), and on the back, with the scene of the Judgement of Solomon (3 Kings iii, 27). Inside, the printed devotional book is an Elizabethan replacement and includes a unique set of prayers printed in 1574.

The pair of panels (**349**) with Latin inscriptions come from the covers of a now-lost girdle prayer-book,

c. 1530–5, representing the Judgement of Solomon and, most unusually, the scene of Susanna accused by the Elders and the Judgement of the young Daniel. The latter is depicted in the portrait of Lady Speke (**352**). Much of the original enamelling on both panels is lost.

The two hat-jewels (**350**, **351**) both represent Christ talking to the Woman of Samaria at Jacob's Well. **350**, with its inscription in English and Renaissance architectural motifs, is datable to the 1540s, whereas the more primitive and smaller version (**351**) can be attributed to the 1530s. D (**350**) 5.7cm

Right **352** Lady Philippa Speke, dated 1592, painted by an unknown artist of the English School in oils on panel (91.5cm × 73.6cm). Born Philippa Rosewell, in 1584 she married George Speke, who was knighted in 1603. She is depicted wearing fashionable jewellery of the 1590s but holding in her left hand a gold enamelled girdle prayer-book, made some 60 years earlier, probably for the wife of Sir Thomas Speke (1508–51), a successful courtier in the service of Henry VIII. Its cover corresponds closely to one of the pair of detached panels above (**349**).

arabesque ornaments in black enamel on the gold but without any initials within the design did survive in the Wyatt family – possibly a third version from Holbein's workshop. The portrait of Anne, Lady Penruddocke, painted by Hans Eworth in 1551 when she was only twenty years old and which remained in the family home at Compton Park until 1930 (see Roy Strong, *The English Icon* (1969), no. 46, p. 102; also an unidentified sitter, no. 51), shows how these miniature girdle prayer-books in their elaborate gold covers were often a prominent item of jewellery.

The men of the early Renaissance seem to have worn jewellery very sparingly; over the dark close-fitting tunic or doublet perhaps a gold chain, the belt fastened with a small enamelled buckle and, unlike the medieval fashion, only two – or at most three – finger-rings. The portrait of the 2nd Baron Wentworth (1525–84), dated 1568, ten years after his surrender of Calais to the French, shows him wearing a narrow belt with a gold enamelled buckle almost identical to **355**, gold buttons on his doublet and a jewel hanging from a blue riband around his neck. The badge or *enseigne* worn in the hat in the late Middle Ages was transformed from a modest affair, usually with religious and amuletic overtones, into a totally new and magnificent type of jewel, often with subjects of Classical mythology rendered in miniature sculpture. Cellini describes how in 1524 the fashion was for the subject to be chosen by the patron and how he vied with his great rival Caradosso (died 1527) to excel in the modelling and enamelling of these miniature scenes in high relief.

The courts of Europe embarked on a new era of formal splendour on an unprecedented scale, led by the Spanish court, rich from its vast possessions in the New World. Bare skin was once more lost behind rich brocades and velvets and mask-like faces and bejewelled hands seem dwarfed amidst stiff ruffs and starched lace collars and cuffs hung with pendant jewels of incredible size and intricate detail. Even the men were encrusted with a profusion of pearls and jewels, as in the half-length portrait of Robert Dudley, painted at the time when he was created Earl of Leicester in 1564 and was striving for the hand of Queen Elizabeth I, whose favourite he was for many years. A spectacular present from James I (1603–25) to one of his more humble subjects, a gentleman of Somerset called Thomas Lyte, has survived; a locket, complete with a Hilliard miniature of the King inside. It affords an opportunity to assess the high artistic standards being achieved in London at this date. By good fortune the jewel was painted in 1611 as it hung on the chest of the proud Thomas Lyte and, instead of the routine pendant pearl, we can see that the goldsmith had ingeniously devised a most unusual pendant of table-cut diamonds ending in a trilobed drop.

The art of the miniaturist was increasingly in demand in the seventeenth century, partly, no doubt, because of the level of perfection to which it had been brought by artists like Nicholas Hilliard in England and François Clouet in France. Led by Jean Toutin and his son, Henri, the goldsmiths of France developed a wonderful technique for painting miniatures in enamel on gold, and some delicate items of jewellery have survived. The earliest date to appear on any of these pieces is 1636 and is accompanied by Henri Toutin's signature

1
362
361
365

Top A group of 16th-century gold jewellery. The openwork pomander (**353**), probably made in England (early 16th century), was once enamelled, but when found in 1854 on the Surrey bank of the River Thames it had lost all trace of colour and 7 of its 12 pearls. This piece, made in two halves, is held together by a central tubular rod and a small ring-topped screw at the top.

The chain (**354**), perhaps worn with a pomander, a girdle prayer-book or, even, a *flohpelze* (a marten or sable fur) at the end, has only 11 of its original polygonal openwork links remaining. Each is enamelled and has pyramidal motifs (around the centre) in the manner of faceted diamonds.

The belt-buckle (**355**), a type worn by men and fashionable at the Elizabethan court, c. 1560–70, is ornamented with an enamelled openwork design. The buckle is fastened by slipping the dome-shaped head of one section into the larger loop on the other. A narrow cloth belt would have been threaded through raised gold bars on the reverse and stitched. H (**353**) 5.2cm

Bottom **356** The Cheapside Hoard of gold jewellery (*c.* 1600–40), found under a house in Cheapside, London (near St Paul's Cathedral), in 1912. Much of the Hoard is in the Museum of London, with a further selection in the Victoria and Albert Museum. This group, in the British Museum, is representative of the main new types of jewellery in the Hoard, which was probably part of a jeweller's stock. Only a few items of the finest court quality were found; much of it would have been suited to the purse of the lesser nobility and the successful late Tudor and early Stuart merchant class – the very kind of jewellery that was universally melted down and reworked as fashion changed. Consequently, unique types and shapes are to be found in the Hoard. The pair of openwork enamelled gold pendants have 20 rose-cut amethysts swinging freely to catch the light; there is a garnet and sapphire pendant, and the four smaller buttons have neat settings for the rubies and diamonds. One of the three 'fan-holders' (centre) is set with emeralds, and in one of the rings is a single cat's eye; most extraordinary is the pendant of bunches of grapes carved in amethyst.

353

354

355

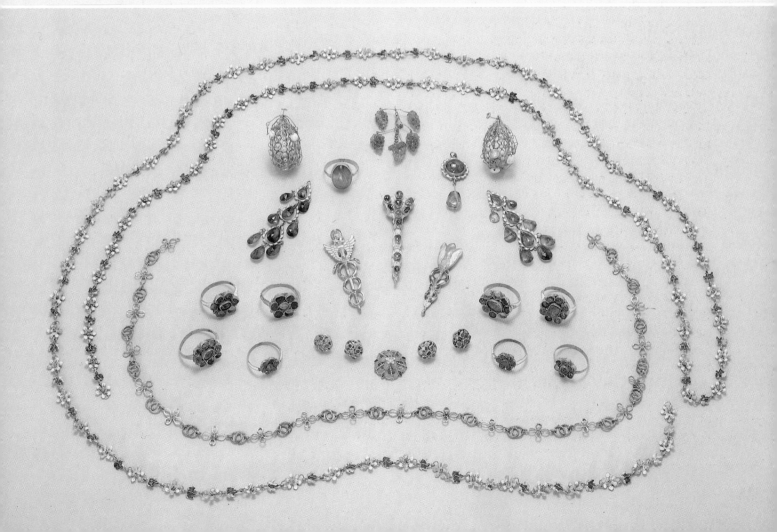

Left and below left **357** Two pendants from the Insignia of the Order of the Garter belonging to William, 1st Earl of Northampton (1567–1630) and made between September 1628 and April 1629. The Earl's insignia is the earliest complete set to have survived and, because of his great wealth, the two pendants are made entirely of enamelled gold, studded with diamonds and rubies. The 'Great George' (*left*) is modelled in the round – a fine example of the continuing technique of *émail en ronde bosse* – and is set with many diamonds of varying cuts. The 'Lesser George' (*below left*) was intended to be worn by a Knight of the Garter on less formal occasions not requiring the wearing of the collar and the rest of the insignia (see **1**), and this openwork specimen is double-sided, with both sides equally richly set with gemstones. H. (of the 'Great George') 7.2cm

Right and below right **358** This English or Netherlandish (Antwerp?) relief of 'Joseph being left in the well by his envious brothers' (*c.* 1540–50), probably made to be worn in a hat jewel, has been reset in the Paris workshop of Alfred André (*c.* 1880–90) as a pendant (comprising a pseudo-Renaissance enamelled frame with its suspension element, still set with a table-cut diamond). On the frame, four blobs of green enamel replace the four gemstones that were originally designed to be secured by the gold bolts which are still clearly visible especially on the reverse (*below right*). The translucent *basse-taille* enamelled oval disc in the centre is in the style of mid-16th century engraved designs by the French artist Jacques Androuet du Cerceau. H. (total) 12.8cm

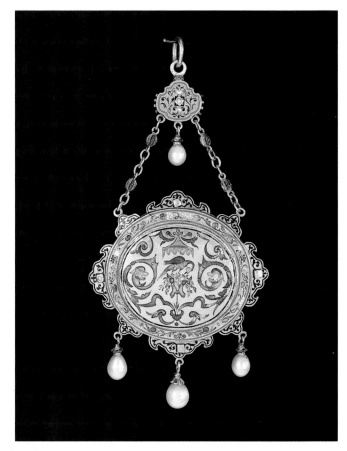

Left **359** A gold enamelled Spanish pendant in the form of a sea-dragon (late 16th century). The body and part of the tail of this fantastic beast consist of two large, irregular-shaped pearls, known as 'baroque' pearls. Smaller pearls mask the join of the tail and the body. Such huge pendants were intended to be worn over rich brocades, particularly for pinning high up on stiff sleeves so that the jewels were free to swing, catching the light as they moved, as can be seen in the portrait of Lady Speke, dated 1592 (**352**). L 10.5cm

Right **360** The 'Phoenix' Jewel; a gold pendant with a bust of Queen Elizabeth I cut out in silhouette (English, *c.* 1570–80). The surrounding enamelled wreath includes red and white Tudor roses. On the reverse, in relief, is the device of a phoenix in flames under the royal monogram, a crown and heavenly rays. The Queen is said to have adopted the phoenix as an emblem of herself; in one painting, she is portrayed wearing a pendant jewel in a form of a phoenix. However, there is no firm documentary evidence concerning the use of this emblem during her reign.

This jewel, which since 1753 has been in the British Museum, is a unique survival. The bust appears to have been freely and individually tooled, engraved and chased, not cut from a medal. w 4.6cm

361 Thomas Lyte (1568–1638), by an unknown artist of the English School. Painted in oils on panel (58.4cm × 45.1cm), the portrait, dated 14 April 1611, includes the inscription giving the sitter's age as 43 years and shows him wearing the 'Lyte' Jewel, which he had received from the King in the previous year. The artist has recorded the exceptional form of the Jewel's original pendant with its trilobe drop; by the 19th century this diamond-set pendant had been replaced by a modern pearl. The portrait remained at Lytescary (Somerset), the family home, until the male line died out in the 18th century.

in full. The minute polychrome scenes and floral decorations are often hidden on the backs of the jewels, and in England and the Netherlands this style was copied in monochrome on the backs of many items of jewellery during the middle decades of the century.

Knowledge of Jacobean and early Carolean jewellery in England is hampered by the acute lack of surviving material, though the evidence recorded in portraits and in the lengthy inventories is valuable. In 1912 the chance discovery near St Paul's Cathedral (London) of the Cheapside Hoard (as it has since been called) provided a new dimension. Although there were jewels of the better known types, like the gold enamelled salamander set with table-cut diamonds and cabochon emeralds, there were many of unparalleled form and design, like the gold hairpin in the shape of a shepherd's crook set with table-cut diamonds and rubies, or the so-called 'fan-holders' of enamelled gold, some set with emeralds. Furthermore, although the Hoard was very large the jewels could be mainly dated to the first three decades of the seventeenth century; fortunately, not all the

Right **362** The 'Lyte' Jewel (English, 1610). A gold enamelled locket set with 29 diamonds. The pierced openwork design of the cover incorporates the monogram IR (for King James VI of Scotland and I of England, who succeeded Queen Elizabeth in 1603).

The four 'Burgundian point-cut' diamonds, set as flowers in the openwork surrounding the monogram IR, date from the fifteenth century, when diamond-cutters at the court of the Duke of Burgundy first created faceted diamonds. They had discovered that diamonds had the property of reflecting the rays of light from pavilion facets set at the correct angles of inclination. Under James I, many of the royal jewels were refashioned and the old gemstones were reset, as on the Lyte Jewel.

Inside the locket is a miniature of James by Nicholas Hilliard (1547 – 1619), the court limner (see **5**, p. 19). The reverse of the cover is brilliantly enamelled in red and blue. The back of the jewel (*below*) is mainly white enamel, with a design in fine gold lines and ruby enamel.

The jewel was given by James I in 1610 to Thomas Lyte, of Lytescary, Somerset (England), as a reward for drawing up an illuminated pedigree of the King. The portrait of Thomas Lyte illustrated opposite (**361**) shows him wearing the jewel. H 6.2cm

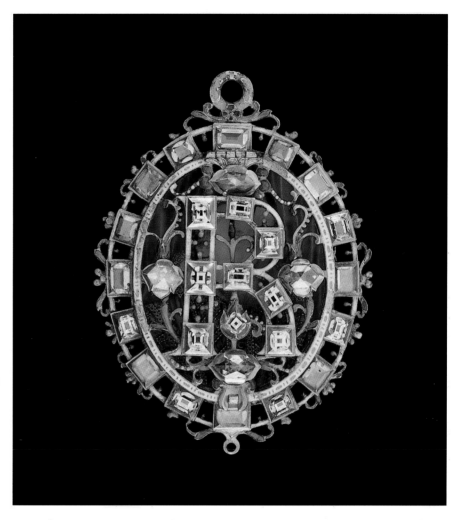

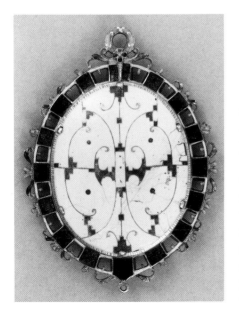

jewellery was of the finest court quality – indeed, some may be typical of the kind worn by the wives of rich merchants and the like. The Hoard's vast range – 35 different chains, 48 finger-rings, 83 pendants, 6 hat ornaments, 2 hairpins, 33 buttons, 12 unmounted cameos, 8 unset intaglios and 5 gems of paste, and a scent-bottle on a suspension chain – is further enriched by 2 watches and various rock-crystal vessels and other associated material. This curious mixture of unmounted gems and of jewellery of varying degrees of expensiveness has led to the suggestion that it was the stock of a jeweller's shop near St Paul's Cathedral and that it was buried in the 1640s, perhaps because of the Civil War. There is still no firm evidence to support this very plausible interpretation but the jewellery itself typifies the change under Charles I towards a lighter style in which faceted stones were suspended swinging within thin, almost flimsy, settings. The diamonds are mainly table-cut but many of the coloured gemstones are faceted briolettes and there are examples of flat rose-cutting. However, the continued use of cabochon gemstones is significant and many of the smaller ones are grouped in clusters within an enamelled setting. Enamelling is profusely used to enrich the effect and the colours are light and gaily delicate, with many backgrounds in a white enamel. The very varied chains illustrate the fashion for delicate enamelled flowers linked by small gemstones.

Perhaps the most interesting aspect of the Cheapside Hoard is the range of engraved gems and the fashion for cameos at this period. Not only Renaissance examples but also ancient and medieval engraved gems and glass pastes were in the Hoard, many without mounts, though some were still in their original settings. Perhaps the most unexpected carved stones are the amethyst grapes hanging in bunches from gold enamelled earrings, presumably of Jacobean or early Carolean date. Equally rare and unexpected is the gold pendant scent-bottle with its combination of enamelled decoration and plaques of carved opaline chalcedony.

Among the very few extant English jewels which can be reliably dated to those few years just prior to the Civil War is the locket of Sir Basil Grenville (1595–1643), the Cornish Royalist General who was killed in the Battle of Lansdowne, near Bath. It contains his portrait painted by David Des Granges, the miniaturist who was employed by both Charles I and Charles II. The gold locket itself is a carpet of brilliant enamelling, with geometric patterns on the reverse but an unrestrained design on the front, filled with pansies, marguerites and leaves interspersed with rubies, opals, diamonds, emeralds and a large sapphire. It is an exquisite rarity, offering sound evidence of English court taste on the eve of the Civil War.

With the change of fashion in the Baroque seventeenth century, vast flowing silken fabrics replaced the stiff tight costumes of the late Renaissance and its great display of formal ceremonial jewellery. The French court, which now set the fashions, tended to frown on the wearing of much jewellery as vulgar and, once again, jewellery became subordinate to the decoration of beauty.   HT

Far left **363** Pendant medal or
Gnadenpfennig (Netherlands, 1627). The
enamelled gold frame encloses a gold
medal of Frederick v, King of Bohemia.
The obverse shows the bust of
Frederick, signed *S.D.R.f* and dated
1627. The reverse (*below left*) is
decorated with Frederick's crest as
Count Palatine – a crowned lion sejant
with orb and sceptre; the five hands
holding the crown represent Bohemia
and the four Protestant provinces
(Moravia, Silesia, Upper and Lower
Lusatia), which had elected him King in
August 1619 in opposition to the
Emperor Ferdinand II. The Imperial
army defeated Frederick's forces at the
famous Battle of the White Mountain,
near Prague, in 1620 and forced
Frederick and his 'Winter Queen',
Elizabeth, daughter of James I of
England, to seek asylum in the
Netherlands. L 4.25cm

Right **364** The 'Grenville' Jewel (English,
c. 1635–40). A gold enamelled locket
containing the miniature portrait by
David Des Granges (signed D D G) of
the Royalist hero, Sir Bevil Grenville
(1596–1643), who was killed while
leading the Cornish Royalist army at
the Battle of Lansdown, near Bath. The
jewel, mentioned in his widow's will in
1647, remained in the family until the
late 19th century. The front is richly
enamelled with a dense 'carpet' of
flowers, some set with rubies and
diamonds; interspersed among the
foliage are emeralds and opals, the
latter in high 'claw' settings to allow the
light through the milky, iridescent
gemstones. In the centre a large
sapphire is set in a raised enamelled
collet. The reverse (*left*) is flat, but the
brilliantly enamelled geometrical
design is exceptionally complex.

365

366

367

Above and *right* Painted enamelling on jewellery of the mid-17th century. These pieces illustrate the genre of enamelled miniatures on gold first made popular by French goldsmiths in the second quarter of the century. The locket (**365**) is by the goldsmith Henry Toutin. The front cover (*above*) shows a naval engagement and inside the cover is a scene of Diana and Actaeon. The reverse (*right*) shows a military siege. This piece,

dated 1636, is one of the earliest signed and dated works by Henry Toutin 'master-goldsmith of Paris'.

The enamelled miniature landscapes on the front of **366** (*above*), in a warm pinkish sepia monochrome, are derived from the style of Claude Lorrain. Between each of the landscapes is an allegorical or mythological figure. In contrast to these delicate landscapes and figures, the

368

365

366

reverse (*above*) is decorated, almost naively, with flowers and foliage in brightly coloured enamels. This necklace may be French, although there were Dutch, German and Scandinavian ateliers working in this manner in the mid-17th century.

The front of **367** (*left*) is set with 35 table-cut diamonds, with an octagonal sapphire and 3 rose-cut diamonds in the pendant; the painted enamelling is confined to the reverse.

Though necklaces of a similar character can be seen in Dutch portraits, including Rembrandt's picture of Saskia, this piece may not have been made in Holland, as both English and French workshops were adopting in this style.

The view (*above*) of a French ribbon slide, dated *c*.1630–40 (**368**), shows the reverse, delicately painted with flowers in coloured enamels. The front is set with an onyx intaglio (illustrated overleaf). H (**365**) 4.5cm

Above A group of 17th-century gold ornaments. The pomander (**369**) is Spanish (*c.* 1600); it consists of a ball of aromatic resin, gum benzoin, studded with small cabochon emeralds set in gold; the settings and the gold mount are enamelled.

The French ribbon slide (**368**), set with a late Renaissance engraved onyx intaglio gem, was in the famous collection of the Earl of Arundel (died 1646). On the reverse, which is colourfully enamelled (see p. 165), are two raised bars for the ribbon to slide through.

The Spanish emerald-set pendant (**370**) is dated to the late 17th century; its baroque style, derived from the French, has its own individuality. H (**369**) 4.4cm

Right **370** On the reverse of the Spanish emerald-set pendant are the insignia of the Holy Office of the Inquisition. By 1680 members of the Court, who were required to attend the Inquisition's *auto-da-fé* in Madrid, appear to have worn pendants of this discreet kind, which to some extent met the requirements of an earlier royal decree requiring the Insignia to be worn.

CHAPTER THIRTEEN

China, Mughal India Tibet and Mongolia

AD 1500–1800

China

This chapter has been devoted entirely to jewellery from China, India and Tibet, as it is less fruitful to explore similarities and comparisons with jewellery from the West at this later period than it was for earlier chapters. With the jewellery from Tibet a completely new style is introduced, while the Chinese, on the other hand, elaborate the themes already initiated (see Chapters 6, 8, 11). From China, prominent as before, are hairpins, and accompanying them are the ornaments in which a man would enclose his knot of hair. Such small caps in jade or gold are known from paintings and from a few excavated examples of the fourteenth to sixteenth centuries. From the Ming period, likewise, date excavated examples of the head-dresses worn by women. A full-size nineteenth-century example is worn by a woman in a painting. Although only comparatively late examples survive, some early paintings suggest that such head-dresses were worn before the Ming period. They bear a close resemblance to the crowns which adorned Bodhisattvas shown in both paintings and sculptures in the very complex forms current from the late Tang period (tenth century AD). 389

Hairpins were sometimes highly elaborate, incorporating small delicate jade flowers in a construction of metalwork. Flowers similar to **383–7** have been found in the pins from the tomb of the Emperor Wanli (AD 1573–1620), his Empress and concubines.

The other major genre of Chinese jewellery, belt ornaments, continued to play an important part. Up to the fifteenth century the main form of the belt set continued to consist of a group of plaques and a buckle ornament. However, while this remained in vogue, new forms were introduced in the Yuan period, which resulted in a greater diversification in general from the later Ming period. The jade belt ornaments illustrate some of the variety which evolved.

To the long familiar themes of animals, birds and flowers were added decorative motifs that referred to China's ancient Bronze Age culture. Coiled or undulating dragons on the plaques, known as *chi* dragons, were copied from designs popular in the Han dynasty (206 BC–220 AD). Such motifs were revised from the Song period (AD 960–1279) when ancient bronzes and jades were widely collected and catalogued. Variety was also introduced with the use of openwork and high relief carving with extensive under-cutting. Many examples of such belt-plaques found in dated tombs make it possible to date

371 A Chinese hair ornament of the Ming Dynasty (14th–15th century AD), carved from a hollowed-out block of jade. The ornament is pierced along its length for the insertion of a pin. It would have been worn by a man to hold a small bun of hair in place. Similar items are shown in paintings of the Song period but the majority of excavated examples, usually in metal or agate, are of the Yuan and Ming periods. L 5.7cm

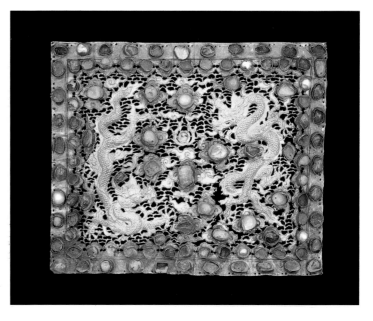

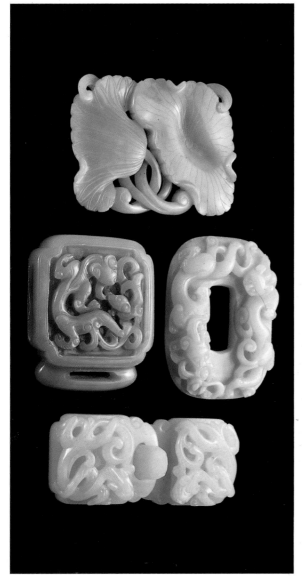

Top left **372** A Chinese hair ornament (14th–15th century AD). Like **371**, it was used to enclose a knot or bun of hair. Much of the ornament is executed in coarse ring-punching, and two side sections have a floral diaper pattern; there is also some chasing. A plain area at the back suggests that a further element was attached through four holes at this point. This ornament is very similar to one excavated from the tomb of the Prince Zhu Tan, who died in AD 1389. H 8.4cm

Above **373** One of a pair of gold Ming-dynasty plaques (15th century AD). Two dragons and a flaming pearl among clouds are worked in relief, with chased detailing. The openwork scrolls were formed by piercing the metal. The border and the clouds are crudely set with semi-precious stones *en cabochon*. The plaque is pierced around the edge for attachment, probably to official or ceremonial robes. H 15cm

Left A group of Chinese jade belt ornaments, illustrating the different forms used between the Ming and Qing dynasties. **374** (right), an early Ming-dynasty plaque (15th–16th century AD), has two dragons with branching tails in high undercut relief.

Also of the Ming dynasty (15th–16th century AD) is **375** (left), a plaque carved with a dragon in high relief with a bifurcating tail, its head turned towards a smaller dragon. The plaque is pierced to allow a leather belt to pass through; a subsidiary portion of the belt hung from the oval loop below.

The ornament carved as two lotus leaves (**376**, top) is also of the late Ming dynasty (16th–17th century AD).

377 (bottom) is a Qing-dynasty clasp, made in two parts (18th century AD). It is decorated in high undercut relief with crouching dragons curled around, their tails touching their heads. L (**377**) 10.3cm

378–82 A group of gold Chinese hairpins. **378** (far right) dates from the 13th–14th centuries AD; its hollow head is in the shape of a seed-pod or gourd. **379** (second from left) is later in date (14th–15th century AD); its head is in the shape of a plumed and crested phoenix, holding a small ball and ring in its mouth.

The three hairpins with filigree decoration are of the Qing dynasty (17th–18th century AD). At the head of **380** (far left) five petals of woven and coiled filigree form a flower enclosing a red semi-precious stone; wires with small heads represent the stamens.

The openwork pin (**381**, second from right) ends in a filigree lizard's head, with a further portion of filigree work below.

The head of the U-shaped pin (**382**, centre) has flowers of fine wire filigree enclosed in a wire framework; further details are executed in wire. The head is inlaid with a semi-precious stone and a pearl. Comparable filigree hairpins have been excavated from a 17th-century tomb near Peking. L (**381**) 13.2cm

383–7 Five Chinese jade flowers of the late Ming dynasty (16th–17th century AD). Elaborate gold and silver hairpins were sometimes set with jade flowers. Examples have been found in 16th-century tombs and in the tomb of the Wanli Emperor (AD 1573–1620). W(**385**, largest) 6.2cm

169

Left **388** A Chinese silver gilt crown-like headdress of the late Ming/early Qing dynasty (mid-17th century AD). Designed to be worn over the forehead and the front part of the head, the crown is constructed as a 'cage' made of thick curved wire and a bandeau decorated in repoussé with scrolling floral designs. To these are attached a multitude of elements: a centrally placed open flowerhead is surrounded by leaves, flowers, finger citron fruit, clouds and a flaming pearl, all on raised wires; amongst this profusion writhe two filigree dragons. Centrally placed on the bandeau is a group containing a phoenix, a dragon and a *shou* symbol against clouds; to the sides of this are separately hooked seven phoenixes, each with a flower on its back. To the back of the crown are hooked four birds resembling peacocks. The leaf or cloud elements attached to the highest strut of the cage are attached to it by coiled wires, so that they 'tremble' on touch or movement. The crown was once brightly embellished with kingfisher feathers and hardstones, a few of the latter remaining. H 18.5cm

389 An anonymous Chinese painting on a hanging scroll, with the portrait of a lady, wearing earrings and an elaborate head-dress (19th century).

these changes in style and technique to the period between the fourteenth and sixteenth centuries.

In the sense that these belts were an important article of dress, and became almost an integral part of the magnificent robes worn by officials and princes, a large gold plaque (one of a pair) can be considered in association with them. The design of dragons is of exceptionally high quality and can be dated quite confidently to the fifteenth century by analogy with designs on blue and white porcelain. It is instructive to compare the detail and high quality of the chased and relief work on the plaques with the much bolder and less refined treatment of the hair ornament which is somewhat earlier in date. Important, too, is the addition of polished gems in rather primitive settings, a characteristic of the Ming dynasty. The use of such boldly placed stones is rare before the Ming period but thereafter becomes an important element in Chinese jewellery.

The most important technical change to take place in the Ming and Qing dynasties is from working predominantly in thin sheets of metal to the use of wire filigree. The plaque illustrates a stage in this

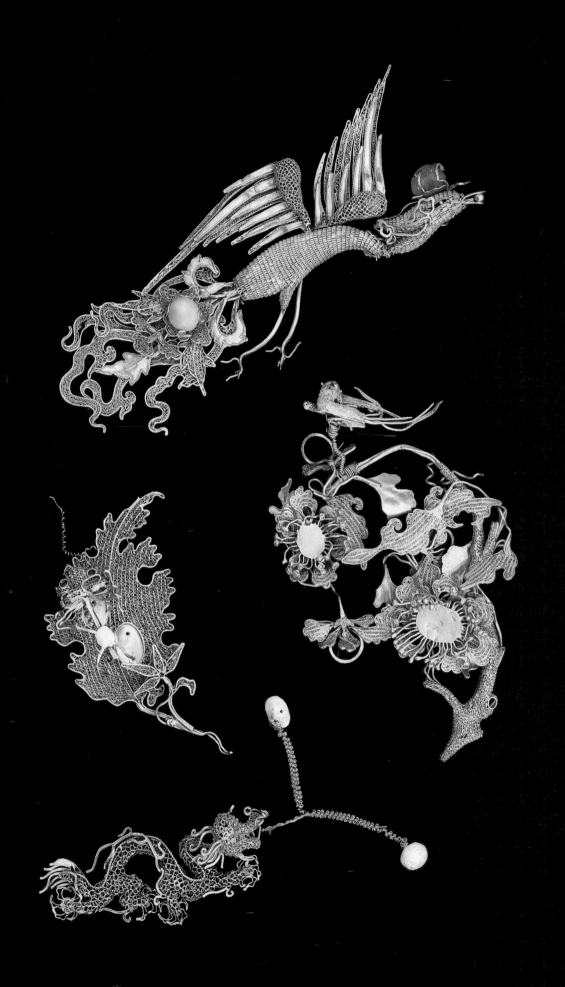

Left **390–3** Four Chinese gold filigree ornaments, of the Qing dynasty (18th century AD) set with semi-precious stones. Similar filigree work has been found as parts of hairpins and head-dresses excavated from Qing-dynasty tombs. L (**390**) 8.9cm

development: on the one hand there is great precision and detail in the execution of the dragons and on the other the effort to achieve an open light effect is arrived at by the pierced work around the clouds and the dragons producing a scroll effect. In the late fifteenth and early sixteenth centuries this trend to finer and more detailed work was continued until in the second half of the sixteenth century such pierced work was replaced by wire mesh and filigree.

An area where this transition can be dated quite accurately is in Jiangsi province in central China. Here two tombs at Nanchang, one dating to the second quarter of the sixteenth century with gold jewellery mainly worked from sheets of gold with pierced details, can be contrasted with a tomb dating from the later part of the sixteenth century in which a magnificent group of jewellery was found. In this latter group the fine detail is executed in elaborate wire mesh. During the seventeenth and eighteenth centuries such wire mesh was used both as a filler in the main elements of the design and as the structure of whole pieces.

Mughal Jewellery of India

The ostentatious display of jewels at the Mughal court mentioned by all visitors to it is borne out by contemporary miniature paintings and a large quantity of extant pieces. Jewellery was worn by both men and women, and was also used in the ornamentation of arms and armour, furniture and vessels. Gems dominate Mughal jewellery. India was a major source and trading centre for precious stones. They were eagerly collected and highly prized by wealthy

394 A miniature painting of the Mughal School (*c.* 1650), depicting Shah Jahan (AD 1593–1666; reigned 1627–58). He holds a fine turban ornament decorated with pearls and a large ruby, and wears another, set with a feather, in his turban. Strings of pearls sprinkled with emeralds and rubies are wound around his turban and also worn as necklaces, bracelets and armbands. More gems are set into his gold sword belt, although the mounts on the sword itself are enamelled. The two rings on his left hand are set with rubies, and he wears a gold thumb-ring (see **600**) on his left hand. 18.9 10.8cm

173

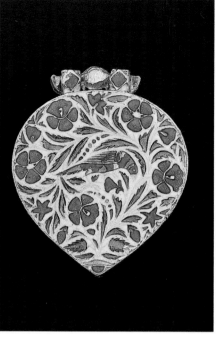

Far right A group of Tibetan turquoise-set jewellery (18th century AD). The ornamental plaque (**398**) is of gold, backed with silver and pierced with five tubular passages for threading or attachment with chains. The leaf and petal-shaped turquoises are set in raised mounts decorated with borders of pearled gold wire and globules.

The amulet-box (**399**) is also of gold. The sides of the lid, which fit closely over the side of the box, are decorated with a floral filigree pattern and flower design encrusted with turquoise.

The pendants (**400**) are made of bronze set with turquoises. Pendants of this type are reported as having been worn formerly by Lhasa women on festive occasions, but they were also generally common in Tibet. when worn, they are turned to the front.
L (**400**) 10cm

Above **395** Gold pendant from Mughal India (17th century AD). One side is decorated with a splayed eagle design. The breast of the bird is inlaid with a faceted diamond; flat-cut rubies and emeralds represent his feathers, against a background of engraved gold floral motifs and more rubies. The other side of the pendant has a champlevé enamelled design featuring a parrot amid a spray of red flowers. H 4cm

members of society; Shah Jahan was famous for his knowledge of gems.

Many gems were bored, strung and worn as necklaces – or as prayer-beads. Others were mounted on gold, which was often worked into an intricate design. Gems were also sometimes inlaid into hardstones, in a design outlined by gold. The stones themselves were frequently left *en cabochon*; stone-cutting does not appear to have been as popular in Mughal India as it was in contemporary Europe.

Enamel was also extensively used in Mughal jewellery. Its origins are unclear (it may have been inspired by European examples), but by the eighteenth century Jaipur was the centre of a thriving enamel industry. Being as colourful as gems, but cheaper and easier to work, enamel was particularly popular for the reverses of pendants and other pieces, decorated on their obverse side with precious stones. Despite their inferior position, Mughal enamels are of the highest quality, and their designs demonstrate the naturalism and botanical detail typical of all Mughal arts.

Tibet

Whereas Chinese Jewellery of this late period is increasingly detailed, the appeal of Tibetan jewellery lies primarily in its bold handling of metal and semi-precious stones. Among the Tibetans the use of jewellery was not confined to women, although 'ladies of good position' wrote Sir Charles Bell, [are] known as *GYEN-SANG-MA*

396 A detail of an armband from Mughal India (Jaipur), dated to the 18th century. The gold centre-piece is decorated on one side with precious stones and on the other with champlevé enamel in a floral design. The silk cords bound with seed pearls would have been tied around the upper arm of a Mughal nobleman. A painted miniature of Shah Jahan shows the Emperor wearing such an armband (**394**).
L (with cord) 39.6cm

397 A lady photographed at Shigatse (Tibet) in 1938. Her horned head-dress shows that she comes from Lhasa. She is wearing strings of seed-pearls, coral, amber and jade beads, a gold amulet-box studded with turquoises and diamonds, and a plaque or brooch of the same sort. The pair of pendants, which are very similar to these illustrated here (**400**, *above right*), were worn, not in the ear-lobe, but hooked into the hair facing the front.

Right **401** The form of this elaborately ornamented object suggests that it is a collar, although its precise function is not clear. It is Tibetan (18th–19th century AD), and is made of gilt bronze. The main section is in two zones: the inner is set with strips of turquoise, lapis lazuli and coral separated by decorated gilt-bronze plaques. The outer zone has incised floral scroll patterns and magical letters, in the *lantsha* character; at intervals are flowers with petals of cloisonné enamel and coral or turquoise centres. This section of the collar ends in two horned dragons' heads. Beyond these are the curved hinged terminals, also in the form of horned Chinese dragons.

(literally 'she with good ornaments'). Their liberal use of self-adornment, indeed, extended to head-dress, and facial and bodily decoration.

The effect of Tibetan jewellery is achieved by an interplay of predominantly turquoise incrustation, sometimes forming elaborate patterns, and metalwork devices such as scrolling with pearled wire and the decoration of settings with abundant false granulation. The metals range from copper alloy, sometimes gilded, through low-grade silver to gold. Turquoise, which in addition to its attractive colour was held to possess talismanic properties, was often of local origin; like the scarcely less popular coral, the use of which was already noted by Marco Polo (1254–1324), turquoise was also imported. Pearls, beads of various stones, coloured glass and lapis lazuli are also used; the inlaid stones, being fixed with a weak adhesive resembling sealing wax, are frequently lost. A similar love of coloured stones can be observed in the silver head ornament from Urga in northern Mongolia.

WZ

402 A Mongolian head ornament (19th century AD): a circlet of silver with two hinged attachments and two openwork pendants, decorated with elaborate scrolling of pearled silver wire and set with coral, turquoises and other stones. The two separate silver hair attachments, which are similarly decorated, were fitted to each of two large stiffened braids of hair. The braids are said to represent cows' horns, reminding married women of the Mongols' descent from a nature spirit and a cow. This head-dress was acquired in Urga by the donor from a Mongol woman who was actually wearing it. D (circlet) 15.9cm

CHAPTER FOURTEEN

West Africa

AD 1500–1850

Benin

Benin, the capital of a kingdom in the humid tropical forest region of southern Nigeria, has been the centre of government of a dynasty which has ruled for six hundred years or more. At the height of its power, by the mid-sixteenth century AD, the imperial authority of Benin was extended by military conquest far beyond the 'tribal' boundary of the kingdom as far as Lagos to the west and the River Niger to the east, incorporating substantial groups of Yoruba and Ibo peoples. Throughout this area the king was able to enforce the payment of tribute, the performance of military service and the safe passage of Benin traders as well as his own personal monopoly of the coastal trade with Europeans. The internal structure of this empire was inevitably complex, with various orders, grades and titles of nobility, a system of territorial administration, trading companies and so on. Considerable skill was demanded of the king in balancing the frequently opposing interests of different factions competing for political favours and power. The king was, however, no ordinary mortal, for at his installation he became the vehicle for those mystical powers by which his dynasty had ensured the survival and continuity of the kingdom.

As in many other cultures, the wearing of personal adornment was not simply a matter of individual taste but was rigorously controlled as a mark of status and rank. The most valued possessions of Benin notables were stiff necklaces of coral beads, conferred upon them by the ruler and returnable upon death. The worst fate that could befall a man was to lose such a necklace, the death of the offender being inevitable. Many other forms of ornamentation such as bracelets and anklets of ivory or cast brass were worn by special classes of courtiers or on particular ritual occasions. Particularly interesting are 'Maltese Crosses' of brass associated with the high god Osa and antedating European influence. Although gilding techniques were known in Benin, very little use seems to have been made of them and they are heavily associated with European motifs.

The production of works of art was organised among various guilds in the capital and their professional activities were controlled by the king. In particular the casting of brass by the Iguneromwan, the brassworkers' guild, and the carving of ivory by the Igbesanmwan, the sculptors' guild, are said to have been carried out only with the king's permission for the exclusive use of the royal court, either as ornaments and furniture for the palace and the royal ancestral shrines, or as regalia for the king and the nobility. Only the king

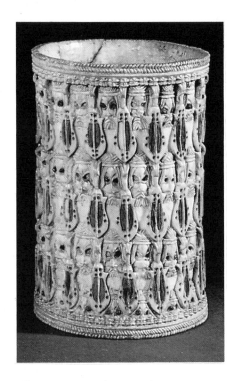

Above **403** One of a pair of Benin ivory armlets, inlaid with copper (16th century AD). Like its pair, it is carved with groups of Portuguese bearded heads alternating with ceremonial swords. L 12.5cm

Opposite, top **404** A pair of Benin ivory armlets, inlaid with copper (16th century AD). Each armlet is carved from a single piece of ivory to form two separate but interlocking cylinders with figures in high relief. On the outer cylinder are figures of the king; on the inner cylinder are elephant heads. L 13.3cm

Opposite, bottom **405** An ivory armlet from Benin (16th century AD). It is carved with European heads and inlaid with cast ornaments of gilt-brass in European style (see the detail, *right*). L 13cm

himself wore and used regalia of ivory. (He claimed the right to one tusk from each elephant killed in the kingdom and the option to purchase the other. Ivory surplus to his ceremonial needs would have been traded with Europeans.)

The late fifteenth to early sixteenth centuries was the period of greatest military success in the history of the kingdom, with increasing power, prestige and wealth at the centre, and it was also during this time that Europeans, beginning with the Portuguese, first established contact. These developments inevitably had their effect on Benin art which, in this period, displays great originality and skill. Portuguese influence was indirect though none the less profound, for Benin artists were clearly stimulated to introduce new forms and motifs by the sight of these exotic human beings with their long hair and long noses. They were stimulated too, perhaps, by the sight of goods in the baggage which can be expected to have included armour and illustrated books from Europe, as well as a variety of wares from India and the Far East. JP/NB

Asante

The Kingdom of Asante was one of the most successful imperial powers to arise in West Africa. Between about 1700 and 1900 this state dominated the central area of the Gold Coast (modern Ghana) and its influence was felt over a far wider area. Its power and prestige were largely founded upon the vast gold resources it controlled. Gold-dust was the sole currency for internal trade and it was also used to obtain European-made goods, such as fire-arms, which served to increase the power of the state.

By the beginning of the nineteenth century the Asante had devel-

Top left **406–8** Asante gold: a group of hammered and chased discs (18th–19th century AD); **407** (bottom right) and **408** (bottom left) also have repoussé ornament. These items were worn as insignia by senior servants of the Asante king. D (**407**, largest) 9.5cm

Bottom left **409–11** Asante gold: three beads cast by the *cire-perdue*, or lost-wax technique (18th–19th century AD). They are probably from a chief's anklet or wristlet. D (**409**, circular bead) 6.2cm

oped an elaborate system of centralised government based on the capital, Kumase, and linked to local chiefs and provincial administrators. Each level of the political and military hierarchy from the Asantehene (overall king) to local chief had its peculiar insignia and regalia. The creation and use of these were, therefore, directly related to the state's political order; and their redistribution followed changes in the pattern of rule. The wearing of gold jewels and gold decorated regalia was restricted to the king and major chiefs, and certain of their senior officials and servants. Gold-dust which had been accumulated during a successful career could only be turned into regalia with the king's permission. All goldwork was produced by professional smiths, some descended from those captured from defeated states in the early days of Asante expansion. In Kumase they worked under the strict supervision of a senior court official. Working for the king and for senior chiefs, they were expected to be inventive and to produce a steady flow of new and striking work. It is even possible that some of the king's gold was recast annually to impress visitors to the yearly Yam Festival by its seemingly infinite variety.

This gold jewellery and regalia was usually seen only on special days in the complex Asante calendar. Senior chiefs appeared in public heavily festooned with gold, and wearing rich silk robes. Imported glass beads were also worn, usually combined with small gold castings and nuggets to form anklets and wristlets. The weight of gold jewels adorning the wrists and arms of kings was sometimes so great that they had to rest them on the heads of small boys who stood in front of them.

Gold jewels also served as badges to show the rank of the wearers and to authenticate their claims to act on behalf of rulers. A particular class of royal servant, the kings' 'souls', were distinguished by circular gold plates, worn suspended around the neck by white cords. Crescentic gold pectorals, and occasionally ones made from imported silver, were given as rewards to the priests of gods who were believed to have helped the Asante, usually in wars against nearby peoples.

Asante goldsmiths were particularly skilled in lost-wax casting; the technique was probably first introduced into the area, perhaps as early as the thirteenth century, by traders from the north travelling in search of gold. By this technique, and by chasing and repoussé work, they produced a wide variety of forms nearly all of which show their liking for elaborately decorated surfaces. Some of the patterns they used seem to have been adapted from imported European silverware and, possibly, ceramics. Their representational work, and in particular the finger- and toe-rings worn by chiefs, was often made to call to mind well-known proverbs or aphorisms. To the Asante, therefore, this art has a verbal dimension.   MM

412 Asante gold: a finger-ring, cast by the lost-wax technique, with three cannon on top (18–19th century AD). D 2cm

413 Asante gold: this lost-wax casting, in the form of a scorpion, was probably broken from a finger- or a toe-ring (18th–19th century AD). L 4.7cm

Right and *below* **414** Asante gold: a lost-wax casting in the form of three elephants surmounted by six birds (18th–19th century AD). This was possibly either broken from a finger- or toe-ring or intended for mounting upon a cap. L 4.7cm

CHAPTER FIFTEEN

Europe

AD 1700–1950

Eighteenth-century jewellery owes much to the discovery in 1725 of a new source of diamonds in Brazil, where the mines operated by the Portuguese soon replaced India as the principal supplier. The availability of diamonds in Europe increased dramatically and changed the look of jewellery: emphasis was placed on the stones themselves, whether diamonds or other gemstones, and settings were kept to a minimum. This had a number of consequences for the construction and wearing of jewellery. Jewels were often made of separate elements that dismantled for use in different combinations: for example, large stomachers or ornaments for the front of the bodice, from the bust to the waist, comprised a series of brooches of decreasing sizes, each of which could be worn individually. Furthermore, large or valuable stones were frequently mounted in removable settings so that they could be taken out and reused in a different jewel or garniture (a set of jewels). Augustus the Strong, Emperor of Saxony, owned an Order of the Golden Fleece made in 1724 with two enormous removable opals; exceptionally, his jewels survive intact in Dresden.

423

Individual stones and complete jewels were also sewn directly to the costume. At the courts of Europe men rivalled women with their gem-set buttons, buckles, badges, shoulder ribbons and sword hilts. In London in 1792, Queen Charlotte wore a petticoat of green silk covered with lace drawn up in festoons with six diamond bouquets, from which hung two large diamond chains and tassels, with further diamond chains on each festoon of drapery. Many jewels were worn in the hair, padded to extreme heights in the 1770s and threaded with strings of pearls, jewels and flowers. A crucial part of such displays was the miniature portrait, a symbol of marriage and allegiance.

Few eighteenth-century gem-set jewels survive in their original state; they were almost always broken up and the stones reset as fashions changed. Imitations, of lesser intrinsic value but superb craftsmanship, often survive better. Jewels set with pastes (stones made of hard lead glass cut to resemble diamonds) were a much sought-after novelty and enabled experiments with cutting that would have wasted too much of a diamond.

By the nineteenth century, the development of the trade and of new materials meant that jewellery was accessible to a far wider audience, permeating all walks of life. It was strongly influenced by two major developments: one was the expansion of archaeological discoveries worldwide and their immediate transmission through the popular press and improved communications; the other was the rise of nationalism and the revival of historic styles – such as Gothic or

437–8

415 Queen Charlotte in her wedding finery. Mezzotint by Thomas Frye, 1761. The young queen wears a diamond diadem and huge earrings, and a diamond collar sewn to a ruched ribbon, from which hangs a huge bow. Strings of pearls are looped at her shoulders. These were the Hanoverian hereditary jewels given to her by King George III when she came from Germany to marry him in London in September 1761.

416–17 Two diamond hair ornaments or aigrettes made in Continental Europe, *c.* 1740–50. The term 'aigrette' (French: tuft of feathers) denotes a hair ornament, often clasping real feathers or resembling feathers in form. The ornament with pearls (**416**) is a rare survival of the asymmetrical rococo style in jewellery. It is close to ornament prints published in Italy in the early 18th century. Pattern books of engraved designs for jewels were circulated across Europe, encouraging international styles and making the origins of such jewels hard to determine. The ribbon-tied spray with emeralds (**417**) may be Spanish or Portuguese. The settings are closed back, permitting the use of metal foils behind the stones to enhance the colour and fire. L (**416**) 8.15cm

418 Badge of the Anti-Gallican Society. English, London, *c.* 1750. Rock-crystals set in silver and an enamelled medallion showing St George spearing the Royal Arms of France surmount a seated figure of Britannia and the motto 'For our Country'. The Anti-Gallican Society was formed about 1745 to promote British manufacturing and trade, and to discourage the import of French goods and customs. This lavish badge was made for a Grand President, perhaps Admiral Vernon (1684–1757), a great English naval hero and early president, who may have added the ships along the top which bear no relation to the Society's arms. H 13.9cm

Renaissance – to establish national identity. In Italy these two influences on jewellery design were combined by the Castellani firm of Rome, who turned their entire production to political purposes. Working during the struggle for Italian unification (achieved in 1861), they reproduced jewels found in Italy from ancient times onwards, creating a visual history of Italy as seen through jewellery to demonstrate that a united country was a great one. 439 434–6

Influences went far beyond Europe: the reopening of trade routes with Japan in the late 1850s prompted the export of Japanese art works that were avidly collected and imitated in the West. At the same time, international exhibitions, starting with the Great Exhibition of 1851 in London, fostered continual artistic and technical invention, from realistic botanical jewels to battery-powered electric cravat-pins for men with flashing 'diamonds'. At the end of the century, ideas of design reform led to led to a new movement in Continental Europe known as *Art Nouveau* or 'new art' (*Jugendstil* in German-speaking countries). Art Nouveau had many interpretations and produced startlingly original jewels, using mainly gold, silver and enamel, or horn heated and moulded into organic forms. 440–3 424–9 444–51

With the twentieth century came the rise of the big jewellery houses; many nineteenth-century firms had signed their creations – Phillips Brothers or Brogden in London, Falize or Wièse in Paris – but they were not brand names like Cartier, Tiffany or Bulgari. In contrast there have been artist designers, working on a small, non-commercial scale yet hugely influential, since the late nineteenth century. The post-war years have seen a burgeoning of individual designer jewellers, many of whom continue to be inspired by the jewels of the past.   JR

Above **419** Marcasite brooch or corsage ornament. English, mid-18th century. Marcasite is a popular name for the mineral iron pyrites, whose lustrous yellow colour led to its being called 'fool's gold'. Fashionable as a substitute for diamonds in the mid-18th century, it was revived for shoe buckles in the Edwardian period and again in the 1930s. This ornament incorporates conjoined hearts with love-birds. It is now fitted with a brooch pin but was probably intended to be sewn onto the corsage. L 15.3cm

420–2 Three brooches with messages in the form of hearts and keys. English, *c.* 1800. **420** Pearls and pink topazes with three tiny heart, key and padlock pendants. **421** A gold hand holding a pearl-bordered heart inset with a compartment containing hair; a miniature key hangs on a chain. **422** A diamond key with a hair compartment in the bow of the key, and two pendant hearts set with a ruby and a turquoise. The combination of ruby and turquoise had denoted a pledge of love since the Middle Ages. The message of these jewels is 'I hold the key to your heart'. Small-scale personal mementoes set with locks of hair or inscribed with sentimental mottoes were beloved by all classes of society. The Prince of Wales, later George IV, purchased jewels almost identical to these around 1800, and when Queen Charlotte gave a lock of her own hair set into a small oval brooch bordered with pearls to her great friend Mrs Delany, its recipient wrote: 'so precious a gift is indeed inestimable'. W (**422**) 3.4cm

Left and below **423** A set of convertible diamond sprays with oak leaves and acorns. English, sold by Hunt & Roskell, London, *c.* 1855. The set comprises three separate ornaments designed for wear in four different ways and was supplied with its gold fittings carefully stored in the base of the box, beneath the velvet pad (shown at the side in the photo). Each spray can be worn individually as a brooch; the two larger sprays can be fitted to the tortoiseshell combs for wear in the hair (shown assembled); all three combine to form a large corsage ornament when fitted to the lozenge-shaped frame; and the circular frame holds the three sprays as a tiara (shown below).

The Viscount's coronet and the initials MP on the lid suggest that the tiara may have been owned by Mary, wife of the 2nd Viscount Portman, who married in 1855. The retailer's name and address can be seen inside the lid of the box. Hunt & Roskell were probably the makers as well; they showed fabulous diamond jewels at the 1851 Exhibition. w of larger sprays 9.3cm

424–9 A group of botanical jewels in coloured gold, ivory, porcelain, pearls and enamel. English, *c.* 1840–60. Coloured gold is achieved by varying the amount of copper for red gold and silver for green gold. When combined with exquisite surface texturing to suggest a velvety pansy or a matt fruit skin, the effect could be remarkably naturalistic. Most of these jewels carry messages derived from the language of flowers, much studied in the 18th and 19th centuries. The meanings would have been immediately understood by both giver and receiver.

424 Bouquet with pansies ('you occupy my thoughts'), forget-me-nots, wild roses and a 'trembler' butterfly, mounted on a sprung wire; this is a hair jewel and the butterfly would have appeared to hover above the head.
425 Peach branch with bird, showing a subtle use of coloured gold inlays for the bloom on the peach. **426** Pink camellia with tinted ivory petals.
427 Pear brooch, the pear in green gold.
428 Vine brooch with threaded seed pearl grapes; identical brooches were shown at the Great Exhibition of 1851.
429 Spray of orange-blossom with green enamelled leaves and porcelain flowers. Queen Victoria wore a wreath of fresh orange-blossom at her wedding in 1840; the flower was chosen because it means 'chastity', or 'your purity equals your loveliness'. It was subsequently worn at all Royal weddings. The Queen owned a set of similar orange-blossom jewellery given her by Prince Albert between 1839 and 1845; it is likely that this brooch was one of a number commissioned by the Queen for members of her family. w (**428**) 7.2cm

430 Turquoise eagle brooch, with ruby eye and diamond beak. English, 1840. This is one of twelve brooches presented by Prince Albert of Saxe-Coburg to each of the bridesmaids at his wedding to Queen Victoria in 1840, in the form of the Coburg eagle. Two other brooches still survive in the families of the original recipients. One is at Woburn house in Bedfordshire, where it was worn by the Marchioness of Tavistock, later Duchess of Bedford; the other is at Hatfield House, where it was worn by the Marchioness of Salisbury. The turquoises are pavé-set, that is, with minimal settings to give an all-over effect. w 4.5cm

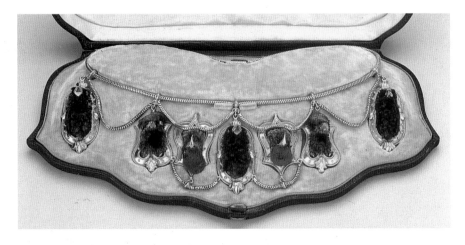

431 Necklace of humming birds' heads. English, made by Harry Emanuel, London, 1865–70. This startling jewel incorporates feathers from the heads of green and scarlet humming birds, imported from Brazil for costume and accessories. Two of the scarlet heads are placed upside down in the box: the colour occurs on the top of the head and the jeweller wanted to create maximum effect on opening the lid. In wear these heads would hang the right way up. Emanuel patented his method for removing the feathers and attaching them to a gold base in 1865. His shop at 18 New Bond Street, the address on the box, closed in 1870. Original boxes often help to date a jewel. w of box 20cm

432 Carved coral parure. Italian, made in Naples, *c*. 1860. This luxurious five-piece set with tiara, bracelet, necklace, brooch and earrings, is a remarkable survival. It is carved entirely from pale pink coral, known as 'angel's skin', which was highly prized in the mid-19th century and much more expensive than dark red coral. Coral has amuletic properties and has been worn for centuries to ward off evil. In the early 19th century strings of large coral beads were widespread. This, however, is an exquisitely decorative piece: the motifs echo the marine origins of coral – mermaids, tritons, dolphins, shells, hippocamps. The carving is consummate and, protected by the original box, has survived in perfect condition. Probably the set was a souvenir of a wedding tour to Italy and hardly worn. L of box 34.8cm

433 Gold bracelet with granulation in the Etruscan style. Italian, made by Giacinto Melillo, Naples, c. 1870. In the early 19th century excavations of the classical tombs around Rome revealed quantities of previously unknown ancient jewellery. Covered with elaborate wirework and minute patterns of tiny gold grains (a technique known as granulation), these ancient pieces inspired modern copies, some faithful or adapted to contemporary taste. This piece reproduces exactly the motifs from cylindrical Etruscan earrings but flattens out the square elements to form a bracelet. Melillo trained in the famous Castellani workshop. L 19.6cm

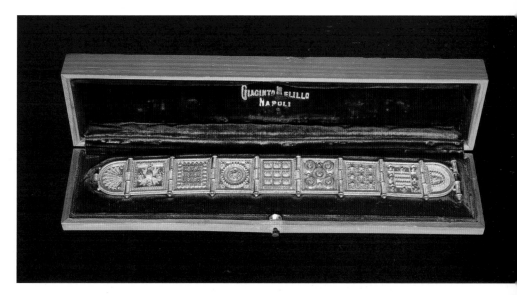

434 Gold and diamond necklace with 'Pompeian-style' medallions. French, made by Eugène Fontenay, Paris, 1867–73. Like Castellani and Melillo in Italy, Fontenay recreated the classical models readily available in Paris from the famous collection assembled in Rome by the Marchese di Campana, sold to Napoleon III in 1861 and displayed in the Louvre. While Castellani slavishly copied the ancient jewels of Italy to demonstrate the national heritage of a country he wished to see united, Fontenay had no such political message to convey. He mixed elements from different periods – here enamel medallions inspired by the Roman wall-paintings at Pompeii are combined with pendant drops and butterflies taken from Hellenistic Greek fringe necklaces to produce a jewel of supreme elegance, scintillating with diamonds not found on any classical piece. D of medallions 3cm

435–6 Two gold brooches by Castellani, Italian, Rome, c. 1860. **435** Brooch in the medieval style with a Lamb of God in micromosaic. The mosaic uses tiny cubes of glass, or gold for the halo; it copies the 12th-century apse mosaic in the church of San Clemente in Rome. The enamel border was taken from a 7th-century brooch owned by Castellani and sold to the British Museum in 1865. D 5.3cm. **436** Brooch with a head of Helios, the sun god, bordered by rays, the hair executed with granulation. Inspired by a Hellenistic Greek ornament in the Campana collection. D 3.25cm

437–9 A group of medieval and Renaissance style gold jewels.

437 (*top*) Brooch with a dragon in a trefoil. French, made by the firm of Jules and Louis Wièse, Paris, late 19th century. The design is inspired by the sculptural decoration on French Gothic cathedrals. A wax model was cast and then worked up by hand. w 4cm

The two pendants with enamel, pearls and gemstones are recreations of jewels depicted in paintings. **438** (*left*) is English, made by Phillips Brothers, London, *c.* 1860–70. It is copied from a portrait in the Royal Collection said to be of the young Queen Elizabeth I and attributed at that time to the Tudor court painter Hans Holbein. L 7.3cm. **439** (*right*) is Italian, designed by Alfonso Rubbiani and made by Luigi Marchi for Aemilia Ars, an Arts and Crafts association in Bologna, 1898–1903. The design copies the jewel worn by St Cecilia in a painting by Raphael then in Bologna cathedral (now in the Art Gallery). L 7.6cm

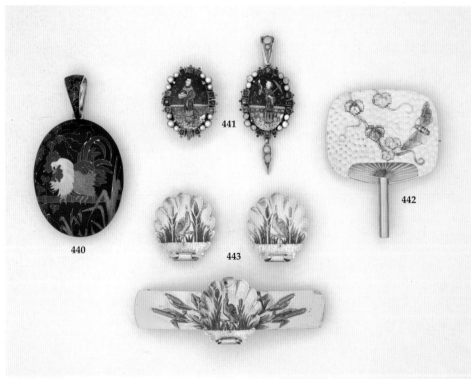

440–3 Gold jewels in the Japanese taste.

440 Locket with cockerel in cloisonné enamel by Alexis Falize, Paris, *c.*1868–75. Cloisonné enamel was used in both China and Japan. Falize was the first to revive and perfect the art in France; other firms imitated cloisonné by casting the design instead of creating the outlines with gold strips. L 5.4cm

441 Brooch and pendant with enamelled scenes and gemstone borders. English, made by E. W. Streeter, London, *c.* 1880. Streeter, author of books on gemstones, ran pearl fishing vessels in Australia and expeditions to Burma for rubies. In 1878 he held an exhibition of Japanese works of art at his Bond Street shop, accompanied by English-made jewels such as these. H (brooch) 2.5cm

442–3 Fan brooch and set of brooch and earrings in coloured gold and platinum. American, Tiffany & Co, New York, *c.* 1880. Platinum is a white metal that does not tarnish, making it an ideal substitute for silver, especially for the rippling pools of water with herons and bulrushes. American hallmarking permitted the use of mixed metals (in the Japanese manner), which European laws in general did not. H of fan brooch 8.3cm

444–8 Art Nouveau jewels from France, all made in Paris around 1900 and illustrating the sinuous lines and wave-like motifs inspired by Japanese art and a fresh approach to natural forms – two of many influences on design at this time.

444 Silver-gilt ensemble: hair comb, necklace and waist-buckle, made by Janvier Quercia. The two-pronged hair comb or *fourche* (fork) and the clip-on waist-buckle that could be transferred from belt to belt were new forms of jewellery. Parisian jewellers were masters of sculptural jewellery: the buckle was made from a wax model, from which a metal die was cast. The size of the die was altered for the comb and necklace with a reducing machine. H of buckle 7.9cm

445 Hatpin with carved horn grass-hopper perched on a corn stalk, by René Lalique. Celebrated in his day, Lalique was one of the most original artist jewellers running a small-scale workshop in the early 20th century. Many of his works were one-off creations for stage divas such as Sarah Bernhardt or wealthy businessmen such as the oil magnate Calouste Gulbenkian. He made horn into a fashionable material by carving it or using heat to mould it. w of grass-hopper 5.1cm

446 Gold and enamel and pearl pendant designed by Edouard Colonna and made by the jewellery workshop of the Maison de L'Art Nouveau, the avant-garde design emporium in Paris that gave its name to the term 'Art Nouveau' for modern-style design. Set up in 1895 by the German entrepreneur Siegfried Bing to provide well-designed objects for household use, it sold furni-ture, ceramics, glass and metalwork as well as jewellery. L of pendant 8.8cm

447 Gold brooch with a head of Marianne, the personification of France, designed by René Bouvet. The face is carved in coral and the cap of liberty is mother-of-pearl. w 5.2cm

448 Gold waist-buckle in the form of leopards biting a cornelian, their feet resting on a cast glass lion's head. Modelled by the sculptor Lucien Hirtz and made by the workshop of G. Espinasse for the firm of Frédéric Boucheron. Boucheron, one of the big Paris houses that survives to this day, showed this design at the Paris Centennial Exhibition of 1900. H 7.8cm

444

445

446

447

448

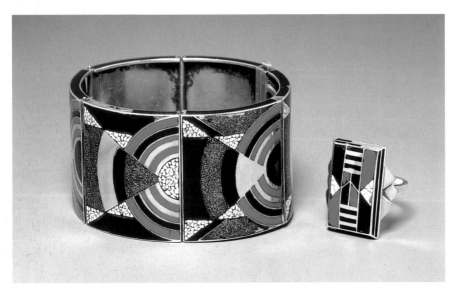

449–51 Art Nouveau or Jugendstil jewels from Scandinavia and Germany.

449 (*top*) Waist-clasp with four dragonflies resting on water-lilies. Danish, 1902. This deceptive piece is made of moulded and painted porcelain, not enamelled metal. It was designed by Christian Thomsen for the Royal Copenhagen Porcelain Factory. W 11.4cm

450 (*below*) Silver waist-clasp with chrysoprase, designed by Patriz Huber, a young member of the Darmstadt artists' colony set up in 1899 to provide good designs for local industry. It was made by the firm of Theodor Fahner in Pforzheim, a jewellery-making centre in Germany with a large export trade: this clasp was sold at Liberty's of London. W 7cm. **451** (*right*) Silver and turquoise pendant also made by Fahner, *c.* 1905, a bold design by C. F. Morawe, one of the firm's in-house artists. L 8cm

452 Silver and enamel buckle designed and made by Nelson and Edith Dawson. Nelson Dawson trained as an architect and painter. In 1891 he turned to enamelling, setting up a studio with his wife, Edith. Together they helped to revive the interest in enamelling in England. Like much Arts and Crafts jewellery, the silver is intentionally oxidised or darkened to enhance the hand-made look. The buckle was formerly owned by Charles Handley-Read, a pioneering collector of Victorian decorative art in the 1960s; he bought it from the Dawsons' daughter. W 5.3cm

453–4 Modernist lacquered silver bracelet and ring. French, designed by G. Sandoz, Paris, *c.* 1926–8. Interlocking circles and triangles suggest the wheels and cogs of a machine, but the technique is traditional: red and black lacquer (a natural resin applied in successive layers) is mixed with eggshell chips, or with powdered shell to give a mottled effect. Used in China and Japan, lacquer was adopted in the 1920s in the West, especially France. It was expensive to do; most of Sandoz's work was made to commission by his father's Paris firm and little survives. H of bracelet 3.7cm

455 Clip brooch with large emerald. English, made by Cartier London, 1936. The antique Indian emerald is carved with a Hindu scene and inlaid with gold and rubies; it was specially mounted by Cartier for the client in an up-to-date diamond setting. The clip brooch, introduced in the late 1920s, had two prongs instead of a standard brooch pin, enabling it to be worn anywhere on the corsage, to edge a dress, or in the hat. Cartier also created jewels around Chinese jades and ancient Egyptian faience, but their Indian-style pieces, loved by Indian and Western clients alike, were a brilliant fusion of Western and Eastern traditions. H 7.2cm

456 Diamond and ruby necklace and earrings. English, made by Cartier London in 1954. The close-fitting rigid collar with a fringe at the front was a popular form in the 1950s. Often lavish pieces like this came apart for wear in different ways. Here the central element of the necklace can be worn as a clip brooch. The stones incorporate many traditional cuts, as well as the long rectangular 'baguette' diamonds, introduced in the inter-war years.

Cartier was founded in Paris in 1847 and had branches in London by 1902 and New York by 1909, each with its own designers and workshops. The production process involved many stages: an initial sketch was followed by a coloured design; from this the stones would be selected, then arranged on wax according to size and quality, to show how the piece would finally look. Once approved, it was passed to the workshop. The London workshop employees were all English; expertise has been handed down from generation to generation, and to this day fathers and sons work side by side. L of central element 4.2cm

CHAPTER SIXTEEN

Amulets

Ancient China

Jade, the name we give to the minerals nephrite and jadeite, had a very special significance in ancient China. It was not only valued as a precious and beautiful stone, but it was believed to have spiritual and even magical qualities. The suits made of jade plaques in the Han dynasty (206 BC–AD 220), which, it was thought, would preserve the bodies of the dead, are the most striking examples of this faith in the magical qualities of jade. The Chinese must have attached such spiritual or magical properties to jade as early as the Neolithic period, for they went to great lengths to transport jade thousands of miles and to manufacture it into discs, rings and arc pendants which are clearly not for practical use, but which must have had some special purpose.

It is impossible to illustrate here the full range of Chinese jades, particularly the ceremonial sceptres, discs and tubes, but a representative group of early carvings in the shape of animals is shown. The jade animals are all pierced so that they could have been attached to robes and presumably they were worn as pendants. While the purpose of the small animal figures is not known, the use of jade suggests that they were more than simply ornamental. Many examples of the Shang and Zhou periods have been found in the tombs of women.

Later jades in the shapes of discs and arcs are definitely known to have been worn as pendants. An exceptional early painting from a tomb of the second century BC has provided important evidence as to the purpose of this type of pendant. Shown in the centre of the painting is a ring similar to **463** and a jade arc similar to **464**. Above is a portrait of the occupant of the tomb, the wife of the Marquis of Dai, and then a complicated picture of dragons, the sun and the moon; here the heavens are portrayed and the occupant of the tomb is shown having reached this abode. The jades thus seem to be important instruments in enabling the dead woman to ascend to the heavens, and to avoid the terrors of the underworld, which are shown with horrifying monsters below.

Such jades are often found placed in the coffin of the dead but they were also worn as part of formal or ceremonial dress, for the clinking sound which they made as the wearer walked is vividly described in contemporary texts. The three pendants illustrated are all decorated with spirals and scrolls which are the hallmark of the late Zhou period. Derived ultimately from bronze designs, such decoration sparkles in the light and was clearly intended to bring out the qualities of this otherwise subtle and subdued stone.

Related pendants of jade were used in later centuries. Precise

Right **458–62** Five Chinese animal pendants. Such small pendants, both three-dimensional and flat have been found in many burials of the Shang and early Zhou periods. They are usually of the same general size and represent the same range of animals. In the top row, the jade buffalo (**458**) and the cicada of turquoise matrix (**459**) are of the Shang dynasty (13th-11th century AD). The other pieces, all of jade, are of the Western Zhou period (11th–10th century BC). The fish (**460**, centre), has details of its eyes, head and fins incised on both sides. The bird (**461**, bottom left), with its large up-curving wings and heavy downward-curving tail, and the stag (**462**) are both shown in silhouette. L (**462**) 6cm

457 A drawing of a Chinese painted silk banner from the tomb of the wife of the Marquis of Dai, near Changsha (2nd century BC). The painting shows two jades and a silk scarf intertwined with dragons, hanging below the platform on which the lady is standing, supported on a stick.

Left **463–5** A group of Chinese jade pendants. These types of pendant have a long history in China. The ring (**463**) is of the Eastern Zhou period (3rd century BC); the arc-shaped pendant (**464**) is of the Eastern Zhou or Han dynasty (3rd–2nd century BC).Such pendants were believed to have supernatural powers to assist the dead.

Also of the Eastern Zhou period (4th–3rd century BC) is the pendant in the form of an s-shaped dragon (**465**). Dragons were benign and in some slightly later tomb-paintings they are shown carrying spirits on their backs. D (**463**) 10.2cm

Below left Stone pendants from the Tell Brak temple in Syria (Jamdat Nasr period, *c.* 3000 BC). They represent a pig (**466**), a ram (**467**) and a fox (**468**). Each has a stamp-seal design cut into the base or back. Many stone pendants of this kind, and cheaper imitations in faience, were found during excavations at Tell Brak. L (**467**) 4.45cm

Below right **469–70** Two pendants of white stone, from Nineveh, Iraq (*c.* 2500–2000 BC). One shows a two-headed bull or ram (**469**) and the other perhaps a bear (**470**). L (**469**) 3.47cm

information on the shapes of the jades used in these late sets is gained from reliefs and sculptures in stone, showing figures and their dress in some detail. Guardian figures along the routes to tombs and attendants shown within tomb chambers wear pendants hanging from the waist.   JMR

Western Asia

Many pendants representing objects or animals have survived from early periods. Although such items are often regarded as amuletic, it is difficult to prove this without supporting written or archaeological evidence. Many of them presumably had decorative and social, as well as amuletic or religious functions, at one and the same time. At the Tell Brak temple in Syria animal pendants in stone and faience with stamp-seal designs were found in great numbers during excavations. These dated to the Jamdat Nasr period (*c.* 3000 BC); they may have been left there as votive offerings, but some were actually embedded in the brickwork. The double-headed animal was an old Mesopotamian device; a white stone pendant from Nineveh may represent a bull, often used to symbolise brute strength. Other common amulets included frogs and flies; a Babylonian myth records that a goddess used to wear lapis-lazuli flies to remind her of the flood that had almost destroyed mankind.

Figures of gods and demons have survived in a variety of materials. A gold pendant of the Old Babylonian period represents the goddess Lama, who was regarded as an intercessor, able to speak with higher gods and convey petitions. The Canaanite fertility goddess, Astarte, who was worshipped extensively in the lands along the eastern Mediterranean coast, is represented as a much

480

486

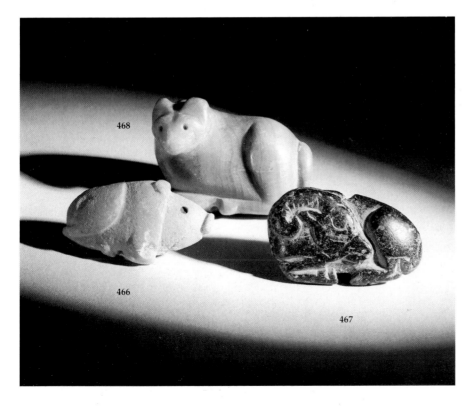

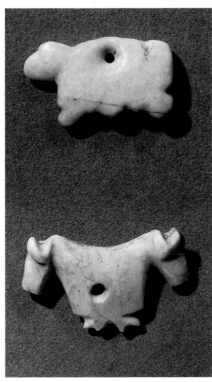

stylised figure embossed on a gold pendant from Tell el-'Ajjul. Another gold pendant is thought to be of a Hittite weather-god: comparable amulets have been found near the Hittite capital of Hattusha (Boğazköy) and elsewhere in the Empire.

A stone plaque of the seventh century BC from Uruk in Iraq is roughly incised with a figure of a demon. This is an unusually crude example of an amulet intended to protect the wearer against the evil Mesopotamian demon Lamashtu, who was a particular threat to women in childbirth. An especially valuable assistant in driving away Lamashtu was the wind-demon Pazuzu: a lapis lazuli pendant shows his head.

Amulets from the Phoenician graves at Tharros display a typically Phoenician mixture of amuletic symbols adapted from Egyptian prototypes. A necklace of gold and cornelian beads includes pendants of cats, hawks, the Egyptian sign for the heart and the Eye of Horus. Many of the Tharros graves contained necklaces of this nature. A hollow gold pendant is embossed with an 'aegis of Bastet', a motif of Egyptian origin (see 492), which is one of many borrowed and adapted by Phoenician merchants. Pendants of this kind were probably intended to hold magic charms or talismans.   JER

Egypt

Most Egyptian jewellery has a magical significance, and it is therefore almost impossible to distinguish the purely amuletic from the ornamental. Moreover, since the Egyptians took their everyday jewellery with them to the grave, it is not always possible to distinguish even funerary jewellery, always amuletic, from secular.

Predynastic amulets are recognisable but it is not until the late Old Kingdom and First Intermediate Period that amulets increase substantially in range of subject and material. Not only the forms represented but also the materials had significance: green felspar or turquoise was the colour of new life, red cornelian or jasper the colour of life-blood, blue lapis lazuli the colour of the heavens. Amulets such as the falcon or bull gave the owner certain powers by assimilation. Others represent the very force to be avoided, such as the scorpion, or the turtle, the animal of death and darkness. Parts of the body endowed the wearer with their particular bodily functions or could act as substitutes. Some amuletic forms gave protection: the cowrie perhaps averted the evil eye from pregnant women as well as bringing fertility; the fish prevented drowning; Thoeris and her dwarf-like helper Bes, a benevolent demon, aided women in child-birth. Sometimes the identity of a deity with its special powers could be assumed.

The scarab was a very potent amulet signifying regeneration. A green jasper heart scarab is inscribed with hieroglyphs from Chapter XXXB of the *Book of the Dead*, a spell intended to ensure that the heart would not give adverse witness against its owner when weighed in the balance to decide whether the deceased should enjoy everlasting happiness in the other world. According to the *Book of the Dead*, the heart scarab should be of green material and was to be placed over

Top right Egyptian amulets from the Old Kingdom and the First Intermediate Period. From the 4th-Dynasty burial of a woman (c. 2550 BC) at Mostagedda comes part of a necklace of gold and turquoise beads (471), with a falcon amulet in gold.

The group of hardstone amulets date from c. 2300–2100 BC. They include: 472 a cornelian right-hand amulet; 473 a cornelian leg and foot; 474 a dark-green jasper turtle; 475 a cornelian amulet in the form of two lions' heads and forepaws set back to back; 476 an amethyst falcon in profile 477 a pink limestone bearded human face.

All of these amulets are typical of this early period. The rare double-lion amulet represents the regions where the dead are reborn to a new life. The falcon amulets may be connected with Chapter LXXVII of the *Book of the Dead*, 'Spell for taking on the form of a falcon of gold'; the gold falcon is an early example of an amulet frequently reproduced in stone, such as 473, and glazed composition. H 1–1.9cm

Bottom right Egyptian bangle and necklace of the Middle Kingdom. The gold bangle (c. 2000–1750 BC) encloses a frieze of amuletic signs and animals alternately in gold and silver (478). The frieze includes a snake gripping a turtle or tortoise by the neck, a *bat* amulet between two two-finger amulets, running hares, seated baboons, falcons, two draughtsmen and a headless serpent, along with a number of *udjats* (eye amulets), *djeds* and *ankh*-amulets.

479, a necklace or girdle (c. 1900–1800 BC), has silver cowrie-shell beads, a cowrie-shell clasp, two beard pendants and two fish pendants of electrum, a silver inlaid lotus-flower pendant and an electrum *heh* amulet; the other beads are of cornelian, amethyst, lapis lazuli, green felspar and electrum. The lotus-flower pendant is inlaid with blue and green glass and cornelian in cloisons. D (478, external) 8.3cm

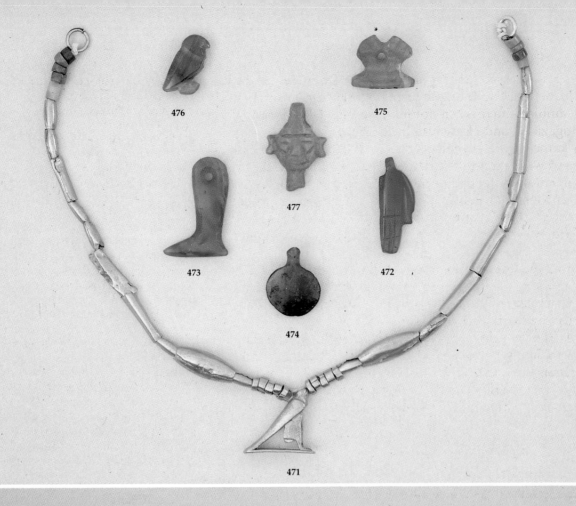

476

475

477

473

474

472

471

478

479

Left **480** Gold pendant of a goddess, dating from the Old Babylonian period (*c.* 2000–1600 BC). The figure is worked on a bitumen core and has a suspension loop at the back. With her horned cap and flounced dress, she can be identified as the goddess Lama. H 3.55cm

Below left **481** A fish pendant of the Egyptian Middle Kingdom (*c.* 1900–1800 BC). The pendant is of gold with green felspar inlay, open on both sides. The central cloison is a strip of sheet metal curved into an oval, with a disc of sheet gold on each side, representing the head; on one side a ring has been soldered for an eye. The tail and fins are soldered onto the cloison; one of the lower fins has been lost. L 2.9cm

Below **482** Fish amulets called *nekhaw* were worn especially by children to protect them from drowning and were usually attached to the end of the side-lock or plait, which symbolised their youth, as shown in this 12th-Dynasty cosmetic container in the form of a little girl kneeling and holding a pot before her to hold the unguent. She wears a girdle of cowrie-shell beads (see **479**).

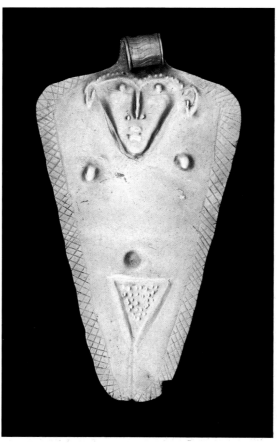

(*Left* Two cylindrical amulets of the Egyptian Middle Kingdom (*c.* 1900–1800 BC). **483** is a tube of sheet gold decorated with granulation. The joins between the individual granules are visible, and they were possibly fixed together before being arranged on the tube. The upper conical cap is removable.

484 is composed of three short cylindrical amethyst beads alternating with three similar gold beads. A copper pin runs down through the centre of the pendant. L (**483**) 6.8cm

Below, centre **486** A gold pendant of the fertility goddess Astarte, from Tell el-'Ajjul, Palestine (*c.* 1600 BC). The naked, crudely stylised figure of the goddess is lightly embossed and incised, the emphasis given to the face, breasts and sexual organs. H 8.9cm

Below right **487** A solid gold Hittite pendant of a god wearing a pointed cap, kilt and long boots, and carrying a short staff (*c.* 14th century BC). There is a loop for suspension at the back. This figure may represent a Hittite weather-god. H 3.94cm

283

484

Above **485** An Egyptian scarab finger-ring (*c.* 1800–1500 BC). The ring is a hollow tube of gold with a green jasper scarab bezel. The base of the scarab is inscribed with a central knot of four uraei and four *ankh*-signs in cartouches. In style the scarab is characteristic of the early 18th Dynasty. Although the base is incised, the scarab itself acts as a powerful amulet. The *ankh*-sign on the base gives eternal life; the uraei could represent a number of goddesses, all beneficient. D (hoop) 2.6cm

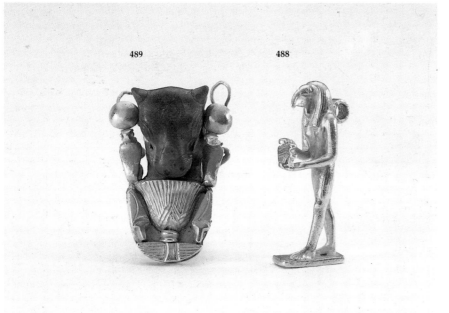

489   488

Above Two pendants: **488**, in gold, is in the form of the ibis-headed Thoth, holding an *udjat*-eye before him (*c.* 1000–900 BC). The pendant was presumably cast and all the details – including those of minute size on the *udjat* – incised. Thoth, the scribe of the gods, is here acting as mediator between Horus and Set, returning the *udjat*, the Eye of Horus, to its owner.

489, with a lapis lazuli bull's head set in gold (*c.* 1300–1100 BC), is a unique piece. The mount is Egyptian: a gold

papyrus head on a basket, flanked by two lotus buds and two uraei wearing sun-discs – familiar Egyptian motifs. The carved bull's head, however, is not of Egyptian style or workmanship: the treatment of the muzzle and eyes with multiple folds is Mesopotamian in character, and the returning spiral on the forehead is also non-Egyptian. The carving, which is Babylonian, or possibly Elamite or Urartian, is clearly an imported piece mounted in an Egyptian setting. H (488) 2.4cm

Above **490** a Mesopotamian amulet of green stone from Uruk, Iraq (*c.* 7th century BC). The plaque is incised with cuneiform signs and the figure of the evil demon Lamashtu, who is represented as a female with the head and claws of a hawk. The writing, on both sides of the plaque, is an illiterate attempt at cuneiform. This amulet would have been worn to protect against Lamashtu and to send her back to the underworld. H 6.25cm

492   491

Above Two openwork blue glazed composition finger-rings from the Egyptian Late New Kingdom (*c.* 1100–800 BC). The design of **491** has five figures of Bes standing on each others' heads. Bes's connection with childbirth suggests that such a ring may well have been worn by a woman.

492 is decorated at the top with an 'aegis of Bastet', with a sun-disc and uraei. The aegis is a deep collar of beadwork surmounted by a lioness's head, but it is linked with the cat-goddess Bastet. Such a ring would have protective qualities. D (**491**) 2.4cm

Above **493** A lapis lazuli pendant in the form of a head of the Mesopotamian wind demon Pazuzu (*c.* 7th century BC). H 1.46cm

Above **494** A gold amulet-case from a Phoenician grave at Tharros, Sardinia (*c.* 7th–6th century BC). It is embossed with an 'aegis of Bastet': the head of a lioness, surmounted by a disc with a uraeus cobra in front, and decorated with granulation and cloisons for inlay. The hollow cylindrical section below would probably have contained a magic charm or talisman. H 4.53cm

Above **495** Necklace from a Phoenician grave at Tharros, Sardinia (*c.* 6th century BC). The cornelian and gold beads are interspersed with stone pendants, fastened with gold wire, representing cats, hawks, the Egyptian sign for the heart and a woman with children on either side. The central pendant consists of a hollow box in gold, representing the Eye of Horus, the contours being defined by cloisons which would once have been inlaid. From this hangs a seated stone cat, to which is attached a pendant; the front of the pendant represents a female head wearing a wig, with a pattern of granulation below. L (pendant) 5.5cm

the heart of the mummy. Apart from its special funerary use, the scarab was often set as a ring bezel, sometimes inscribed with further amuletic signs. Other amulets such as the frog and cat, both connected with fertility, also formed bezels.

Some types of amulets are peculiar to particular periods: for example, faces, legs and hands are typical of the late Old Kingdom and First Intermediate Period. Oyster-shells, affording their wearer health, and knot-clasps are especially Middle Kingdom in date. Also typical of the Middle Kingdom are beads and clasps in the form of metal cowrie-shells, being worn apparently in girdles rather than necklaces, to judge from several female statuettes. Metal fish pendants (called *nekhaw*) are equally typical, usually being attached to the

485
85

47

479

481

side-locks of children and most often made from a green stone, to judge from the number of known examples. *Heh* amulets are common from the Middle Kingdom until Roman times; the god Heh is always shown kneeling with his arms raised, a pictogram in which he wishes the wearer millions of years. Cylindrical amulet pendants, probably to protect women and children, are also characteristic of the Middle Kingdom, but some types continue into the New Kingdom and later. In the case of **483** the quality of the granulation suggests a Middle rather than a New Kingdom date. The hollow cylinders were probably used as amulet cases: one example of late date still contained three amulets, others contain spells written on papyrus. A gold bangle containing an amuletic frieze is a rare type; the only other comparable form of bangle is dated to the First Intermediate Period. Its frieze-like procession of animals and amulets is similar to those found on contemporary amuletic ivory wands. Small figures of gods in precious metal are often of the later periods. CA

The Mediterranean

Though amulet pendants containing inscriptions or other magical material were in use in the Greek and Roman world, it is not always easy to define a separate class of amuletic jewellery in these cultures, since religious and superstitious considerations governed the design and selection of a high proportion of the ornaments worn. The

496 A gold bracelet and a detail of two gold necklaces from a treasure found at Backworth, Northumberland (England). The full contents of the treasure are unknown but the other items included five finger-rings and two brooches. The three pieces illustrated each have similar wheel and crescent pendants (only the wheel pendants are shown); the wheel of the lower necklace has a central button of green glass. The chains are made of figure-of-eight links, twisted at the neck through a right angle.

The Backworth jewellery is of British make (possibly late 1st or early 2nd century AD). While much of its ornament reflects both native and Roman traditions, the bracelet and necklaces are purely Roman in style.

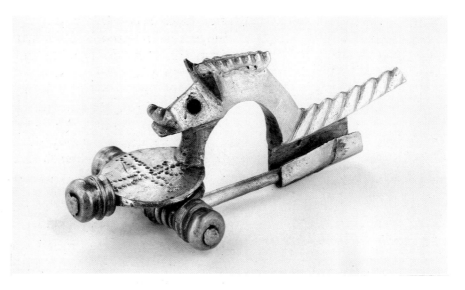

Above left **497** Late 4th-century AD Christian gold ring from Suffolk (England). The octagonal bezel is engraved with the Christian monogram in reverse and the figure of a bird perched in a tree, pecking at fruit. The deep engraving has never had any inlay, so the ring was almost certainly a seal-ring. D (internal) 2.1cm

Above right **498** A Romano-British silver and parcel-gilt brooch (*c.* 400). The bow is ornamented with the head and mane of a boar with eyes of blue glass. On the disc at the head of the brooch is chased a monogram from the Greek letters *chi* and *rho*. These are the first two letters of Christ's name in Greek. By the 4th century AD, when Christianity was the official religion, the monogram had become specifically Christian, and was often associated with *alpha* and *omega*, the first and last letters of the Greek alphabet. L 6.6cm

deities and other devices engraved on gemstones were not haphazardly chosen, and many of the motifs which seem to us purely ornamental may have had an additional role in averting evil and protecting the wearer. For example, the widespread Hellenistic and Roman fashion for rings and bracelets in the form of snakes was based not only on the decorative possibilities of this creature, but on its associations with the underworld and its connection with healing deities such as Asclepius. Other protective motifs include knots of Hercules, phallic symbols, and moon-crescents and sun-wheels. The latter were used throughout the Roman Empire, but where they occur in the Celtic northern provinces their religious significance is underlined and augmented because the wheel is also symbolic of a major Celtic god, Taranis. Ornaments such as the Backworth necklaces are thus wholly within the mainstream of Roman jewellery styles, and yet peculiarly appropriate for the Celtic milieu in which they were worn, and probably made.

The rise of Christianity did not change the attitude to the amuletic function of jewellery: signs and symbols continued to be used in personal ornaments, but were given special significance for Christians. Some of these are specific, such as the Chi-Rho monogram seen on two fine late Romano-British pieces, a silver crossbow brooch from Sussex and a superb gold ring from Suffolk. Other motifs are more ambiguous. Direct representations of pagan deities were unacceptable to Christians, but there was nevertheless a shared iconography. The palm-branch of Victory, the peacocks of Juno and the doves of Venus are three of the many images which were used symbolically, though differently perceived, by both pagans and Christians; whether these symbols were worn for purposes of identification, devotion or protection against misfortune cannot, however, be established. As a result of the Edict of Milan in AD 313 , when the Emperor Constantine the Great gave official recognition to Christianity, the more sumptuous jewellery began to include Christian images and motifs, but the jewellers also brought into their repertoire new shapes, like pectoral crosses, and new types for carrying holy relics.   CJ

OPPOSITE

Top left **502** Ottonian gold brooch (late 10th century AD), incorporating a late Antique onyx cameo with a Greek inscription which can be roughly translated as 'Good fortune attend the wearer'. The loops around the circumference of the oval brooch originally held a string of pearls. D (max.) 3.55cm

Top right **503** Byzantine gold and cloisonné enamel reliquary cross (10th century AD), hinged to open and reveal a relic, most probably a fragment of the True Cross. Believed to have been found in the Great Palace in Constantinople, the reliquary had lost the enamel plaque from its face. On the back the Mother of God stands in an attitude of prayer between half-figures of St Basil and St Gregory the Miracle-worker. H 6cm

Bottom **504** Two views of a Byzantine gold and cloisonné enamel pendant reliquary depicting two military saints (13th century AD). It incorporates an 11th-century Constantinopolitan enamel medallion of St George with a Greek inscription translating as '[The bearer] prays that you will be his stout defence in battle'. The medallion was converted into a reliquary, probably in 13th-century Thessaloniki, by the provision of a receptacle with a hinged flap enamelled with a depiction of St Demetrios lying in his shrine in the church of his name in Thessaloniki; the flap opens to reveal a gold effigy of the saint and the space for the relics. Round the edge of the reliquary runs a Greek inscription in enamel, 'Anointed with your blood and myrrh'. According to a Georgian inscription engraved on a hinged annular half-cover, the reliquary later contained a fragment of the True Cross belonging to St Kethevan, Queen of Georgia (died 1624). D 3.25cm

Top **499** Byzantine gold bracelet (*c.* AD 600), said to have been found in Syria. The hinged clasp is embossed with a bust of the Mother of God in an attitude of prayer; the empty settings on either side would originally have held gems or coloured glass. The hoop of the bracelet is pierced and embossed with peacocks and swans facing each other over vases of vine-tendrils, motifs associated with life after death. D (external) 7.1cm

Above left **500** Byzantine nielloed silver finger-ring (6th or 7th century AD). The bezel is engraved and punched with a crude Medusa-like face, from which radiate seven serpents; above is a small cross. On the hoop is a partly abbreviated Greek inscription, 'Lord protect the wearer'. D (hoop, external) 2.1cm

Above right **501** Byzantine gold medallion, probably made in the Holy Land (*c.* AD 600). It comprises two embossed gold discs, mounted back to back. One side shows the Adoration of the Magi with, above, a flying angel and the Star of Bethlehem and, below, a Greek inscription 'Lord, protect the bearer. Amen.' The other side shows the Ascension. D 5.8cm

North of the Alps

Jewellery with magical or amuletic properties (often associated with specific hardstones) was important to the pagan Germanic folk of Northern Europe, and continued to be made and worn well into the Christian period, as is shown by the magical runic inscriptions on certain gold and agate finger-rings of the ninth and tenth centuries AD. In the pagan period amuletic jewellery seems to be particularly favoured amongst women and children, as the tooth and crystal-ball pendants would seem to suggest, but magical formulae and symbols also occur on weapons and on other male possessions, like the Christian-period finger-ring with a double bezel from the River Nene at Peterborough (England).

Throughout the Middle Ages there was a widespread belief that precious stones and engraved gems possessed magical virtues. Accounts of stones and their virtues, known as lapidaries, survive. This evidence, combined with references in inventories to such gems, shows that this belief was not merely theoretical but was a part of everyday life. Stones had particular powers – for example, the jacinth increases riches and the carbuncle inspires. The toadstone, in reality a fragment of fossil but thought to be grown in the forehead of a toad, was sometimes used to detect poison. Some stones had religious virtues; for instance, contemplation of the deep blue of the sapphire could raise men's souls to the contemplation of the heavenly kingdom. However, several medieval lapidaries record the belief that the sins of the wearer impair the virtues of the stones. *The Lapidary of Sir John Mandeville* states that it often happens that a good diamond loses its virtues by the sins of him who bears it.

Relics of Christ and the saints were objects of devotion in the Middle Ages. A pilgrim sign showing the shrine of St Thomas of Canterbury demonstrates how relics such as the body of St Thomas

Below left A group of jewellery with rock-crystal and agate (Merovingian and, perhaps, Lombardic (**506**), 6th and 7th centuries AD). The buckle (**505**) is of rock-crystal and silver; the pendants of crystal (**507**) and of agate (**506**) have gold slings. As well as imported garnet, Germanic jewellers of the period incorporated other semi-precious stones (**588**). Beads of amethyst were exotic imports, but rock-crystal and agate may have been found and worked more locally, although the sources of the raw material remain obscure. Rock-crystal was commonly believed in antiquity and in medieval times to have amuletic properties. Large spherical beads occur on the Continent and in England at this period in rich graves, and in some cases the metal mounts survive.

Below **508** A beaver-tooth pendant set in a gold mount, from a late 7th-century Anglo-Saxon woman's grave at Wigber Low, Derbyshire. The teeth of various carnivores, mostly dog, wolf, bear and boar, were worn as protective amulets by a number of Germanic tribes, mostly it appears, by women. Beaver-tooth amulets are rarer, later, and seem to be commoner amongst children, perhaps as a substitute for the more overtly pagan associations of the carnivore teeth. L 3.8cm

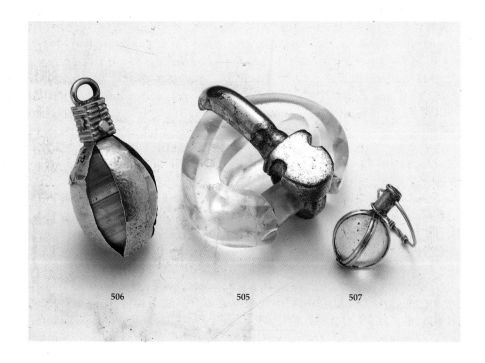

509 Two views of a reliquary of the Holy Thorn. This French gold reliquary consists of a central leaf and two covers; within the central leaf is the thorn. The exterior is formed of two pieces of rock-crystal with a coloured backing that creates the effect of an amethyst. The Holy Thorn was taken from the Crown of Thorns purchased by St Louis from Baldwin, the Emperor of Byzantium. The setting probably dates from the second quarter of the 14th century. On the inside of the covers and on one side of the central leaf are six scenes in translucent enamel from the life of Christ (shown above are the Crucifixon and the Descent from the Cross). On the other side of the central leaf is a manuscript illumination of the Nativity and the Annunciation to the Shepherds. Behind this is the thorn, mounted in crystal and with an inscription at one side DE SPINA : SANCTE : CORONE (Thorn of the Holy Crown). H 3.8cm

were provided with elaborate bejewelled shrines. Relics were sometimes exposed for veneration but there had developed a tradition of wearing relics on the person and so they were set in jewels. One such reliquary pendant is constructed around a thorn, from the crown of thorns worn by Christ at the Crucifixion, set in crystal amidst enamelled scenes of the life and passion of Christ. The cross from Clare (Suffolk, England) shows how the relics (a fragment of wood and stone) could be contained in an appropriately shaped box, itself engraved with the Crucifixion motif. We do not know the relics contained in a reliquary from Devizes (Wiltshire, England), but the inscription suggests that it was intended to preserve the wearer against sudden death.

In the same way that relics came to be worn rather than exposed, a prayer was inscribed as a talisman rather than spoken. *Ave Maria*, the beginning of a salutation of Gabriel to the Virgin at the Annunciation, was often inscribed on jewels, brooches, purse mounts and other objects. The name of Jesus was in itself a protection from all evils. The names of the Three Kings (the wise men who came to the Epiphany) were a common prophylactic inscription on cups and jewels. It was sometimes thought helpful against epilepsy or fever. Amuletic inscriptions were common on rings. The Coventry ring includes the Three Kings in its inscription together with the words *ananyzapta tetragrammaton*, the first a charm against the falling sickness and the second one of the unwritable names of Jehovah. Occasionally verses from the Bible were used as prophylactic inscriptions and the wearing of a gold noble of Edward IV (1461–83) as a pendant was probably for protection against the dangers of travel by sea and land, especially against attack by robbers. Its efficacy as a charm was, no doubt, thought to reside in the inscription on the coin, which is taken from Luke iv, 30. Travellers have for centuries continued to seek protective intervention from saints, like St

524
521
515
516
514
523

510

511

514

513

512

Top left A group of English amuletic finger-rings (12th–15th century). **511** is silver-gilt, the others are of gold. Three of these examples illustrate the use in finger-rings of precious stones as amulets: jacinth (**512**), carbuncle (**511**) and toadstone (**510**). The 'Cannington' ring (**513**) is inscribed with the Angelic Salutation around the hoop. Its high openwork bezel is set with a cabochon sapphire.

514, from Coventry, Warwickshire (15th century), is engraved on the exterior with Christ standing in the tomb with the instruments of the Passion behind. The words around the hoop describe the Five Wounds of Christ, a popular subject for personal devotion at the end of the Middle Ages. The inscription engraved on the inside is magical rather than devotional. D (**514**) 2.7cm

Bottom far left **515–16** Two early 14th-century English amuletic brooches. The gold ring brooch (**515**) is set with a ruby and an opal. It has the inscription + AVE I MARIA G.

The silver octagonal brooch (**516**) is inscribed on one side IHESUS and on the other NASERRENE. The name of Jesus was thought to be of special value against epilepsy. D (**516**) 4cm

Bottom left **517** A silver 14th-century pendant showing Christ blessing the Virgin and (below) six saints, including Peter, Paul, John the Baptist and John the Evangelist. It may have been produced either in northern Italy or in Germany. Around the edge is an inscription which includes the phrase: *mentem santam spontaneam honorem Deo patrie liberationem* (the holy mind, honour freely rendered to God, and liberty to the country), indicating its amuletic properties. Originally enamelled, the silver figures would have stood in reserve against a coloured background. D 5cm

518

519

520

Above A group of pilgrim badges (14th–15th century). Such badges were sold at shrines for pilgrims to wear on their return home. Two of the badges are English (**518**, **519**); these are lead badges of St Thomas of Canterbury. **518** is remarkable, since it shows the actual shrine of St Thomas at Canterbury, Kent (England), which was elaborately decorated with jewels; **519** is a bust of the saint. L (**518**) 5.1cm

520 is a French silver pilgrim badge of the shrine of Our Lady of Hal, in Belgium (14th–15th century). D 3.8cm

Christopher, and their images have often been introduced into jewellery of modern times. Similarly, it was believed that a caul had amuletic properties which would help to preserve the wearer from death by drowning; pendants containing a caul were frequently worn by mariners, even as late as the nineteenth century.   530

Coral is a material to which in the ancient world great amuletic powers had been attributed. It was said, according to Greek mythology, to have originated as the spurts of blood gushing forth after Medusa's head had been severed by Perseus. At an early stage coral was thought to be a protection against magic spells and in Italy, especially around Naples, it was carved in a wide variety of symbolic   529
forms, such as the bull's head, to promote strength. The talismanic agate 'eye', found in jewellery of the Roman period, was not infrequently recreated in glass and other forms in modern jewellery –   531
indeed, the vogue continues to the present day. The wearing of the fist-shaped amulet as a protection against the 'evil eye' was not uncommon, and pendants with the hand in the characteristic position

521

522   523

Above **524** A gold 15th-century reliquary cross found on the site of Clare Castle, Suffolk (England). The front has a panel with the Crucifixion, against a ground which has traces of red enamel, with an inscription INRI in black. Inside the cross is a fragment of wood and granite, perhaps of True Cross and the Rock of Calvary. H 3.8cm

Right Group of 16th- and 17th-century amuletic jewellery. The ivory hand, wearing gold rings set with an emerald and a garnet (**525**), is mounted in filigree enamelled gold to form a pendant; it is Spanish (16th century). The *mano cornuta* was directed against the Evil Eye.

The gold enamelled reliquary cross (**526**) is also Spanish, but probably of the early 17th century. The reverse is hinged to allow relics to be placed behind the oval vitrines.

The coral pendant (**527**) is Italian (17th century) and is carved in relief with the rare scene of the young Jesus between Mary and Joseph and the Holy Dove (above) returning after the Dispute in the Temple; the other side has the Annunciation. Coral was widely thought to have great amuletic powers, particularly against magic spells. H (**527**) 4.3cm

of the thumb and first finger forming the *mano cornuta* was another potent gesture against evil. Several fine Spanish examples have survived, including a wood and enamelled silver pendant that has been considered an 'ex-voto' of Charles V of Spain (reigned 1519–53) and several portraits of Spanish *Infantas* record the wearing of this particular form of amulet, alongside enamelled gold crosses containing holy relics, coral, a horn, even an animal's foot. LW/JC/HT

527

526

525

Left English amuletic jewellery. The 15th-century gold reliquary (**521**) is from Devizes, Wiltshire. One side shows a bishop, the other St John the Baptist with the Lamb of God, and the legend A MON DERREYNE. The word 'derreyne' (a form of *derrière*) signifies the last moment of existence.

522, a 14th-century gold pendant, shows the Virgin and Child on one side and the Crucifixion on the other. The figure style and drapery are typical of the East Anglian school of manuscript illumination (*c.* 1300).

The coin pendant (**523**) is set with a gold rose noble of Edward IV (1461–83). This coin was worn as an amulet on account of the inscription, taken from Luke iv, 30: *Ipse autem transiens per medium illorum ibat* (but he, passing through the midst of them, went his way). The words were very generally used as a charm against the dangers of travel, especially against attack by robbers. H (**521**) 4.6cm

Right **528** A portrait of the Infanta Anna, by Juan Pantoja de la Cruz (1602). It shows the Spanish custom, especially among royal children, of wearing many amuletic items, such as the pendant 'higa' (or clenched hand), coral and rock-crystal and small reliquaries.

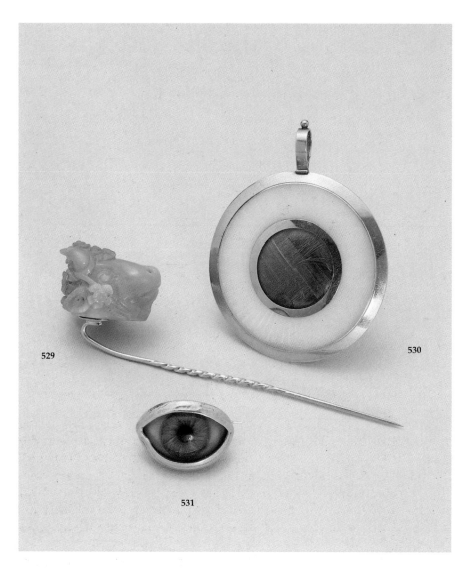

529

530

531

A group of early 19th-century talismanic jewellery. The Italian gold cravat pin (**529**) has a carved coral bull's head, the horns garlanded with flowers. In amuletic terms the bull's head signifies strength.

The gold and glass amulets are of English origin. The 'eye' brooch (**531**) may be based on the agate 'eye' in ancient Roman amuletic jewellery. The opaline glass pendant (**530**) has one compartment with plaited hair and another (on the reverse) containing a caul under glass. It was believed that a caul could prevent death by drowning and, hence, was a popular amulet among sailors. D (**530**) 4.6cm

Buddhist and Islamic Amulet-Cases

The use of amulets is widespread in Buddhism, just as it is in various religions of the east, including Islam and Hinduism. The purpose of wearing amulets varies considerably from country to country in the Buddhist world, from protection against malignant spirits, as in Tibet, to Japan where, among many other uses for amulets, certain types help to protect motorists on the road.

In Thailand, Burma and other parts of mainland South-East Asia, amulets can range in medium from diagrams or pictures on paper, to clay, metal or stone images, tattoos of sacred symbols, fragments of old manuscripts, and many other materials. Unusual natural objects, such as a tiger's tooth or some peculiar object, may also serve as amulets. The holiness of the amulet-maker himself, usually a monk, is of special importance in making the amulet effective; the blessing of an amulet by holy monks also assists the power of the object to aid the wearer.

The ancient kingdom of Gandhara, roughly equivalent to the valley of the Kabul River in modern Pakistan, lay on a long-established trade-route which linked China and the Far East with the

One Buddhist and three Persian amulet-cases. The Persian pieces date from the 11th to the 13th centuries AD; two of them are silver, enhanced with gilding and nielloed. All three are designed to be worn strung around the neck. 532 is part of an amulet-case found at Nihavand with other possessions of a Turkish official (see also 333, 334). Both sides are decorated with a peacock in repoussé, surrounded by a Quranic inscription in Kufic script: 'Say: He is God, One God, the Everlasting Refuge, who has not begotten, and has not been begotten, and equal to Him is not any one' (*Sura* CXII). On the end is the figure of a lion in high relief.

533 is decorated on three of its sides with an animal in repoussé; the other two sides have an Arabic inscription in Nashki script: 'Glory and prosperity'.

534 is gold; it is engraved with palmette motifs and nielloed.

The eight-sided gold cylinder (535), from a *stupa* at Ahin Posh near Jalalabad (Afghanistan), is Gandharan (2nd–3rd century AD). Garnets are used to back the oval openings along each of the eight faces and, again, on the two ends; one of the leaf-shaped openings still contains a green-black stone. One of the ends is designed to be opened.

L (535) 7.3cm

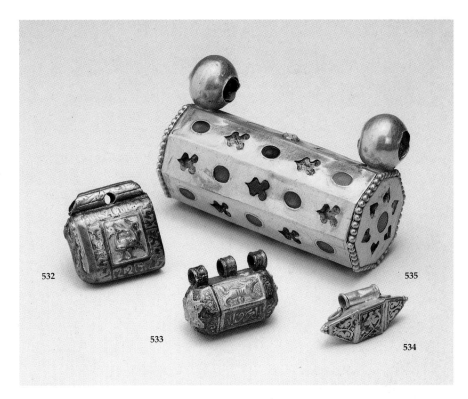

532   535

533   534

Mediterranean world. Buddhism reached Gandhara as early as the third century BC. Cylindrical amulet-cases, like a gold example of the second or third century AD from a *stupa* near Jalalabad (Afghanistan), can be seen on Gandharan sculptures of Bodhisattvas, where they are depicted worn on a cord running over the left shoulder and passing under the right armpit. These images of Bodhisattvas, with their rich jewels, are undoubtedly based on wealthy Gandharan laymen or nobles.

In Tibet Buddhism is notable for the great prevalence of magic, deriving from the native belief in malignant spirits responsible for illness and other misfortunes. Amulet-boxes were worn by men and women for protection, especially when travelling. They also served as badges of rank; officials above a certain grade had to wear boxes in a topknot of the hair. The example illustrated (399) is recorded as having been worn on the pigtail of an official's servant. Amulet-boxes are sometimes in the form of miniature shrines with openings showing stamped and painted plaques with Buddhist images; otherwise they may contain woodblock-printed charms on paper, grains, pebbles and pieces of cloth or silk. They are more usually rectangular or round and offer wide scope for the traditional devices of Tibetan ornamentation.

In Islam the most potent amulet is the written word: verses from the *Quran* (especially the five verses of protection), miniature *Qurans*, the names or attributes of God, the names of holy men, and charms written on paper are inserted into amulet cases and worn by men, women, animals or anything needing protection. They can also be inscribed over doors, on household objects and on to the amulet case itself: 532 has *Sura* CXII repeated on its front and back; 533 wishes glory and prosperity on its owner.   RK/WZ/RW

CHAPTER SEVENTEEN

Cameos in Jewellery

Cameos are precious or semi-precious stones on which the design has been carved in relief – the exact opposite of the much older engraved (or intaglio) gem, which is also frequently set in jewellery, especially in signet-rings. Both cameos and engraved gems were mostly cut in the same method (i.e. on the wheel), but instead of hollowing out the design the stone of a cameo was cut away to leave the design standing in relief. Whereas the engraved gem was highly functional, since it could be impressed into damp clay and wax to indicate ownership of sealed goods, for example, the cameo was purely ornamental and so it is perhaps not surprising that, although the engraved signet-stone (in some form or another) can be traced back to the Sumerian period in Mesopotamia and even back to about 5000 BC in some parts of Western Asia, the cameo does not make its appearance until the Hellenistic period (about the third century BC).

Its emergence in the Greek world following the conquests of Alexander the Great (333–323 BC) had led to the suggestion that it may be due, in part, to influences from the newly acquired territories of the former Persian Empire. Certainly, at this time the Greeks acquired the Oriental fashion for mounting precious stones in their jewellery and both the onyx and sardonyx were stones admirably suited for cameo treatment, since both have stratified layers of light and dark stone. The opportunity to create decoration in relief – albeit in miniature – would have accorded with Greek taste and may, therefore, account for the flowering of the cameo as an art-form in the Hellenistic age. Unfortunately, none of the Hellenistic cameos in the British Museum is set in contemporary jewellery.

An early example from Sumeria (c. 2000 BC) demonstrates the long-standing interest in banded stones in Western Asia. Although it shows a simple form of cutting and polishing to accentuate the concentric circles, it has not been cut away to leave a surface-pattern in relief. This smooth polished treatment of banded stones remained popular in the eastern Mediterranean; for example, a massive late Antique gold finger-ring, set with a colourful sardonyx of this type, was found at Tarvis in Illyria and probably dates from the third century AD. There is even evidence among the jewellery from Ur (c. 2500 BC) that some of the cornelian beads had been artificially given white patterns, reminiscent of the white strata in a banded stone. The effect was produced by drawing a pattern on the bead with an alkaline solution, generally soda, and subsequently heating it; the alkali would then penetrate the stone, leaving the pattern indelibly marked upon it in white. Either the beads or this technique

536 A cornelian bead from a tomb at Sumerian Ur (c. 2500 BC). It has been artifically patterned by the use of an alkaline solution, which has partially penetrated the stone (as shown by a chipped section, lower centre), leaving a permanent design in white. Such beads were probably imported from the Indus Valley, where the technique was practised.

537 A group of agate, gold and cornelian beads from Sumerian Ur (*c.* 2200–2000 BC). Banded stones became increasingly popular in the later 3rd millennium, and the central bead here, cut so as to give concentric circles of different colours, may be regarded as a distant ancestor of the cameo. L 9cm

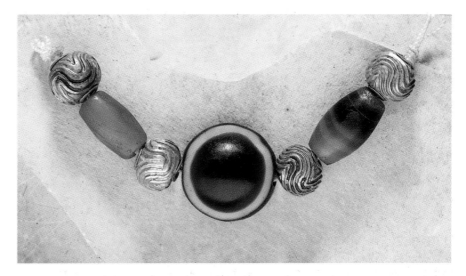

538–9 Two gold Roman finger-rings, each set with a cameo depicting a head of Medusa (2nd–3rd century AD). **538** (right), found in a tomb near Patras, in the Peloponnese, has a hoop made of eight flattened beads, with an oval sardonyx cameo.

539 (left) is one of four gold finger-rings found with a hoard of gold and silver coins at Sully Moors, near Cardiff (Wales). Only about 30 cameos are known from Roman Britain, and the most common design on them is Medusa. In this case the onyx cameo shows Medusa surrounded by a wreath of serpents. D (**538**) 2.4cm

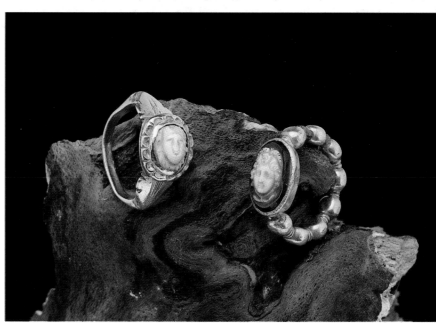

540 A garnet cameo pendant set in a gold frame, found at Epsom, Surrey (England). The cameo depicts a bearded man in a Phrygian cap. Pendants set with large cabochon garnets came into use among the Anglo-Saxons during the 7th century AD. Most are plain polished gems, but a very few, of which this is an outstanding example, are set with carved stones. The cameo is of late Antique origin, and had been cut down before setting into the Anglo-Saxon mount. L 3.85cm

541 The 'Noah' Cameo: the onyx cameo, mounted in a heavy gold pendant frame, is carved with a representation of Noah and his family leaving the Ark. On the doors of the Ark is incised: LAVR MED (added when in the possession of Lorenzo de' Medici).

This gem, one of the great masterpieces of the art of cameo-cutting, has been attributed to antiquity, to the court workshop of Frederick II Hohenstaufen (died 1250), to the circle of Ghiberti (1378–1455) and to a Florentine gem-cutter of the time of Lorenzo de' Medici (1449–92). Although opinions about its true date still differ, it is now accepted that it cannot be antique and the least controversial view is that it is a product of the court workshop of Frederick II Hohenstaufen (c. 1204–50) in Sicily or southern Italy.

The finely pounced floral motifs on the reverse of the gold mount (*left*) are characteristic of French and Burgundian goldsmiths' work of the 15th century, L 5.3cm

of bleaching the cornelian beads may have been brought to Ur from the East, but even at this early date it is indicative of the Oriental fascination with the natural beauty of stones and their variegated markings, which is most fully realised in the cameo technique at its best.

By the end of the second century BC the cameo had been generally accepted by the Romans, both as an ornament, especially for furniture, and as personal adornment; the Roman Emperors wore them, according to Pliny, as insignia with ceremonial dress. Stylistically the Roman cameo is a direct continuation of the Hellenistic, and for about two hundred years the art flourished; by the end of the second century AD the Roman cameo begins to disappear except for one class with inscriptions, mainly dedicatory but sometimes amuletic.

502

Curiously, the British Museum's fine collection of classical cameos contains few that have survived in their original mounts and settings – indeed, the only items of jewellery set with cameos are finger-rings. A typical example is the ring set with an onyx cameo of a Gorgon's head, which was reputedly found near Patras and dates from the second century AD. A slightly later example found near Cardiff (Wales) is one of about thirty cameos known to have a Romano-British origin, and, significantly, the only ones found mounted in jewellery are those set in finger-rings. Furthermore, this ring is also set with a Medusa or Gorgon's head, a subject that seems to have been much the most common among the Roman cameo finger-rings, due to some amuletic belief.

538

539

After the Roman period cameos were evidently highly prized but only very rarely are they to be found in contemporary gold settings, like the 'Epsom' cameo pendant. During the Middle Ages, as the late Professor Hans Wentzel has shown, the carving of cameos was not as rare as previously thought. However, much uncertainty remains about the location of the workshops and the date of their productions, as, for example, in the case of the magnificent 'Noah' Cameo, which had entered the Medici collections before 1465. At some stage, probably around 1400, the owner had the brilliantly harmonious and dignified mount made in heavy gold; only the reverse is given a delicate pointillé decoration that catches the light in its sinous, three-dimensional effects.

540

With the Italian Renaissance in the fifteenth century the art of the cameo blossomed under the patronage of eager collectors, like Pope Martin V (1417–31), Leonello d'Este of Ferrara (1407–50), Dandolo of Venice, Giustiniani of Genoa, Cardinal Francesco Gonzaga, Pope Paul II (1464–71) and perhaps the greatest of all, Lorenzo de' Medici. The names of the gem-engravers begin to be known, though more is known about those of the sixteenth century, such as Valerio Belli and Domenico Compagni in Rome. By that time every court in Europe had followed the Italian fashion, and many employed Italian artists for this purpose. Matteo dal Nassaro, of Verona, worked in France for François I, training both Italians and Frenchmen, while Jacopo de Trezzo became gem-engraver to Philip II of Spain.

Of course, many of these creations were not intended to be worn as jewellery, and of those that were mounted a fair proportion have since been separated. Consequently, the number of cameos that remain in their original settings as items of jewellery is not large and, perhaps, one of the rarest is a double-sided gold pendant set with diamonds and rubies that was preserved since the sixteenth century in the famous Piccolomini cabinet in Rome. During the sixteenth century, especially in Italy, the art of the cameo-cutter and of the goldsmith became most sophisticatedly conjoined in a class of jewellery that is frequently described as *commessi* – an Italian term for jewels in which the gold and cameo elements are unified into a single composition. Fewer than twenty of these distinctive jewels are known to have survived, and, although it has been suggested that they are French and perhaps all from one workshop, the variations in quality and in design are too great. The most strikingly beautiful examples from the late sixteenth century, as in the case of the famous 'Leda and the Swan' *commesso* in the Kunsthistorisches Museum, Vienna, are composed of chalcedony and similar hardstones but, exceptionally, shell-cameos were also used.

In Tudor England the fashion for Renaissance cameos was eagerly followed by Henry VIII, who had, in the person of Richard Atsyll (or Atzell), an official 'graver of stones', and from the manuscript lists it is clear that the King possessed jewels set with engraved gems, though whether the latter were of Roman or Renaissance date is seldom clear – unlike the finger-ring owned by the Lord Privy Seal, Thomas Cromwell, whose inventory in 1527 includes 'a gold ring set with an antique child's head . . . 6s 8d'. Throughout the Elizabethan period, the demand for cameos undoubtedly grew, but little is known about the handful of artists who worked in this field in London, and it is not yet possible to identify the master who created the cameo portraits of the Queen, several of which have survived, some in their original settings (finger-rings and pendants). Another group, now more confidently attributable to a workshop in England, depict a lady wearing an Elizabethan-style dress with a high collar; the quality of the execution is never high, as with the two unmounted examples that were part of Sir Hans Sloane's collection in 1753 when the British Museum was founded. Very recently another was found near Framlingham Castle (Suffolk) and purchased in 1984 by the Museum, but fortunately this cameo had survived in its original gold enamelled pendant. Though the enamel had suffered from burial, the workmanship is unmistakably Elizabethan and strikingly similar to a gold enamelled locket pendant containing a shell-cameo of two busts back to back (from the Earl of Carlisle's collection). This popular Renaissance cameo subject, in which one bust is carved in the highest possible relief whilst, in contrast, the second bust is carved in the most subtle low relief, can be found repeated on another shell-cameo in the Sloane collection of 1753 (now in the British Museum) – a further demonstration of this form of virtuosity.

French master goldsmiths of the seventeenth and early eighteenth centuries often provided extremely accomplished settings for contemporary cameos, like a Louis XIII openwork pendant of enamelled gold in the fashionable 'pea pod' design and set with precious stones, or the more restrained design of an enamelled ring set with a beautiful ruby cameo, carved in low relief with a female head

542

552

547

548, 549

545

554

OPPOSITE

Top **542** A double onyx cameo in a gold enamelled pendant, enriched with diamonds and rubies (Italian, *c.* 1520–30); given by Pope Clement VII (died 1533) to the Piccolomini family in Rome. The obverse (*left*) has a bust of Hercules wearing a lion's skin around his neck, cut entirely in the dark blue stratum of the stone. On the reverse (*right*) is Omphale, wearing a lion's skin on her head.

The lion's skin worn by Hercules was taken from the lion of Nemea killed as one of his Labours. Hercules is said to have become enamoured of Omphale, a Lydian queen whom he served for three years, when he allowed himself to be dressed in women's clothing and let Omphale wear the lion's skin. W (with frame) 4.5cm

Bottom left **543** An onyx cameo of Diana mounted in an enamelled gold frame. The stone is perforated through its length and may originally have come from the East in the form of a bead. The frame may be French (mid-16th century); however, the reverse is covered by a more recent gold plate engraved with floral designs. L (with frame) 4.8cm

Bottom right **544** A pendant in the form of a miniature altarpiece (probably Italian, *c.* 1560–80). Mounted within the enamelled gold triptych is an onyx cameo of the Pietà at the foot of the Cross, accompanied by kneeling angels. On the doors, enamelled in black, are the emblems of the Passion (on the inside) and St Peter and St Paul (on the outside). The reverse comprises a cabochon rock-crystal beneath which is painted the head of Christ in profile. H (pendant) 4.9cm

Above **545** French pendant (*c.* 1630) containing an onyx cameo of Lucius Verus, the adopted son of the Roman emperor Antoninus Pius. After Antoninus died in AD 161, Lucius, until his own early death in AD 169, shared the Imperial title with his adoptive brother Marcus Aurelius (reigned AD 161–180).

The pendant's openwork gold frame is richly enamelled and jewelled. The distinctive design of the pendant is in the style of engravings by Pierre Marchant of Paris (1623); the enamelled flower design on the reverse (*right*) illustrates the vogue for stylised naturalism. H 2.4cm

Left **546** A pendant set with a heliotrope cameo showing a bust of Christ wearing the Crown of Thorns (Italian, second half of the 16th century). The red flecks in the stone are here used to indicate drops of blood on the head and face. Contemporary accounts indicate that heliotrope became popular with Italian Renaissance cameo-carvers, like the gifted Matteo dal Nassaro, of Verona. The gold gem-set pendant frame is richly enamelled, especially on the reverse, where the insignia of the Society of Jesus (founded 1540) are seen against a background of flowers. The two pendant opals and the pendant skull *memento mori* may be later additions. W 4.9cm

547–51 Late 16th-century cameos and jewels of English (?) origin. **547** is an openwork pendant of enamelled gold set with garnets, with (at the centre) an onyx cameo of Queen Elizabeth I.

Three of these cameos depict the bust of a lady in court attire: **548** and **549** are unmounted onyx cameos in the Sloane Collection (pre-1753) and may be from an Elizabethan workshop in London; **549** (top left) corresponds closely to the third example set in a gold enamelled pendant (**550**) and recently found in the soil near Framlingham Castle, Suffolk (England); the enamel had suffered from burial. **551** (centre) is a well-preserved example of the same kind of goldsmiths' work, with similar distinctive filigree enamelling and pounced goldwork as on **550**. It is set with a large, poor-quality shell cameo of a popular Renaissance subject.

The English origin of this group proposed here is currently the subject of further research.

once thought to be a portrait of Mme de Maintenon. The Napoleonic classicism in France brought cameos once more into fashion, not just the splendid diadems, bandeaus, belts, bracelets and combs set with cameos that the Empress Josephine and her contemporaries, the Duchesses de la Rochefoucauld and de la Valette can be seen wearing in the paintings of Gérard and David in 1807 and 1808, but throughout Europe and at almost all levels of society. The lady of modest means would be able to buy a shell-cameo in a simple gold setting, but throughout the nineteenth century cameos were produced, especially in Italy; the jewellers both there and in the capital cities of Europe devised the elaborate settings, often studded with pearls and gemstones or colourfully enamelled, but by the middle of the century more probably set in plain gold, fashioned in the rather ponderous 'archaeological' style with filigree and granulation. The workshop of the Saulini family in Rome produced many of the spectacular cameos of the middle decades of the nineteenth century. Of the three cameos set into a massive 'archaeological-style' 560 bracelet, the one in the centre with a Medusa head is signed by Tommaso Saulini (1793–1864). Both he and his son Luigi exhibited in the International Exhibition in London in 1862.

One of the gifted Italian cameo artists to come to England at the end of the Napoleonic Wars in 1815 was Benedetto Pistrucci, who

Left **553** The 'Flora of Pistrucci', from the Payne-Knight collection (1821). This gold finger-ring is set with a fragment of cornelian breccia, carved in high relief with the head of Flora wearing a wreath of roses, poppies and marguerites (?), by the Italian engraver Benedetto Pistrucci (1784–1855), who settled in England in 1815. L 2.3cm

Right **555–9** A group of jewellery of the 19th century, set with hardstones and engraved gems. **555** (right) is an onyx cameo by the Italian gem-engraver Antonio Berini (1770–1830), which may represent Alexander the Great, mounted in a French enamelled gold brooch, enriched with diamonds and pearls.

The agate cameo (left) of the Roman emperor Augustus (63 BC–AD 14) was engraved in England (*c.* 1830) by the Italian engraver Benedetto Pistrucci, and mounted in a contemporary enamelled and chased gold openwork frame (**556**).

557 (bottom) is an Italian gold brooch-pendant with a ropework border in the 'archaeological' style, containing a panel of hardstone inlays set into marble to create a flower-spray. This type of work, known as *pietra dura*, had long been a speciality of Florence. This piece dates from the mid-19th century.

558 (centre), a gold brooch, set with a glass mosaic panel, is by the Castellani firm of Rome and Naples (*c.* 1860). The Greek letters in the centre mean 'bravo' or 'well done'. The Castellani firm may have based their design of this brooch on the central element of Byzantine bracelets of the 6th and 7th centuries AD.

559 (top) is an enamelled gold brooch in the form of entwined snakes, the four heads being set with diamonds; in the centre is a plasma cameo of the head of Medusa. It may have been made in Italy in the early 19th century.

Top Left **552** A portrait 'commesso' jewel. The Italian term, *commesso*, is generally applied to a rare class of Renaissance jewel in which gold and cameo elements are unified into a single composition. In this piece (late 16th century) the bearded head is executed in shell-cameo; the ornate armour is enamelled gold. The gold back is plain, with three loops for attachment. H 3.1cm

Above (left and right) **554** An early 18th-century gold finger-ring set with a ruby cameo of a female head in the classical manner. The ring is finely enamelled on the hoop and on the underside of the bezel. By the mid-19th century this ring with its rare ruby cameo had acquired a romantic but fanciful association: the cameo was thought to depict Mme de Maintenon, the last mistress of Louis XIV, and the ring said to have been given to her by the king when she retired to a convent. D 2.2cm

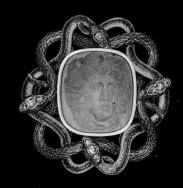

560 An Italian gold bracelet in the heavy 'archaeological' style, decorated with gold filigree. It is set with three contemporary onyx cameos by Tommaso Saulini (1793–1864), of Rome. The photo shows the head of Venus after a celebrated classical marble statue in Rome. The other two cameos are Medusa, in the centre, and a male head, possibly Hymen, god of marriage. L (bracelet) 18.9cm

settled in London and from 1817 to 1849 was Chief Engraver at the Mint. Not long after his arrival he was at Sir Joseph Bank's house in London, when Richard Payne-Knight, the famous collector of Classical antiquities, showed a cameo which Pistrucci recognised as his 'Flora'. When he claimed that he had cut this cameo before leaving Italy for the dealer Bonelli, Mr Payne-Knight refused to believe that it was not ancient. Pistrucci, to support his contention, made several 'Floras' – without convincing Mr Payne-Knight, whose manuscript catalogue (now in the British Museum with his Bequest) contains a deprecatory comment on Pistrucci, vigorously expressed in Latin.

In the late eighteenth to nineteenth centuries in England the passion for cameos and intaglios led James and William Tassie to make faithful copies in glass paste, whilst Josiah Wedgwood produced a loose variation of the art in his jasperware and black basalt medallions and intaglios. These became popular at other European ceramic factories, like Sèvres, Berlin and Fürstenberg – even in Portugal where the Lisbon porcelain works produced 'cameos' of Queen Maria I and Don Pedro; rare examples modelled by Joao Figueireido are dated 1782 and 1783 respectively. Indeed, this model of the Maria portrait was used by John Flaxman in 1787 when he was preparing the medallion for Josiah Wedgwood. Like many others, the firm of Wedgwood is still today meeting the undying demand for cameo heads, but rarely are cameos to be found in jewellery of modern design after the late 1930s and the art of true cameo-cutting has had few protagonists in this century. HT

CHAPTER EIGHTEEN

Functional Finger-Rings

563
565
566
561
564
562

Left A group of gold finger-rings from the Classical world. The earliest is a Minoan signet-ring from Crete (16th century BC), engraved with a scene of two wild goats mating (**561**).

Two of the rings are Etruscan: one, of the 6th century BC, is engraved on its bezel with a winged horse and sphinx (**562**). The second is of the 5th century BC (**563**); it has a sard gem engraved in 'globolo' style with a man on a horse. The ornate bezel has a design of animals and dolphins in repoussé, with filigree ornaments and fine granulation.

564 is a Greek signet-ring of the 4th century BC with an engraved scene of Aphrodite holding a dove.

565, from Rhodes, is Mycenaean (14th century BC). In the British Museum is a three-piece steatite mould from Enkomi of about the same date; this produces a cast with a similar bezel.

The massive gold ring set with a plain sardonyx (**566**) is Roman (3rd century AD); it is said to be from Tarvis in Illyria (in modern Yugoslavia). D 4cm

The difficulties of classifying finger-rings have been recognised and stressed by eminent authors in the past, for the ring often serves more than one purpose and its appearance frequently does not proclaim them. The further back in time, the less documentation about the use of rings has survived and their function becomes increasingly conjectural.

Probably the most ancient purpose of the finger-ring was simply to be decorative, as the gold and lapis lazuli finger-rings from the graves at Ur (*c.* 2500 BC) would seem to indicate: ten rings were worn on the hands of Queen Pu-abi. Decorative finger-rings range from the simplest of designs, like the early Mycenaean ring found at Rhodes or the La Tène silver wire ring (**167**), to the massive gold and sardonyx late Roman example and the delicately chased and engraved

26

gold hoop found at Poslingford (Suffolk), which was made in Anglo-Saxon England before the Norman Conquest – and to this day finger-rings have been made for this, and no other, purpose. Amuletic rings, like those with runic inscriptions and magical symbols, have already been mentioned in the wider context of amuletic jewellery (chapter 16). However, there have been, at different times through the ages, finger-rings specifically designed for a practical function: for example as signet-rings; archers' thumb-rings; marriage, betrothal and love rings; mourning and commemorative rings. All these rings were essentially personal and are, therefore, included here; there were, however, others – official rings, rings of investiture, and so on – that have been excluded for the reasons given in the Introduction. Two royal Anglo-Saxon rings of exceptional character have been tentatively included as early examples of commemorative finger-rings but, in the absence of written evidence, an official purpose for these two rings cannot be excluded.

Although many of these functional rings have also been designed to be highly decorative, their use has been the primary consideration; others, made as purely decorative rings, have subsequently been given a special use, as in late medieval and Elizabethan England, when rings set with gems were frequently used by the rich as 'marying' rings – these 'wedding-rings' were, no doubt, quite indistinguishable from the purely decorative rings of the same type. Nevertheless, some brief outline of these main types of finger-ring seems justified, despite the fact that clear divisions frequently do

A group of Anglo-Saxon gold finger-rings of the 9th and 10th centuries AD. **567** and **568** are unique survivals of a class of royal gift rings presented by the monarch as a mark of royal favour, and, though found as far apart as Wiltshire and Yorkshire, by an extraordinary coincidence they are linked dynastically. **567** is engraved with the name of King Æthelwulf of Wessex (AD 839–58) and **568** (on the interior) with that of his daughter, sister of Alfred the Great, Queen Æthelswith of Mercia (AD 853–88). Both also carry explicitly Christian designs inlaid with niello: Æthhelwulf's ring with a Tree of Life and peacocks motif, Æthelswith's with the *Agnus Dei*.

569 and **570** had a different, magical function. The former, from Greymoor Hill, near Carlisle, has an untranslatable runic inscription which reads: *ærkriufltkriurithonglæstæpontol*. Two other rings of the period with similar inscriptions survive, proof of the popularity of what must have been regarded as a powerful charm.

570 was found in the River Nene at Peterborough. Most unusually it has two bezels, one decorated with an elaborate 'endless knot', the other with three interlacing triangles, both symbols with religious and magical significance.

571, from Poslingford, Suffolk, is purely decorative, with engraved panels of animal, plant and interlace decoration. D (**569**) 2.9cm

Below right **572** An impression from a lapis lazuli cylinder-seal found in a grave at Sumerian Ur (*c.* 2100 BC). The seal is carved with two scenes of combat between animals and heroes. The inscription, which has been intentionally erased, would have given the name, father's name and profession of the original owner. The seal is illustrated on p. 31.

Below left **573** A black stone seal pendant of the Halaf period (*c.* 5000 BC) from Arpachiyah, Iraq. Seals of this kind were impressed into damp clay to indicate ownership of or responsibility for sealed goods. Stamp-seals worn as pendants remained popular in parts of Western Asia throughout the prehistoric and early historical periods. H 2.25cm

not exist and, in the absence of reliable documentary evidence, many finger-rings in the British Museum's collections cannot now be reliably classified under specific headings, although there is a strong possibility that they had a special function at one time.

The two most securely identifiable categories are discussed first, followed by the problems concerning the other two categories, and mention is made of a few significant examples.

Signet Finger-Rings

Although the finger-ring designed to be used as a signet does not seem to have emerged until much later, the wearing of small pendants, which could be used as stamp-seals, seems to date back in parts of Western Asia to about 5000 BC. Cylindrical seals were soon to become the standard form of signet in southern Mesopotamia; on them the incised inscription would give the name, family name and profession of the owner, and, by rolling it on damp clay, goods could be sealed and identified. These cylinder-seals were hollowed out and worn on a cord or chain around the neck or attached to toggle-pins, as found in some of the graves at Ur (*c.* 2500–2100 BC). Occasionally these cylinder-seals have been found with gold mounts, which, as in the case of a lapis lazuli example from Ur, transform an essentially functional object into a highly decorative and attractive piece of jewellery. That their cylindrical form was found attractive as well as practical is demonstrated by a massive and beautiful Egyptian gold ring (*c.* 1400 BC), which is set with a revolving glass cylinder in place of the bezel. The blue glass, which imitates the lapis lazuli stone, is not engraved and was evidently intended to be worn purely as an ornament.

The cylinder-seal was unknown in the Minoan and Mycenaean civilisations, although Babylonian and Hittite cylinders were clearly imported in considerable numbers and later placed in the tombs, as the excavations in Crete and Cyprus have shown. Minoan draftsmen engraved the gold bezels of their fine rings; **561** demonstrates the high quality achieved at this early date (*c.* 1600–1500 BC).

In Egypt, even as early as the Twelfth Dynasty (*c.* 1800 BC), the scarab had become the bezel of the finger-ring. By mounting the

scarab so that it could be swivelled round, the Egyptians made it ideally suited to the signet-ring, for not only could it be worn as a potent amulet (the scarab was the symbol of the resurrection in the Other World), but it could also be engraved on the flat underside and so serve as the signet of the owner whenever required; an example bearing the prenomen of Queen Hatshepsut dates from the beginning of the fifteenth century BC. By engraving on the underside of the scarab a further advantage is gained, because the signet is worn against the skin and, therefore, protected from the risk of scratches and surface damage.

About this time the swivelling bezel became a fashionable element in the design of Egyptian finger-rings; the fine engraving found on both sides of the thin glass plaques often set into these bezels is a remarkably skilful feat. The deeply engraved bezels of gold and other metals also make their appearance about 1400 BC and, simultaneously, a new and inexpensive technique of setting into the bezel an inlay of a different material (one example is a plain ivory ring set with a blue glazed composition) also makes its debut in Egyptian signet-rings of the Eighteenth Dynasty. Although the latter may have been intended for use, it is less likely that the cheap glazed composition rings of Tutankhamun and his wife, Ankhesenamun, were functional; if, as has been suggested, they were merely intended for distribution at festivals or court occasions, then these so-called 'signet-rings' would not really qualify for inclusion in this section.

A new form of signet-ring is introduced into Egypt during the Saite Period (c. 600 BC), in which the thick bezel is raised above the shank and cut away on the underside to allow room for the finger. As might be expected, contemporary Phoenician signet-rings are often much influenced by the older Egyptian tradition, especially the use of the swivel bezel set with an engraved stone.

In the Greek world the art of engraving the gold bezel was reintroduced by about 600 BC and a beautiful Hellenistic example shows the skill to perfection. The Greek tradition for engraving gemstones goes back to about 700 BC, but it was not before about 600 BC that the practice of mounting them in finger-rings became general. Like the Greeks, the Etruscans mounted engraved gems in the bezels of finger-rings, sometimes subordinating the gems within a most ostentatious and elaborately worked gold setting, apparently using them less as signets and more as ornamental additions to the purely decorative ring. However, in Rome the practice of wearing finger-rings for sealing purposes is well documented and, for example, by the end of the third century BC, Roman consuls were wearing signet-rings with a distinctive device. It was about this time that both the sardonyx and the garnet became popular in Rome as a seal-stone, but many signet-rings continued to have intaglios cut in metal bezels (gold, silver or base-metal). Romano-British finds include three silver rings found at Amesbury in Wiltshire with a hoard of coins, the latest having been issued in AD 402–50.

In the Early Christian era there was no break in the tradition and, although the bezels were occasionally set with intaglio gems, more frequently the flat surface of a metal bezel was engraved; such signet-rings were much favoured at the Byzantine Imperial Court in

A group of Egyptian signet-rings. The two glazed composition rings date to the 18th Dynasty (c. 1361–1352 BC); **574** bears the name of Tutankhamun, **575** that of Ankhesenamun, Tutankhamun's wife. Such glazed composition signets were probably distributed at festivals or court occasions.

The owner of the silver signet (**576**) was, judging from its hieroglyphic inscription, a priest of one of the 22nd-Dynasty Sheshonqs (presumably Sheshonq I), as well as of Psammetichus I, founder of the 26th Dynasty. It is noteworthy that the funerary cult of a revered king was still being maintained 300 years after his death. The form of this ring (dated c. 600 BC is characteristic of the 26th Dynasty: it has a thick oval bezel raised well above the hoop, with a curved section cut away on the underside.

577, a gold ring of the same period, is similar in form, also with a cut-away bezel. It is inscribed: 'Chief Steward of the God's Adorer, Sheshonq'; its owner was a high-ranking official in the administration of the High Priestess of Amun at Thebes.

The gold stirrup-shaped ring (**578**) is dated c. 250–200 BC and is inscribed: 'The Son of Re, Ptolemy, Living forever, Beloved of Ptah'. Although four of the Ptolemaic rulers bore the epithets 'Living forever' and 'Beloved of Ptah', this inscription probably refers to Ptolemy III Euergetes.

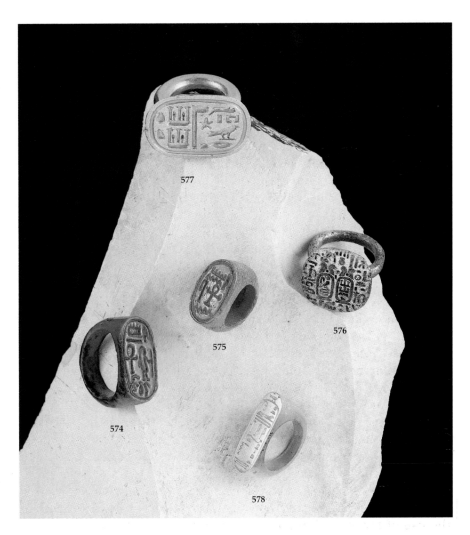

Constantinople and in the early Sasanian Empire to the east. The late Antique practice of wearing a signet-ring deeply cut with the portrait-busts of a man and a woman beneath a small cross suggests that in the Early Christian era there was a new fashion for combining the love or betrothal ring with the signet finger-ring. This custom may have spread to Gaul and lived on under Frankish and Merovingian rule, as demonstrated by the 'Dromacius and Betta' signet-ring from Mulsanne (France).

The fashion for engraved gems set in the bezels of signet-rings did not die in the Eastern Empire as it had in Rome during the Imperial period, and north of the Alps, during the sixth and seventh centuries, Roman engraved gems were highly prized and given elaborately worked gold settings. In this period widespread illiteracy made the seal indispensable, and the signet-ring continued without a break through the early Middle Ages in the West.

With the development of heraldry in the later Middle Ages in Europe as a means of identification, all who were entitled to bear arms wore signet-rings engraved with their armorial bearings. Thus, the signet-ring gained a new lease of life. By the fourteenth century very fine examples from Italy occur frequently, but until the following century it is rare to find French or English armorial signets of

580 579

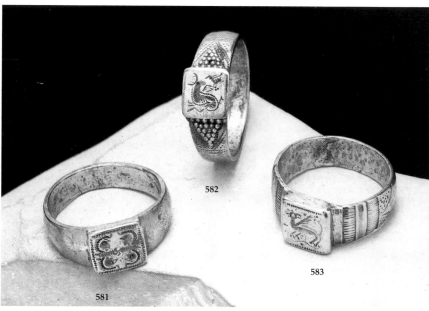

582
581
583

Top left Two gold Phoenician finger-rings (*c.* 6th century BC). In **579** the cornelian scarab shows Isis suckling Horus, with Osiride figures on either side and a winged disc above. This signet was probably not worn on a finger, but attached to a string or necklace.

The green glass scaraboid (**580**) represents two winged sphinxes on either side of a sacred tree. A swivel of gold wire passes through the scaraboid and is attached to a disc at either end of the hoop of three gold wires. The ring could be worn on the finger, with the design against the skin, if so desired, to prevent it from becoming damaged. L (bezel) 1cm

Centre left Three silver signet-rings (*c.* AD 400), found at Amesbury, Wiltshire (England), inside a pot with a hoard of coins, the latest being issues of Theodosius II (AD 402–50). Each ring has a chased or engraved design on its bezel: **581** has four helmeted heads; **582** a recumbent stag looking over its shoulder at a bird; **583** a griffin looking over its shoulder. The similarities in style and technical execution suggest that the three rings were made by the same craftsman, perhaps for the same customer on commission. D (each ring) 2.5cm

Bottom far left **584** A Sasanian agate finger-ring (*c.* 4th century AD), with a Pahlavi inscription *b'nwky*, perhaps a proper name. The design of a wolf suckling two children recalls the story of Romulus and Remus, founders of Rome, and is one of many Sasanian borrowings from the West. The use of stone rings themselves, however, is characteristically Sasanian. D 2.1cm

Bottom left **585** A late Antique gold signet-ring from Usküdar (Scutari), near Istanbul (4th or 5th century AD). The bezel is engraved with the seated figure of Orpheus playing the lyre to two recumbent animals; a retrograde Greek inscription may be deciphered as 'Seal of John, the crowned saint'. D (external) 2.5cm

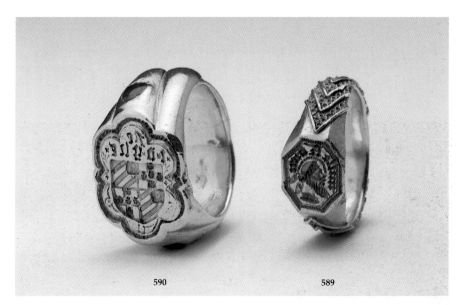

590 589

Above **586** A late Antique gold marriage-ring of *c.* AD 500. The bezel is deeply incised with a male and a female bust beneath a small cross. Engraved and nielloed male and female busts alternate on the seven medallions which make up the hoop. All the males wear the *chlamys* fastened at the right shoulder with a type of brooch indicative of high rank; on the bezel the brooch is shown on the left shoulder, indicating that this is a signet-ring. D (external) 2.45cm

Top centre **587** A Merovingian gold signet-ring, from Mulsanne, Sarthe, France (late 6th–7th century AD). Around the bezel are the inscribed and nielloed names, Dromacius and Betta. The figures of a warrior and woman on the bezel are of uncertain interpretation. At each shoulder is a pair of profiled heads of birds-of-prey with cruelly curving beaks, conjoined at the back by a nielloed frame; when they are viewed together from the front they form an animal mask. The weight, in excess of 24 grammes, is the equivalent of between 5 and 6 standard Byzantine *solidi*. D 2.5cm

Top right **588** A Merovingian gold finger-ring, possibly from the south of France (6th–7th century AD). Here the gemstone is a reused Roman nicolo of the late Republican period. It depicts Romulus and Remus in a cave beneath a tree, with a shepherd to the right. The heavy gold setting, enriched with pellets and granulation at the shoulder, is characteristic of an ostentatious display of wealth associated with the high nobility of the period. D 3.6cm

Above Two gold signet-rings. **589**, a 15th-century French ring, was found in Selby, Yorkshire (England). Its bezel is engraved with a Saracen's head and the inscription *nul si bien*. As is the case with many signet-rings, the owner has not been identified.

590, a massive late 14th-century signet, is set with a ruby on each shoulder and is engraved on the bezel with a shield including the arms of the de Grailly family. Above the shield the letters *E.I.D. Gre* have been interpreted as 'E[st] [Sigillum] I[ohannis] D[e] Gre', meaning, 'this is the seal of Jean de Grailly. D (external) 2.8cm

comparable quality, as in the Fishpool Hoard (buried in 1464), although one splendid and massive gold stone signet-ring from France may date from the late fourteenth century. Thought to be the ring of Jean de Grailly, who was a companion-in-arms of the Black Prince and created a Knight of the Garter in 1364, a recent study of the arms suggests that it may have been made for another member of the family rather than Jean himself. A great refinement among armorial signets was to reproduce not only the coat-of-arms but the correct tinctures; this was achieved by engraving the coat-of-arms in crystal; they were repeated in colour on the reverse side and the crystal would then be set in the gold bezel. Although the engraved surface could be used for impressions, the colours would not wear

328j

away. The signet-ring of Mary, Queen of Scots (beheaded in 1587) is probably the most interesting example of this type; it was evidently made in France, where this technique was especially practised and popular.

Men who were not entitled to bear arms were allowed to seal with a simple device, and many merchants' rings in bronze and base metal have survived, engraved on the bezel with a merchant's mark, often incorporating the initials of the owner's name. This custom was to be developed and became fashionable in the nineteenth and twentieth centuries, as in the Elizabeth Barrett Browning amethyst finger-ring. Although the need for the signet-ring gradually became less essential after the eighteenth century, there remains even to this day a vogue for them, however rarely they are actually put to use.

The Archer's Thumb-Ring

Another type of finger-ring which was primarily functional, but often very decorative as well, was the bow-ring worn by archers on the thumb. Again, there is a long history attached to these rings, for with the early development of the crossbow thumb-rings of this shape often appear, but in certain countries and at certain periods they are especially beautifully worked and designed. Three are illustrated here, spanning more than two thousand years and offering three very different solutions. Indeed, the European medieval example is trebly functional, for it is also a fine signet-ring and incorporates an amuletic text on the exterior of the hoop, which is the same as the text on the fifteenth-century coin pendant. The gem-studded jade examples from India are particularly ornamental and are occasionally depicted in contemporary Mughal miniatures. Simple bronze or ivory versions are not uncommon and were extremely functional.

Marriage, Betrothal and Love-Rings

The *fede*, or hand-in-hand, ring appears in Roman times, when the two clasped hands (*dextrarum ivnctio*), represented a contract. The Roman symbolism of two hands clasped in troth was, of course,

Below left A group of archers' thumb-rings from China, India and medieval Europe. The Chinese ring, of brownish-green jade (**599**), dates from the 5th century BC (Eastern Zhou period). The oval spreading shape of this ring seems to have been general in ancient China from the period when the cross-bow was developed. This example is decorated with dragons' heads in profile formed by modelled C-scrolls, with incised details.

The Indian ring (**600**) dates from the 17th century AD (Mughal period). It is made of grey-green jade, inlaid with rubies and emeralds in gold settings. In a miniature painting (*c*. 1650) Shah Jahan is shown wearing an archer's thumb-ring on his right hand (**394**).

The gold and nielloed Venetian example (**601**) also acts as a signet-ring, the bezel being engraved with the armorial seal of the Donati, an old Venetian family. On the outside is engraved a personal badge or device (see detail *below*); on the hoop is a Latin inscriptions taken from Luke, iv, 30, which was widely used as a charm against the dangers of travel, especially robbery (see also **523**). The inside of the hoop is also engraved, with a badge in the form of a column upon a mount, cut by a scythe, from which issues a scroll with the legend AIDA MEDIO. This exceptional amuletic piece, found at Aegium in the Peloponnese, can be dated to the 14th century AD. L (**599**) 4.5cm

Top 16th- and 17th-century signet-rings. **591**, an early 16th-century merchant's ring of brass (once gilded), was found at Gloucester (England). The bezel is engraved with a merchant's mark combining the letters R, P, S, E and A. Inside the hoop is an enamelled motto: *Y leve yn hope*.

592, an Elizabethan gold signet-ring with armorial bearings engraved on the bezel, belonged to a member of the Ravenscroft family of Bretton in Flintshire, possibly Thomas Ravenscroft, recorded in 1580 as Sheriff of Flint and head of the family.

593 was made for Mary, Queen of Scots (1542–87), probably at the French court between 1548 and 1558. In the bezel is a crystal skilfully engraved with the Queen's achievement; the correct tinctures appear through the crystal on a field of blue. On the underside of the bezel is the cipher for Mary and François (the Dauphin, to whom she was betrothed from 1548 to 1558). There was no other time when the simultaneous use of this cipher and of those armorial bearings would have been as correct as in those ten years. This large gold ring is finely ornamented with flowers, once brightly enamelled.

594 is a rich example of the late 17th-century form of private signet-ring, in which the bezel is set with a contemporary gem – here an amethyst engraved with an Roman altar scene. This enamelled gold ring belonged to Henry Howard, 4th Earl of Carlisle (1694–1758), a well-known collector of engraved gems.

Bottom 19th-century signet and commemorative finger-rings. Elizabeth Barrett Browning's silver-gilt signet-ring (**595**) is set with an amethyst engraved: EBB. Elizabeth Barrett married Robert Browning in 1846; she died in 1861. Robert had the ring enlarged for his daughter-in-law Fanny. Robert's gold finger-ring (**596**), with the inscription *Ba* (Robert's nickname for Elizabeth), has a compartment for hair and an engraved inscription within the hoop: *God bless you, June 29 1861*.

Also commemorative is the black enamelled gold ring (**597**) with brown hair and a gold crown under the crystal bezel, the underside of which is engraved: *CR 1st* (under a royal crown). The hoop bears the legend: PLUS.QUAM.VICTOR.1648. The ring probably dates from the opening of the coffin of Charles I in St George's Chapel, Windsor Castle, in the presence of the Prince Regent in 1813.

Of exceptional interest is the small commemorative ring with a locket bezel (**598**), containing, under the hinged enamelled gold cover, the gold laureate head of Napoleon in low relief. It is said to be one of six rings made for the chief conspirators in the Emperor's escape from the Isle of Elba in 1815. Only one other example is known to be in England (in private possession). L (bezel) 0.35cm

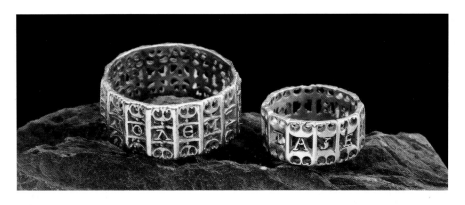

Left above **602–3** Two gold finger-rings from Roman Britain (2nd–3rd century AD). Polygonal openwork rings incorporating an inscription are a distinctive type found throughout the Empire. The pierced technique is especially typical of late Antique jewellery, but this class of ring appears to have come into use in the 2nd century AD. In many cases the mottoes on the panels are in Greek: that on **602** (left), from Corbridge, Northumberland, reads: 'the love-token of Polemios'. The Bedford ring (**603**, right) has a Latin motto: EUSEBIO VIVAS ('[long] life to Eusebius'). Such rings must clearly have been made to special order, which seems to argue against any single place of manufacture.
D (**602**) 2.5cm

Left below **604–5** Two gold Romano-British finger-rings (4th century AD). **604** (left) was excavated in the late Roman fort of Richborough, Kent in 1935, while **605** (right) was found at Thetford in Norfolk. Each has similar decoration on the shoulders of double spirals of beaded wire and an oval bezel within which is set a plaque embossed with a design of clasped right hands (*dextrarum iunctio*), most likely representing, in this context, a betrothal. D (**604**) 2.8cm

highly applicable to the Christian betrothal or marriage-ring and the magnificent gold example excavated at the Late Roman fort of Richborough (Kent, England), in 1935 is thought to be no earlier than the fourth century AD and, therefore, probably a betrothal finger-ring.

Fede-rings have continued in use throughout Europe up to the present day and sometimes they bear a religious, or even magical, inscription, making them fall into both the amuletic and betrothal categories, for it is impossible to know which had the greater significance for the original owner.

Another late Roman innovation was the openwork finger-ring incorporating letters which form an appropriate inscription. From the second century AD onwards the Christian betrothal ring was usually made of gold, and the delicate polygonal example excavated at the Roman fort at Corbridge, Northumberland, in 1935 is a rare survival from Roman Britain. Although the interior is smooth, the sixteen openwork panels are each divided into three horizontal zones, the middle containing a letter; the Greek inscription, which indicates that it was a betrothal ring, suggests that it was made in the Eastern Roman Empire. Byzantine marriage-rings of the sixth and seventh centuries are often elaborately engraved, and depict the bride and bridgroom; on one example they are being blessed by the figures of Christ and the Virgin, and accompanying Greek inscription may be read as 'Harmony'.

There is no reliable information about the form of wedding-ring used in Britain during the early Middle Ages but it is interesting to note that in medieval times the wedding ceremony took place at the church door, not at the entry to the chancel, as is normal today. The

606 A Byzantine gold and niello marriage-ring (7th century AD). The bezel is engraved and nielloed with figures of Christ and the Mother of God blessing a bridegroom and a bride respectively; below the figures is inscribed, in Greek, the word 'Harmony'. The octagonal hoop is engraved and nielloed with scenes from the life of Christ. D (external) 2.7cm

607 A Flemish oil-painting on panel by Petrus Christus, dated 1544, depicting a young wealthy couple with St Eligius, patron-saint of goldsmiths, in the shop of a jeweller-goldsmith. Petrus Christus (died 1473) was active in Bruges. Among the jewellery in this painting can be seen the finger-rings neatly stored on rolls of paper(?) in a small box.

Above Two 15th-century love-rings.
608 is an English ring from Godstow Nunnery, near Oxford. Its broad gold hoop was formerly enamelled; the outside is chased with flowers and foliage and engraved with the Trinity, the Virgin and Child, and a male saint. In the interior is engraved the legend: *Most in mynd and in myn hert/Lothest from you ferto depart.*

609 is Italian. On the shoulders is the legend, enamelled in black, *Lorenso * a Lena Lena*. The bezel is set with a diamond crystal. D (**608**) 1.9cm

Below A group of 18th- and early 19th-century love- or marriage-rings. The two gold puzzle-rings with multiple hoops are early 19th-century and are identically composed, except that **614** (shown apart) has five hoops interlacing at the back and joined at the front with an applied ornament of two hands clasped over a heart; **615** has seven interlacing hoops.

616 is probably French (late 18th century); set in the bezel under glass(?) is a white plaque painted in brown with a motif of hearts and doves, encircled with the inscription: L'AMOUR

NOUS UNIT.

617, although English (*c.* 1760), has an enamel inscription around the hoop in French: FIDELITE MERITE AMOUR. This gold ring has a heart-shaped faceted sapphire set in the bezel.

618 also has an enamelled inscription around its hoop: UNIS A JAMAIS. The bezel, with its pair of billing doves, is enamelled and set with a small ruby. This French ring (*c.* 1760–70) was probably made as a betrothal gift.
w (bezel) 1.2cm

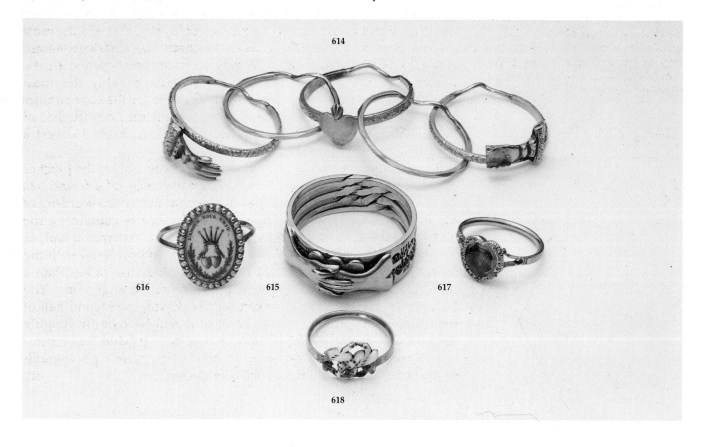

Left A group of marriage-rings. **610** and **611** are of a late 16th-century German type, made of two gold, gem-set and enamelled interlocking rings which cannot be separated. Their double form has led to them being widely called 'gimmel' rings (from Latin *gimmellus*, 'twin'). On the inner surfaces of each ring, when opened, can be read the enamelled inscription (in Latin on **610** and in German on **611**): 'whom God hath joined together let no man put asunder'. A considerable number of rings of this type have survived but some are products of the 19th-century fakers. Few can be traced back as far as the 1850s; **610**, however, was not only purchased by Lord Braybrooke in 1856, but it bears a French restricted warranty mark in use between 1819 and 1838.

612 and **613** are examples of Jewish marriage-rings only worn during the wedding ceremony. Their date and place of origin is much disputed, but it seems likely that an Eastern European, perhaps Transylvanian, origin in the last 150 years is the most likely. **612** has bosses around the hoop with applied filigree work and enamelling. The enamelled pyramid on its bezel is hinged, and has on its gold base-plate the initial letters of the phrase *Mazzāl tōb*, meaning 'good luck'.

613 has pierced enamelled scenes from the Garden of Eden over the cylindrical ground. The identical scenes are to be found on another ring in the Waddesdon Bequest in the British Museum. W (**613**, hoop) 2.1cm

custom of the bride to give as well as to receive, a wedding-ring is another obscure aspect, and certainly few such rings can now be recognised. In early Tudor times the English custom, still common today, of having a plain gold hoop as a wedding-ring is apparently well attested, for J. G. Nichols when editing the *Chronicle of Queen Jane* (1850) quotes from an account of Mary I's marriage in London to Philip II of Spain in July 1554: 'The Quenes marriage-ring was a plain hoope of gold without any stone in it; for that was as it is said her pleasure, because maydens were so maried in old Tymes'.

The presence of an inscription occasionally establishes beyond doubt that the ring was made for a marriage, as with the gimmel finger-rings and the well-attested Jewish wedding custom of using a large ring during the actual ceremony. However, many finger-rings are simply tokens of love – from the so-called 'Fair Rosamond's ring' 608 of the late Middle Ages to the eighteenth-century finger-ring with a 616 pair of doves and the words '*L'amour nous unit*'.

Commemorative and Mourning Rings

A particularly interesting group of commemorative rings were worn by the adherents of the British royal house of Stuart and these 'Jacobite' rings usually have set in the bezel a portrait of one of the Stuart kings – Charles I (the Martyr), Charles II, James II or the Old Pretender. Occasionally the portrait of the last reigning Stuart monarch, Queen Anne (died 1714), is set in the bezel of finger-rings 620 and the example illustrated is exceptional in being executed in gold foil, with embossed details. The fashion for wearing (after the monarch's death) a commemorative ring with his or her portrait has continued to this century, whilst others were made to be worn during the monarch's lifetime as a token of loyalty. Perhaps the most curious example is the ring made to commemorate Charles I, whose 597 coffin in St George's Chapel, Windsor Castle, was opened in the presence of the Prince Regent in 1813, and probably the most evocative is the ring, said to be one of six made for the conspirators 598 concerned in the escape of the Emperor Napoleon from the Isle of Elba, which contains (under the hinged gold enamelled cover) a gold relief portrait of the Emperor.

Since the fourteenth century, and possibly even earlier, the practice of wearing rings as a memento of a deceased relative or friend has existed. These rings are usually easily recognized by the wording of the inscriptions. However, finger-rings with bezels containing the hair of the loved one, have survived without any inscription and, as in one case where the bezel has a piece of silk embroidered with the 627 hair, it is not always clear that it is a mourning ring rather than a token of love – or just a bizarre form of decorative finger-ring. The fashion for mourning rings began to fade during the second half of the nineteenth century, largely because it had become thoroughly debased and universal. The cheap versions, mass-produced in centres like Birmingham, often designed to hold an imperfect photograph in the bezel, represent the last phase in the story. HT

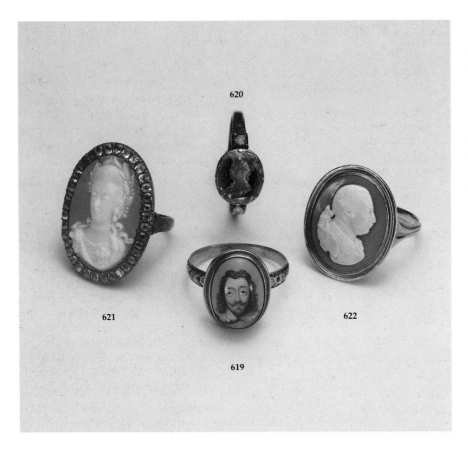

A group of commemorative rings for monarchs. **619** is a mid-17th-century ring with a painted enamel portrait of Charles I, made either following his execution in 1648, or after the Restoration of the monarchy in 1660 when it was once again safe to show Royalist allegiance.

620, an English ring (*c.* 1715), contains a portrait of Queen Anne in embossed gold foil on a ground of black hair; on either side of the bezel is a diamond in a square setting.

621 is set with a Lisbon porcelain 'cameo' portrait of Queen Maria I of Portugal (1734–1816), bordered by crystal pastes; this silver-gilt ring may have been made before her death, as ceramic cameos of the Queen were modelled by Joao Figueireido in 1782 and would have been available during her lifetime.

622 is a gold ring set with a glass-paste portrait of King George III of England (died 1820). This cameo may have been produced by William Tassie (1777–1860), nephew of James Tassie (1735–99), during the King's lifetime, since the ring contains no reference to his death.

A group of English memorial finger-rings. **623** commemorates the death of George III: the bezel contains an onyx cameo urn and the inscription *G III Obt. Oct. 1820*. However, the monogram LR (repeated three times), combined with other royal emblems in gold filigree over the black enamelled hoop, remains a mystery.

624 is an earlier memorial ring of black enamelled gold set with 24 diamonds and ornamented with skulls and cross-bones, even within the bezel with its plait of hair. Made in 1773, the inscription records the death of Evelyn Pierrepont, 2nd Duke of Kingston, who in 1745 had raised a regiment of Horse to oppose the Jacobite army of Bonnie Prince Charlie.

625 is a plain 17th-century gold ring, set with a 'baroque' pearl. Inside the hoop is engraved: *None can prevent the Lord's intent*; the deceased's name and date of death (underside of the bezel) can no longer be read.

626, dated 1788, commemorates a certain William Hanley Esq., aged 69; the bezel has an enamelled gold urn and a simple inscription: IN MEMORY OF A FRIEND.

627 is a late 18th-century form of memorial ring, with a piece of silk in the bezel embroidered with hair to imitate a moss-agate; the bezel is bordered with sapphires.

628 is enamelled gold, made in London in 1823 by Ebenezer Taylor and John Kennard upon the death of a Mary Attwood, aged 38; the bezel is in the form of a diamond-set snake encircling a compartment for hair.

629 is excellently enamelled and designed; it was made in London in 1847 by Thomas Eady of Clerkenwell to commemorate the demise of Hugh, Duke of Northumberland, whose device is on the shield-shaped bezel.
L (**629**, bezel) 1.4cm

Select glossary

Achievement In heraldry, complete display of armorial bearings.

Ajouré Any variety of open pattern, such as one formed by cutting out portions of metal with a chisel. Gems were also set ajouré (open-back setting), allowing light through the stone, to maximise the effect of colour.

Aigrette (from the French, 'tuft of feathers'). Originally a hat or hair ornament in the form of jewelled feathers or a brooch to support a feather, in use in Renaissance Western Europe, Persia and Mughal India. By the 18th century a variety of forms had developed, including flower bouquets or crescent sprays, worn by ladies as hair or corsage ornaments.

Ankh-**sign** The Egyptian hieroglyphic sign for 'life'.

Annealing Reheating worked metal to remove its brittleness.

'Archaeological style' This term is used here to describe designs and forms in 19th-century jewellery directly inspired by archaeological discoveries, especially at Pompeii, Herculaneum and in the Etruscan tombs in the vicinity of Rome.

'Baroque' pearl A large and irregularly shaped pearl, usually of fantastic shape, much favoured by Renaissance goldsmiths.

'*Basse-taille* enamelling', see **enamelling**

Beading The visual effect of beading can be achieved by:
a. arranging single solid gold grains in lines to form a border;
b. placing wire between two blocks in a groove cut with hemi-spherical depression. The blocks are hammered, while the wire is turned.

Bezel A term now generally applied to the upper part of a finger-ring (ie. excluding the hoop and the shoulders). More widely used as a term for the metal rim or ring for holding in place another material (such as a glass or rock-crystal in a watch-case cover).

Bracteate A sheet-metal disc whose main decoration is executed in repoussé. Often suspended by means of a cylindrical attachment and worn as a pendant.

Briolette A drop-shaped stone faceted all over, usually with triangular facets.

Bulla A gold pendant of Etruscan origin, worn as an amulet, usually consisting of a hollow convex gold disc. The *bulla* was worn on a broad band around the neck.

Cabochon A precious or semi-precious stone which is merely polished, without being cut into facets.

Calibré-cutting A stone cut into a specific shape to fit its setting exactly.

Cameo A hardstone or gem into which a design is cut in relief, often making use within the design of the contrasting colours occurring naturally in the stone. Several types of shell producing contrasting layers are also suitable for shell-cameos. Shell is easier to work than hardstone, being cut with a point or a sharp-edged tool and not drilled.

Carbuncle A large red stone polished *en cabochon*, usually a garnet, but sometimes a ruby.

Cartouche
a. In Egyptian hieroglyphic texts, an elongated oval in which names of kings and queens appear.
b. An area, often roughly shield-shaped and contained within a frame of fanciful design. Occasionally found blank, but more often decorated with armorial devices, initials, trophies and scenes.
c. Additionally, a specialist use of the term to describe the tiny decorative suspension plaque from which hang the short suspension chains attached to the pendant jewel below.

Champlevé enamelling, see **enamelling**

Chasing A technique of working metal from the front using a tool with a rounded end so that the pattern is indented into the surface.

Chi-Rho monogram The first two letters of Christ's name in Greek (Christos), *chi* and *rho,* used in monogram form.

Chip-carving Deeply cut designs, often geometric, deriving much effect from the interplay of light and shadow on their angled surfaces, which are frequently gilded.

Cire-perdue The 'lost-wax' process of casting. A wax or wax-coated model is embedded in clay which is then baked so that the wax melts and is lost, leaving a mould into which the molten metal can be poured. The mould has to be broken to retrieve the object.

Cloison A cell formed of thin strips of metal soldered to a metal base. In inlaid work the cloison is designed to hold the inlay of stone or glass (or a man-made imitation). A design made up of a network of cloisons for inlays or enamels is described as cloisonné. See also **enamelling (cloisonné)**

Demi-parure, see *parure*

Electrum A naturally occurring alloy of gold and silver.

Embossing, see **repoussé**

Enamel A coloured glass, or a combination of vitreous glazes, fused onto a metallic surface. The general term 'enamels' is often applied to a class of objects heavily decorated with some form of enamelling.

Enamelling:
  cloisonné A technique in which a network of cloisons forming the outlines of a decorative pattern or a picture is soldered to a metal surface (particularly gold); the coloured enamels are laid into the cloisons in powdered form and fired. When cool the enamel is polished and forms a smooth surface level with the cloisons.
  champlevé A technique of enamelling in which the surface of the metal is gouged away to create troughs and channels, each separated from the other by a thin ridge. The coloured enamels are laid into the troughs in powdered form and fired. When cool the enamel is polished and forms a smooth surface level with the metal ridges. Thick sheet metal is required, so copper and other base metals are ideal for this technique.
  basse-taille A sophisticated version of **champlevé** enamelling Within an area that has been cut away to receive the enamels a design or scene is chased in low relief. The translucent enamels used 'flood' the chased work, so that they lie in varying thicknesses. Light is reflected back through the enamels from the metal (usually gold or silver) in varying degrees, producing rich tonal effects which can give the impression of three-dimensional modelling to figural scenes.
  émail en ronde bosse ('encrusted' enamelling) A technique in which small objects or figures fashioned in the round or in very high relief (usually in gold) are covered with translucent or opaque enamels.
  painted enamels A technique evolved during the 15th century AD to create pictorial scenes. The metal, usually copper, was cut from a thin sheet and slightly domed. A layer of enamel was applied in wet powdered form over the front and back and fired, providing a base on which to apply subsequent layers and to delineate the composition, often by drawing with a needle through the wet enamel.
  enamel miniature-painting A technique evolved in France in the second quarter of the 17th century and related to the Renaissance technique of **painted enamels**. The metal, often gold, was covered by a white or light-coloured enamel; onto the smooth surface thus created the enameller applied coloured enamels, using such techniques of the miniaturist as stipple-painting.
  filigree enamelling Similar to **cloisonné enamelling**, except that the cells are formed by the filigree (ie. twisted gold wire), and the enamel does not form a smooth surface level with the filigree.

Engraving A technique of cutting patterns into a surface with a sharp tool.

Faience A glazed composition used in the ancient world; formed from a fused mass of crushed quartz and glazed in various colours, often imitating semi-precious stones.

False filigree A term here used to describe the fine cast-gold openwork jewellery of pre-Columbian Central and South America.

Fibula A brooch of safety-pin form.

Filigree A decorative pattern made of wires, sometimes soldered to a background, but often left as openwork.

Filigree enamelling, see **enamelling**

Fire-gilding The application of a mixture of gold and another substance, particularly mercury, to an object; when heated the mercury or other admixture is given off and the gold is deposited on the surface. Mercury gilding was the main form of gilding used on European metal artefacts from late Roman times until the mid-19th century.

Gilding The application of gold to the surface of an object made of another material. See **fire-gilding** and **parcel-gilt**.

Granulation Decoration consisting of minute spherical grains of metal soldered to a background, usually in gold. The ancient method, which left no solder visible between the grains and the surface of the gold, was rediscovered only in the 20th century.

Intaglio A sunk pattern or a design cut into a flat surface, usually metal or a hardstone. When intended to be used as a seal, the device would be executed in reverse.

Heliotrope (bloodstone) A dark-green variety of chalcedony with red flecks.

Jacinth The name for a reddish-orange stone, either a variety of garnet or a zircon.

'Loop-in-loop' chain A type of chain used in antiquity, made by folding the oval links in half and threading each one through the looped ends of its neighbour. The more complicated double form can be made by threading the bent link through the looped ends of the two preceding ones, and this can be cross-linked with another to form a chain of up to 8 sides with a characteristic herringbone pattern.

'Lost-wax' casting, see *cire-perdue*

Lunula A crescent-shaped sheet of gold.

Memento mori (Latin: 'Remember that you must die') A term to describe objects incorporating emblems of mortality, designed to remind the onlooker of the inevitability of death.

Millefiori Tiny cubes or tesserae formed by fusing together glass rods of different colours and cutting slices across the section.

Nefer-sign An ancient Egyptian hieroglyph, meaning 'good' and 'beautiful'.

Nicolo A term used to describe a type of onyx engraved either in intaglio or in cameo.

Niello A black compound of silver, lead, copper and sulpher – the exact composition varies – fusible at low temperatures; it is applied to metal (usually silver) in much the same way as enamel but is not vitreous.

Openwork, see **ajouré**

Opus interrasile A type of intricate pierced decoration executed by cutting out a pattern in sheet gold using awls or tiny chisels.

Parcel-gilt A term used to describe silver objects which have been partially enriched with gilding. See **fire-gilding** and **gilding**.

Parure A matching set of jewellery, usually consisting of a necklace, earrings, brooch or bracelet. A *demi-parure* is a set containing fewer items, such as a brooch and earrings or a necklace and earrings.

Pectoral A form of ornament worn on the chest.

Penannular brooch A brooch in the shape of an incomplete ring, having two terminals close together and often highly decorated.

Pietra dura A technique of inlaying shaped hardstones and other materials into a hardstone or marble background, often creating a pictorial effect.

Plasma A translucent green variety of quartz.

Pointillé A form of decoration in which tiny dots form the design.

Pomander (from French *pomme d'ambre*, 'perfume apple', or 'musk ball'). Originally a mixture of spices or perfumes rolled into a ball. Substances used included musk, ambergris, civet or gum benzoin. Early pomanders were enclosed in simple cases, usually spherical, and pierced to allow the scent to escape.

Pouncing A term here used to describe the surface patterning produced by the technique of stippling.

Repoussé (embossing) A technique of working sheet metal from behind with punches to raise the pattern, which stands in relief on the front.

Ring-punching Sometimes described as ring-matting; a form of matt surface decoration produced by means of a tool with a concave circular tip, resulting in an overall pattern of small circles.

Rose-cut A type of cut developed especially for faceting diamonds; it could have 24 triangular facets on a flat base, or 48 triangular facets, 24 on each face.

Sard A translucent brownish-red variety of quartz, distinguishable from cornelian only by its darker colour.

Scarab Egyptian amulet, its upper side in the shape of the dung-beetle, symbol of regeneration and resurrection, its flat underside often used for inscriptions.

Scaraboid Egyptian amulet with a flat underside bearing inscriptions, similar to the **scarab** except that the upper side takes the shape of an animal or good luck symbol.

Shibuichi A technique used by Japanese metalworkers of inlaying a dark-grey or silver alloy with coloured metals. In the related technique of *shakudo* a black copper alloy is used.

Shell-cameo, see **cameos**

Spinel A gemstone occuring in many colours, especially deep red, a compound of magnesium and alumina.

Table-cut One of the earliest styles of gem-cutting, based on the natural octahedron, one of the forms in which diamond crystals occur. The top of the octahedron is cut off to leave a flat surface, with the pointed half of the octahedron below.

Tincture In heraldry, the colour used in a coat of arms.

Torc (or torque) A metal collar or neck-ring, worn particularly in Bronze Age and Iron Age Europe.

Wesekh-**collar** In ancient Egyptian jewellery, a broad collar composed of multiple strings of beads.

Uraeus The representation of the head of a rearing cobra, a symbol of royalty in ancient Egypt.

References for the illustrations

All the jewellery illustrated in this book is in the collection of the British Museum. The reference numbers given are to the British Museum accession numbers. The abbreviations refer to the Museum Departments, as follows:

EA   Ancient Egypt and Sudan (formerly Egyptian Antiquities)

ETH   Africa, Oceania and the Americas (formerly Ethnography)

GR   Greek and Roman Antiquities

MLA, PRB   Prehistory and Europe (incorporating the former Medieval and Later Antiquities and Prehistoric and Romano-British Antiquities)

OA   Asia (formerly Oriental Antiquities)

PD   Prints and Drawings

WAA   Ancient Near East (formerly Western Asiatic Antiquities)

Object numbers with the prefix HG refer to the catalogue of the Hull Grundy Gift (Tait 1984).

Most of the items illustrated here were published in the catalogue of the British Museum exhibition *Jewellery through 7000 Years* (Tait 1976). Fuller descriptions of many of the objects, as well as bibliographical references up to 1976, may be found there.

Some of the comparative illustrations are from other sources. The publishers would like to thank the copyright holders for permission to reproduce their photographs.

Half-title illustration see **436**

Frontispiece WAA 1980-12-14,1 *Bibl.* J. Curtis and J.E. Reade (eds), *Art and Empire: Treasures from Assyria in the British Museum* (London 1995); Rudoe 1983/4

Page 4 see **430**

Contents page MLA 1991,1-7,1. Gift of R.C. Kwok

---

1 Reproduced by permission of the Trustees of the Wallace Collection.

2 WA 121201

3 EA 920

4 OA. Stein painting 46 (Ch. lvii. 003)

5 ML Waddesdon Bequest *Bibl.* See **362**

6 Palazzo Vecchio, *Studiolo*, Florence (© Scala/Firenze)

7 WAA 121441; 122310–12; 122318A; 122325; 122343; 122364; 122411–15; 1929.10–17.320 *Bibl.* Tait 1976, no. 11

8 WAA 120851 *Bibl.* Tait 1976, no. 12i

9 Drawn by Susan Bird

10 WAA 122444 *Bibl.* J. Reade, *Early Etched Beads and the Indus–Mesopotania Trade*, British Museum Occasional Paper No. 2 (1979), p. 12

11 WAA 121425 *Bibl.* Tait 1976, no. 12f

12 WAA 121426 *Bibl.* Tait 1976, no. 12g

13 WAA 121424 *Bibl.* Tait 1976, no. 12h

14 EA 62150 *Bibl.* Tait 1976, no. 3; Andrews 1981, no. 41

15 EA 35528 *Bibl.* Tait 1976, no. 9; Andrews 1981, no. 198

16 EA 62468 *Bibl.* Tait 1976, no. 18; Andrews 1981, no. 276

17 EA 63444 *Bibl.* Tait 1976, no. 20; Andrews 1981, no. 314

18 WAA 127814 *Bibl.* Tait 1976, no. 1

19 WAA 123596 *Bibl.* Tait 1976, no. 7

20 EA 37532 *Bibl.* Tait 1976, no. 6; Andrews 1981, no. 132

21 EA 51178 *Bibl.* Tait 1976, no. 8; Andrews 1981, no. 158

22 EA 62221 *Bibl.* Tait 1976, no. 2a; Andrews 1981, no. 10

23 EA 62223 *Bibl.* Tait 1976, no. 2b; Andrews 1981, no. 17

24 EA 63088 *Bibl.* Tait 1976, no. 5; Andrews 1981, no. 89

25 WAA 121361 *Bibl.* Tait 1976, no. 12b

26 WAA 121378 *Bibl.* Tait 1976, no. 455

27 WAA 121372 *Bibl.* Tait 1976, no. 12c

28 WAA 122206–8 *Bibl.* Tait 1976, no. 13a

29 WAA 121487 *Bible.* Tait 1976, no. 13b

30 WAA 120583 *Bibl.* Tait 1976, no. 15

31 WAA 122216 *Bibl.* Tait 1976, no. 400

32 WAA 122243 *Bibl.* Tait 1976, no. 16a

33 WAA 122217 *Bibl.* Tait 1976, no. 16b

34 WAA 122433 *Bibl.* Tait 1976, no. 16c

35 WAA 122202 *Bibl.* Tait, 1976, no. 16d

36 WAA 122213–14 *Bibl.* Tait 1976, no. 16e

37 EA 63709 *Bibl.* Tait 1976, no. 17; Andrews 1981, no. 326

38 EA 63438 *Bibl.* Tait 1976, no. 19; Andrews 1981, no. 325

39 Cairo Museum (photo Hirmer Photoarchiv, Munich)

40 EA 65281. Sir Robert Mond Bequest *Bibl.* Tait 1976, no. 25; Andrews 1981, no. 406

41 EA 40928 *Bibl.* Tait 1976, no. 21a; Andrews 1981, no. 394

42 EA 54460 *Bibl.* Tait 1976, no. 23; Andrews 198, no. 554

43 EA 59194 *Bibl.* Tait 1976, no. 27; Andrews 1981, no. 558

44 EA 57699–700 *Bibl.* Tait 1976, no. 30a; Andrews 1981, nos 577–8

45 EA 57698 *Bibl.* Tait 1976, no. 30b; Andrews 1981, no. 574

46 EA 7876 *Bibl.* Tait 1976, no. 345

47 EA 3084 *Bibl.* Tait 1976, no. 24a; Andrews 1981, no. 539

48 EA 32220 *Bibl.* Tait 1976, no. 24b) Andrews 1981, no. 541

49 EA 3082 *Bibl.* Tait 1976, no. 26; Andrews 1981, no. 545

50 WAA 121416 *Bibl.* Tait 1976, no. 41

51 WAA 132116 *Bibl.* Tait 1976, no. 42

52 WAA 130762 *Bibl.* Tait 1976, no. 43a

53 WAA 130763 *Bibl.* Tait 1976, no. 43b

54 WAA 130764 *Bibl.* Tait 1976, no. 43c

55 WAA 130767 *Bibl.* Tait 1976, no. 43d

56 GR 92.5–20.8 *Bibl.* Tait 1976, no. 32; *GRJ*, p. 66, pl. 6B

57 GR 92.5–20.7 *Bibl.* Tait 1976, no. 33; *GRJ*, p. 66, pl. 7B

58 GR 92.5–20.13 *Bibl.* Tait 1976, no. 34; *GRJ*, p. 63, pl. 3D

59 GR 97.4–1.34–5. Turner Bequest *Bibl.* Tait 1976, no. 36; *GRJ*, p. 86, pl. 12H

60 GR 97.4–1.239–40. Turner Bequest *Bibl.* Tait 1976, no. 38; *GRJ*, p. 86, pl. 12H

61 GR 97.4–1.604. Turner Bequest *Bibl.* Tait 1976, no. 39

62 GR 97.4–1.356. Turner Bequest *Bibl.* Tait 1976, no. 40; *GRJ*, p. 76

63 PRB 1940.4–4.1–2 *Bibl.* Tait 1976, no. 44

64 PRB 45.1–22.1 *Bibl.* Tait 1976, no. 45

65 PRB 90.4–10.1 *Bibl.* Tait 1976, no. 46

66 EA 37984

67 EA 14693 *Bibl.* Tait 1976, no. 51a

68 EA 66840–1 *Bibl.* Tait 1976, no. 51b; *Egypt's Golden Age*, no. 325

69 EA 66718

70 EA 29255 *Bibl.* Tait 1976, no. 48a

71 EA 29263 *Bibl.* Tait 1976, no. 48b

72 EA 29264 *Bibl.* Tait 1976, no. 48c

73 EA 68531 *Bibl.* Tait 1976, no. 48d

74 EA 2895 (a pair with EA 48064) *Bibl.* Tait 1976, no. 48e

75 EA 14508 *Bibl.* Tait 1976, no. 48f

76 EA 57516 *Bibl.* Tait 1976, no. 48g

77 EA 63347 *Bibl.* Tait 1976, no. 48h

78 EA 64186 *Bibl.* Tait 1976, no. 48i

79 EA 66827 *Bibl.* Tait 1976, no. 47

80 EA 59416–17 *Bibl.* Tait 1976, no. 49a

81 EA 49717 *Bibl.* Tait 1976, no. 403a

82 EA 14349 *Bibl.* Tait 1976, no. 403b

83 EA 2922 *Bibl.* Tait 1976, no. 401

84 EA 32723
Bibl. Tait 1976, no. 404b; *Egypt's Golden Age*, no. 333

85 EA 2923. Anastasi Collection
Bibl. Tait 1976, no. 346a

86 EA 54459
Bibl. Tait 1976, no. 56

87 EA 59334
Bibl. Tait 1976, no. 53

88 EA 3359
Bibl. Tait 1976, no. 54

89 EA 2864
Bibl. Tait 1976, no. 55a

90 EA 14346
Bibl. Tait 1976, NO. 55b

94 EA 54317–18. Franks Bequest
Bibl. Tait 1976, no. 55d; *Egypt's Golden Age*, no. 294

92 EA 65617
Bibl. Tait 1976, NO. 57b

93 EA 65616
Bibl. Tait 1976, no. 57a

94 EA 14594–5
Bibl. Tait 1976, NO. 58

95 PRB P1974.12–1.269
Bibl. Tait 1976, NO. 60

96 PRB 68.12–28.341
Bibl. Tait 1976, NO. 61

97 PRB 1939.5–1.3
Bibl. Tait 1976, no. 67

98 PRB 1954.10–2.4
Bibl. Tait 1976, no. 68

99 prb 1916.6–5.300
Bibl. Tait 1976, no. 69

100 53.4–12.16–18
Bibl. Tait 1976, no. 70

101 PRB 53.4–12.15
Bibl. Tait 1976, no. 457

102 PRB 38.1–28.1
Bibl. Tait 1976, no. 71

103 PRB WG23. Collection of Canon William Greenwell
Bibl. Tait 1976, no. 73

104 PRB WG20. Collection of Canon William Greenwell
Bibl. Tait 1976, no. 77

105 PRB 49.3–1.8
Bibl. Tait 1976, no. 76

106 PRB 74.3–3.9
Bibl. Tait 1976, no. 74

107 PRB WG22. Collection of Canon William Greenwell
Bibl. Tait 1976, no. 75

108 PRB P1974.12–1.342–6
Bibl. Tait 1976, no. 62

109 PRB 1900.7–27.1
Bibl. Tait 1976, no. 66

110 PRB 85.6–13.3
Bibl. Tait 1976, no. 79

111 PRB 34.12–22.1
Bibl. Tait 1976, no 80

112 WAA 130683. Raphael Bequest
Bibl. Tait 1976, no. 81a

113 WAA 132927
Bibl. Tait 1976, no. 81b

114 WAA 132057
Bibl. Tait 1976, no. 81c

115 WAA 132025
Bibl. Tait 1976, no. 81d

116 WAA 35072–85
Bibl. Tait 1976, no. 84; J. Curtis, *Nush-i Jan: the Small Finds*, 1–21 (London 1984)

117 WAA 132825
Bibl. Tait 1976, no. 82

118 WAA 135588
Bibl. Tait 1976, no. 83

119 WAA 124563

120 WAA 135782. Castellani collection
Bibl. Tait 1976, no. 85

121 WAA 133392 (part)
Bibl. Tait 1976, no. 86a

122 WAA 133334
Bibl. Tait 1976, no. 86b

123 GR 1960.11–1.18–19
Collection of the 7th Earl of Elgin
Bibl. Tait 1976, no. 88; *GRJ*, p. 98, pl. 14E

124 GR 1960.11–1.46–7
Collection of the 7th Earl of Elgin
Bibl. Tait 1976, no. 89; *GRJ*, p. 100

125 GR 84.8–4.2
Bibl. Tait 1976, no. 90; *GRJ*, p. 112, pl. 18D

126 GR 61.4–25.3
Bibl. Tait 1976, no. 92; *GRJ*, p. 116, pl. 19E

127 GR 1907.12–1.9
Bibl. Tait 1976, no. 94; *GRJ*, p. 120, pl. 22E

128 GR 67.5–8.485. Blacas Collection
Bibl. Tait 1976, no. 95

129 GR 62.5–12.16. Blayds Collection
Bibl. Tait 1976, no. 97; *GRJ*, p. 146, pl. 38A

130 GR 1358F, 1359F. Franks Bequest 1897
Bibl. Tait 1976, no. 98; *GRJ*, p. 144, pl. 36

131 GR 81.5–28.2. Bale Collection
Bibl. Tait 1976, no. 103; *GRJ*, p. 140, pl. 32A

132 GR 40.2–12.1
Bibl. Tait 1976, no. 99; *GRJ*, p. 147, pl 39B

133 GR D219

134 GR 56.6–25.17.
Bibl. Tait 1976, no. 102; *GRJ*, p. 143, pl. 34

135 GR 1841.3–1.13. Campanari Collection
Bibl. BMCJ, no. 2292; *GRJ*, pl. 41A

136 GR 72.6–4.667
Bibl. Tait 1976, no. 108;, *GRJ*, p. 129, pl. 28

137 GR 93.11–3.1
Bibl. Tait 1976, no. 106; *GRJ*, p. 125, pl. 24E

138 GR 94.11–1.450–1
Bibl. Tait 1976, no. 107; *GRJ*, p. 126, pl. 25G

139 WAA 124017. Franks Bequest
Bibl. Tait 1976, no. 109a

140 WAA 123927. Franks Bequest
Bibl. Tait 1976, no. 109e(i)

141 WAA 123933. Franks Bequest
Bibl. Tait 1976, no. 109e(ii)

142 WAA 123940. Franks Bequest
Bibl. Tait 1976, no. 109e(iii)

143 WAA 123941. Franks Bequest
Bibl. Tait 1976, no. 109e(iv)

144 WAA 124041. Franks Bequest
Bibl. Tait 1976, no. 109c

145 WAA 123924. Franks Bequest
Bibl. Tait 1976, no. 109d

146 WAA 124012. Franks Bequest
Bibl. Tait 1976, no. 109f

147 WAA 124026. Franks Bequest
Bibl. Tait 1976, no. 109b(i)

148 WAA 124036. Franks Bequest
Bibl. Tait 1976, no. 109b(ii)

149 WAA 124045. Franks Bequest
Bibl. Tait 1976, no. 109b(iii)

150 WAA 124048. Franks Bequest
Bibliography Tait 1976, no. 109b(iv)

151 WAA 135089
Bibl. Tait 1976, no. 110

152 OA 1945.10–17.215. Raphael Bequest
Bibl. Tait 1976, no. 126b. For animal-shaped plaques in gold and silver from Inner Mongolia and Xinjiang and Shaanxi provinces see *Wenwu* 1980.7, pp. 1–10, pls 2, 3; *Wenwu* 1981.1, pp. 18–22, pl. 8; *Wenwu* 1983.12, pp. 23–30, pls 4, 5

153 OA 1945.10–17.87
Bibl. Tait 1976, no. 127c

154 OA 1973.7–26.42
Bibl. Tait 1976, no. 127a

155 OA 1936.11–18.254
Bibl. Tait 1976, no. 127b

156 PRB 1939.5–1.12
Bibl. Tait 1976, no. 131

157 PRB 1939.5–1.22
Bibl. Tait 1976, no. 132

158 PRB 1939.5–1.7
Bibl. Tait 1976, no. 133

159 PRB P1974.12–1.334
Bibl. Tait 1976, no. 134

160 PRB 80.8–20.25
Bibl. Tait 1976, no. 135

161 PRB 80.12–14.8
Bibl. Tait 1976, no. 138

162 PRB 1907.10–24.2
Bibl. Tait 1976, no. 141

163 The National Museum, Copenhagen (photo Lennart Larsen)

164 PRB ML1710. Morel collection
Bibl. Tait 1976, no. 111

165 PRB ML1711. Morel collection
Bibl. Tait 1976, no. 113

166 PRB ML1621. Morel collection
Bibl. Tait 1976, no. 117

167 PRB 1926.3–13.12
Bibl. Tait 1976, no. 458, Stead 1984, p. 62, fig. 20, no. 3

168 PRB POA165
Bibl. Tait 1976, no. 137

169 PRB P1970.9–1.1
Bibl. Tait 1976, no. 139

170 PRB 1932.7–6.2,5,19,22
Bibl. Tait 1974, no. 121

171 PRB 1960.5–3.1
Bibl. Tait 1976, no. 119

172 PRB 1960.5–3.2
Bibl. Tait 1976, no. 120

173 PRB 1969.1–3.5
Bibl. Tait 1976, no. 124

174 PRB 1951.4–2.2
Bibl. Tait 1976, no. 125

175 PRB 1946.4–2.1
Bibl. Tait 1976, no. 146

176 PRB 38.7–14.3
Bibl. Tait 1976, no. 145

177 PRB 1951.4–2.1
Bibl. Tait 1976, no. 122

178 PRB 60.6–9.3. Egger collection, Budapest, 1860
Bibl. Tait 1976, no. 142

179 ETH 1929.7–12.1
Bibl. Tait 1976, no. 147

180 ETH 1913.10–20.1
Bibl. Tait 1976, no. 150

181 ETH 1921.3–21.1
Bibl. Tait 1976, no. 148

182 ETH 1952.Am 10.1
Bibl. Tait 1976, no. 149

183 ETH 194. Am 7–31.13

184 ETH 1960.Am 6.1
Bibl. Tait 1976, no. 151

185 ETH 1909.Am 12–18.16

186 GR 72.6–4.815.. Castellani Collection
Bibl. Tait 1976, no. 152; *GRJ*, p. 158, pl. 45A

187 GR 67.5–8.537
Bibl. Tait 1976, no. 154

188 GR 1914.10–16.1
Bibl. Tait 1976, no. 157

189 GR 77.9–10.16–17
Bibl. Tait 1976, no. 155

190 GR 72.6–4.660. Castellani Collection
Bibl. Tait 1976, no. 156; *GRJ*, p. 165, pl. 49B

191 GR 72.6–4.670. Castellani Collection
Bibl. Tait 1976, no. 162; *GRJ*, p. 179, pl. 5B

192 GR 14.7–4.1203. Townley Collection
Bibl. Tait 1976, no. 161

193 GR 1903.7–17.3
Bibl. Tait 1976, no. 158; *GRJ*, p. 177, pl. 54F

194 EA NG1269

195 GR 1946.7–2.2
Bibl. Tait 1976, no. 164

196 WAA 125019

197 WAA 124097
Bibl. Tait 1976, no. 179

198 WAA 135207
Bibl. Tait 1976, no. 180a

199 WAA 132933
Bibl. Tait 1976, no. 180b

200 WAA 1921.6–28.1
Bibl. Tait 1976, no. 129

201 OA 1923.7–12.1
Bibl. Tait 1976, no. 181; Robert Knox, 'Jewellery from the Nilgiri Hills, a model of diversity', *South Asian Archaeology* (1983), in press

202 OA 86.5–15.6,7,14
Bibl. See **201**

203 OA 92.11–3.13
Bibl. Tait 1976, no. 182

204 EA 57323
Bibl. Tait 1976, no. 173

205 EA 65684
Bibl. Tait 1976, no. 174a

206 EA 67399
Bibl. Tait 1976, no. 174b

207 EA 26328
Bibl. Tait 1976, no. 178

208 EA 34264
Bibl. Tait 1976, no. 177a

209 EA 14457
Bibl. Tait 1976, no. 177b

210 PRB 1934.12–10.21
Bibl. Tait 1976, no. 167

211 PRB OA245
Bibl. Tait 1976, no. 165

212 PRB 83.5–9.2
Bibl. Tait 1976, no. 168

213 PRB 1883.5–9.2

214 PRB POA 201
Bibl. Tait 1976, no. 166

215 PRB P1981.2–1.5
Bibl. Johns and Potter 1983, p. 83

216 PRB P1981.2–1.7
Bibl. Johns and Potter 1983, pp. 84–5

217 PRB P1981.2–1.23
Bibl. Johns and Potter 1983, p. 95

218 PRB 1994.4–8.11–12 and 25–8
Bibl. R. Bland and C. Johns, *The Hoxne Treasure, An illustrated introduction* (London 1993)

219 PRB 1962.12–15.1
Bibl. Tait 1976, no. 171; R. Higgins, *Greek and Roman Jewellery* (London 1961), p. 192, pl. 64C

220 MLA AF323–30. Franks Bequest, 1897
Bibl. Tait 1976, no. 186

221 MLA 1984.5–1.1
Bibl. David Buckton, 'The beauty of holiness: *opus interrasile* from a Late Antique workshop', *Jewellery Studies* 1 (1983–4), pp. 15–19, col. pl. I; David Buckton, 'Byzantine coin-set pendant, AD 324–88', *National Art-Collections Fund Review* (1985), pp.

92–3 (with full bibliography)

222 MLA 1916.7–4.2–6
Bibl. Tait 1976, no. 191

223 MLA 1916.7–4.1
Bibl. Tait 1976, no. 190; Katharine R. Brown, *The gold breast chain from the Early Byzantine period in the Römischgermanisches Zentralmuseum* (properly: *Three Byzantine breast chains; ornaments of goddesses and ladies of rank*) (Mainz 1984), esp. pp. 17–20, fig. 12, pl. IV

224 EA 1877.11–12.34

225 MLA 1981.1– 4.3

226a–i MLA 1923.7–16.12, 54, 59, 58, 55, 108, 8, 111, 29. Delagarde collection.
Bibl. Tait 1976, nos 192c (**e**), 192a (**g**), 192e (**h**). Cf. Arrhenius 1985

227 MLA 93.6–1.219. Durden Collection
Bibl. Tait 1976, no. 193

228 MLA 1963.11–8.101

229 MLA 1859.5–12.1
Bibl. Tait 1976, no. 364; Jessup 1974, p. 50, pl. 2.3

230 MLA 1145.70

231 MLA 67.7–29.5
Bibl. E. Bakka, 'On the beginnings of Salin's Style I in England', Universitetet Bergen Årbok, Historisk-antikvarisk rekke, 3 (1958), pp. 16–19; C.J. Arnold, *The Anglo-Saxon cemeteries of the Isle of Wight* (London 1982), pp. 52–3

232 MLA 1921.11 1.221
Bibl. Cf. Arrhenius 1985

233 MLA 91.10–19.24
Bibl. Cf. Arrhenius 1985

234 MLA 65.3–18.1
Bibl. Arrhenius 1985, pp. 120, 123, fig. 61

235 MLA 1978.5–3.1
Bibl. Arrhenius 1985

236 MLA 1921.11–1.365. Curle collection
Bibl. Tait 1976, no. 195

237 MLA 1921.11–1.363. Curle collection
Bibl. Tait 1976, no. 203. *Cf.* B. Nerman, *Die Vendelzeit Gotlands* II (Stockholm 1969); I (Stockholm 1975, ed. A. Lundström)

238 MLA 1912.6–10.1
Bibl. J. Werner, 'Slawische Bugelfibeln des 7. Jahrhunderts', in G. Behrens and J. Werner (eds), *Reinecke Festschrift* (Mainz 1950), pp. 158, 164, 168–72, pl. 34:3

239 MLA 1985.3–1.1–2; 1926.5–11.2
Bib. Cf. J. Hampel, *Alterthümer des Frühen Mittelalters in Ungarn* I (3 vols, Braunschweig 1905), pp. 355–8

240 MLA 83.12–14.1
Bibl. Tait 1976, no. 200; G. Speake, *Anglo-Saxon Animal Art and its Germanic Background* (Oxford 1980), pp. 52–5, pl. 7f

241 MLA 51.8–6.10
Bibl. Tait 1976, no. 199, H. Roth, *Die Ornamentik der Langobarden in italien*

(Bonn 1973), pp. 78–81, pl. 11:1

242 MLA 1939.10–10.4–5
Bibl. Tait 1976, no. 197, Angela Care Evans, *The Sutton Hoo Ship-Burial* (London 1986)

243 MLA 1939.10–10.6–11,17,18
Bibl. Tait 1976, no. 198; Angela Care Evans, *The Sutton Hoo Ship Burial* (London 1986)

244 Drawn by Eric Eden

245 MLA 76.5–4.1
Bibl. Tait 1976, no. 201

246 MLA 65.7–12.1. Castellani Collection
Bibl. Tait 1976, no. 202

247 MLA 1952.4–4.1
Bibl. Tait 1976, no. 207; Backhouse, Turner and Webster 1984, cat. no. 11, pp. 30–1

248 MLA 1904.11–2.3. Forster Bequest, 1904
Bibl. Tait 1976, no. 209; J. Graham-Campbell, 'Bossed penannular brooches: a review of recent research', *Medieval Archaeology* 19 (1975), pp. 33–47

249 MLA 1980.10–8.1–6
Bibl. D.M. Wilson, *Anglo-Saxon Art* (London 1984, p. 96, pl. 120

250 MLA AF542. Franks Bequest, 1897
Bibl. Tait 1976, no. 210

251 MLA 1901.7–18.1
Bibl. Tait 1976, no. 208

252 MLA 54.7–14.96
Bibl. Tait 1976, no. 204

253 MLA 88.7–19.101. From Lord Londesborough's collection
Bibl. Tait 1976, no. 206

254 MLA 56.3–20.1
Bibl. Tait 1976, no. 205

255 OA Stein painting 47 (Ch. 1vii 002)

256 OA After Beijing 1980, p. 17, fig. 2

257 OA 1938.5–24.221–5
Bibl. Tait 1976, no. 212. Elaborately granulated goldwork has been excavated from an Eastern Han tomb at Ganquan in Hanjiang Xian, Jiangsu province; see *Wenwu* 1981.11, pp. 1–11, pl. 3. Later examples have come from an Eastern Jin tomb in the northern suburbs of Nanjing; see *Wenwu* 1981.12, pp. 1–7, pl. 1. For northern China see *Wenwu* 1973.3, pp. 2–28, pl. 1

258 OA 1938.5–24.252
Bibl. Tait 1976, no. 213. For a comb-back worked in exactly the same way ,found in a hoard excavated at Hejiacun near Xi'an, Shaanxi province, see Beijing 1972, p. 61. Compare also elaborate jewelled and granulated work reported in the following: *Wenwu* 1959.8, pp. 34–5, fig. 2; *Wenwu* 1966.3, pp. 8–15, pl. 4; *Wenwu* 1973.8, pp. 41–7. 62; *Wenwu* 1983.10, pp. 1–23, fig. 49; *Wenwu* 1984.4, pp. 1–9, pl. 5.4; *Wenwu* 1985.2, pp. 83–93, pls 5, 6. The survival of these techniques into the Song period is documented by an elaborate ornament from a Song tomb

reported in *Kaogu* 1962.8, pp. 418–19, pl. 10:13

259 OA 1938.5–24.284
Bibl. Tait 1976, no. 215. For a similar example excavated in Hunan province, see *Kaoqu* 1957.5, pp. 40–8, pl. 7:9

260 OA 1936.11–18.242–3
Bibl. Yetts 1930, nos B162, B163, pl. XLVIII. For the belt from the tomb of Fuma Zeng see Beijing 1958, pl. 107:3. Compare also plaques from a 10th-century tomb at Suzhou, see *Wenwu* 1981.2, pp. 37–45, fig. 15

261 OA 1937.4–16.129–37
Bibl. Tait 1976, no. 214

262 OA 1938.5–24.238
Bibl. Tait 1976, no. 216

263 OA 1938.15–24,243–4
Bibl. Tait 1976, no. 217

264 OA +1141
Bibl. Tait 1976, no. 220

265 OA +1143
Bibl. Tait 1976, no. 221

266 OA +1140
Bibl. Tait 1976, no. 218

267 OA +2686

268 OA +1142
Bibl. Tait 1976, no. 219a

269 OA 1940.12–14.320
Bibl. Tait 1976, no. 219b

270 Drawn by Susan Bird

271–4 ETH. Pomona Loan, 1950
Bibl. Tait 1976, no. 222c

275 ETH. Pomona Loan, 1950
Bibl. Tait 1976, no. 224

276 ETH. Pomona Loan, 1950
Bibl. Tait 1976, no. 222

277 ETH +4076
Bibl. Tait 1976, no. 227

278 ETH 1938.10–21.25. Gann Bequest, 1938
Bibl. Tait 1976, no. 225

279 ETH 9685
Bibl. Tait 1976, no. 228

280 ETH 1938.10–21.24. Gann Bequest, 1938
Bibl. Tait 1976, no. 229

281 ETH 8382
Bibl. Tait 1976, no. 230

282 ETH 1952.AM 2.1
Bibl. Tait 1976, no. 231

283 ETH 1952.AM 11.2
Bibl. Tait 1976, no. 232

284 ETH 1938.10–21.51. Gann Bequest, 1938
Bibl. Tait 1976, no. 235

285 ETH 1930.F.476
Bibl. Tait 1976, no. 236a

286 ETH 1938.10–21.201. Gann Bequest
Bibl. Tait 1976, no. 236b

287 ETH 1920–118
Bibl. Tait 1976, no. 237

288 ETH Add. Ms 39671, f. 80

289 ETH 1920.10–13.2a,b
Bibl. Tait 1976, no. 238

290 ETH 1920.10–13.4a,b
Bibl. Tait 1976, no. 239

291 ETH 1904.10–31.1
Bibl. Tait 1976, no. 240

292 ETH +5802
Bibl. Tait 1976, no. 242

293 ETH 1902.6–23.1
Bibl. Tait 1976, no. 243

294 ETH +5804
Bibl. Tait 1976, no. 249

295 ETH +5803
Bibl. Tait 1976, no. 248

296 ETH 1910.12–2.5
Bibl. Tait 1976, no. 246

297 ETH 1954.W.Am 5.1589
Bibl. Tait 1976, no. 251

298 ETH +344–5
Bibl. Tait 1976, no. 253

299 ETH 44.7–29.1
Bibl. Tait 1976, no. 244

300 ETH 1904.7–18.2
Bibl. Tait 1976, no. 245a

301 ETH 1904.7–18.1
Bibl. Tait 1976, no. 245b

302 ETH 1955.Am 6.1–2
Bibl. Tait 1976, no. 252

303 ETH +1669
Bibl. Tait 1976, no. 256

304 ETH +7834
Bibl. Tait 1976, no. 257

305 ETH 1914.3–28.1
Bibl. Tait 1976, no. 466

306 MLA 56.7–1.1461
Bibl. Tait 1976, no. 258; Westermann-Angerhausen 1983–4, pp. 20–36

307 MLA. Townley Collection, 1814
Bibl. Tait 1976, no. 259; Steingräber 1957, p. 26, fig. 10; Westermann–Angerhausen 1983–4, pp. 26–7, Abb. 16, Kat. Nr. 10

308 MLA 81.8–2.3
Bibl. Tait 1976, no. 260. *Cf.* T.I. Makarova, *Peregorodchatye Emali Drevnei Rusi* (Moscow 1975)

309 MLA 1907.5–20.1–19 (selection)
Bibl. Tait 1976, no. 261; K. Reynolds Brown, 'Russo-Byzantine Jewellery in the Metropolitan Museum of Art', *Apollo* CXI, no. 215 (London, January 1980), pp. 6–9 (with bibliography)

310 MLA 1966.7–3.1
Bibl. Tait 1976, no. 268; I. Toesca, 'Lancaster e Gonzaga: il fregio della sala del Pisanello nel Palazzo Ducale di Mantova' *Civiltà mantovana* XI (1977), p. 351; *Splendours of the Gonzaga*, (exh. cat.) Victoria and Albert Museum (November 1981–January 1982), no. 8, p. 106

311 Reproduced courtesy of Henry M. Trivick

312 MLA 85.6–15.1
Bibl. Tait 1976, no. 462; Wart *et al.* 1981, no. 119, p. 62

313–18 MLA 54.8–20.1–6
Bibl. Tait 1976, no. 463; Ward *et al.* 1981, nos 111–114, pp. 60–1

319 MLA 1929.4–11.1
Bibl. Tait 1976, no. 263

320 MLA 1937.6–8.1
Bibl. Tait 1976, no. 262a

321 MLA 1937.6–8.2
Bibl. Tait 1976, no. 262b

322 MLA AF2683. Franks Bequest, 1897
Bibl. Tait 1976, no. 264

323 MLA AF2702. Franks Bequest, 1897
Bibl. Tait 1976, no. 265

324 MLA AF2703. Franks Bequest, 1897
Bibl. Tait 1976, no. 266

325 MLA AF2767. Franks Bequest, 1897
Bibl. Tait 1976, no. 267

326 MLA AF2802–3, AF2812, AF2817–20, AF2823–4, AF2840. Franks Bequest, 1897
Bibl. Tait 1976, no. 271

327 MLA AF2811
Bibl. Tait 1976, no. 271a

328 MLA 1967.12–8.1–9
Bibl. Tait 1976, no. 270 (**a–e**), no. 421

329 MLA AF2851. Franks Bequest, 1897
Bibl. Tait 1976, no. 272

330 MLA AF2894. Franks Bequest, 1897
Bibl. Tait 1976, no. 273a

331 MLA AF2891. Franks Bequest, 1897
Bibl. Tait 1976, no. 273b

332 MLA AF2889. Franks Bequest, 1897
Bibl. Tait 1976, no. 273c

333 OA 1937.3–13.9–19 (complete set)
Bibl. R. Ettinghausen, 'Turkish elements on silver objects of the Seljuq period of Iran', *Communications presented to the First International Congress of Turkish Arts* (Ankara 1961), pp. 128–33; B. Gray, 'A Seljuq hoard from Persia, *BMQ* 13 (1939), pp. 73–9

334 OA 1937.3–13.20–38 (complete set)
Bibl. Tait 1976, no. 274. See also **333**

335 OA 1925.5–12.2–3

336 OA 1981.7–7.2

337 OA 1954.4–12,1
Bibl. Tait 1976, no. 464

338 OA AF2448

339 OA 1938.5–24.356–7, 363–4,369,377
Bibl. Tait 1976, no. 277

340 OA 1938.5–24.204–5
Bibl. Tait 1976, no. 279. Song and Ming examples, in *Kaogu* 1962.8, pp. 418–19, pl. 10:7; *Wenwu* 1982.2, pp. 28–33, fig. 10

341 OA 2441/AF2392. Franks Bequest, 1897
Bibl. Tait 1976, no. 465a

342 OA 2451/AF2402. Franks Bequest, 1897
Bibl. Tait 1976, no. 465b

343 OA 2452/AF2403. Franks Bequest, 1897
Bibl. Tait 1976, no. 465c

344 OA 1938.5–24.328
Bibl. Tait 1976, no. 278

345 OA +615 (centre); 1938.5–24.433,528
Bibl. Tait 1976, no. 280

346 MLA. Waddesdon Bequest, 1898
Bibl. Tait 1976, no. 289; Hackenbroch 1979, p. 141, fig. 357; Tait 1981, p. 50, col. pl. xa; Tait 1986, cat. no. 3, col. pl. vic and figs 42–5

347 PD. Sloane Collection, 1753

348 MLA 94.7–29.1
Bibl. Tait 1976, no. 286; Hackenbroch 1979, p. 281, fig. 748; Tait 1980, cat. no. 11, pp. 48–50; Hugh Tait, 'The "Tablett": an important class of Renaissance jewellery at the Court of Henry VIII', *Jewellery Studies* 2 (1985–6)

349 MLA AF2852–3. Franks Bequest, 1897
Bibl. Tait 1976, no. 285; Hackenbroch 1979, p. 281, fig. 749; Tait 1980, cat. no. 12, pp. 50–1, col. pl.; Hugh Tait, 'The "Tablett": an important class of Renaissance jewellery at the Court of Henry VIII', *Jewellery Studies* 2 (1985–6)

350 MLA 1955.5–7.1
Bibl. Tait 1976, no. 288; Tait 1963, p. 147, fig. 1; Hackenbroch 1979, p. 278, fig. 746; Tait 1980, cat. no. 9, p. 48, col. pl.

351 MLA 1983.11–2.1
Bibl. Tait 1962, pp.230–1, pl. XXXIXd–e; Tait 1963, pp. 147ff., fig. 2a–b, col. pl.

352 Private collection (photo courtesy of Victoria and Albert Museum)

353 MLA 54.1–24.1
Bibl. Tait 1976, no. 284

354 MLA 1959.4–3.1
Bibl. Tait 1976, no. 291

355 MLA 1960.2–2.1
Bibl. Tait 1976, no. 292

356 MLA 1912.7–24.1–5; 1914.4–23.1–20
Bibl. Tait 1976, no. 296; Tait 1980, cat. no. 120, pp. 87–9, col. pl.

357 MLA 1980.2–1.1–4
Bibl. Hugh Tait in *Princely Magnificence* (exh. cat., Victoria and Albert Museum, 1980), pp. 96–8, cat. no. 127

358 MLA 1956.10–7.1
Bibl. Tait 1976, no. 290; Tait 1974, p. 167, col. pl.; Hackenbroch 1979, p. 279, figs 753A–B; Somers Cocks and Truman 1984, p. 72, fig. 1

359 MLA. Waddesdon Bequest, 1898
Bibl. Tait 1976, no. 295; Hackenbroch 1979, fig. 887 (no text); Tait 1981, p. 52, fig. 30, col. pl. XB; Tait 1986, cat. no. 28, col. pls XXII–XXIII and fig. 143

360 MLA. Sloane collection, 1753
Bibl. Tait 1976, no. 294; Tait 1974, p. 229; Hackenbroch 1979, p. 295, fig. 790; Tait 1980, cat. no. 35, p. 59, col. pl. reversed; Tait 1986, cat. no. 36, fig. 174

361 Somerset County Museum, Taunton Castle

362 MLA. Waddesdon Bequest, 1898
Bibl. Tait 1976, no. 298; E. Auerbach, *Nicholas Hilliard* (London 1961), pp. 167–8, pl. 165; Tait 1974, p. 171, col. pl.; Roy Strong, *Nicholas Hilliard* (London 1975), p. 117; Hackenbroch 1979, p. 297, fig. 794, col. pl.; Tait 1981, p. 55, figs 32–5, col. pl. XIA; Tait 1986, cat. no. 33, col. pls XXIV–XXV and figs 160–1

363 MLA AF2876. Franks Bequest, 1897
Bibl. Tait 1976, no. 300; Tait 1986, under cat. no. 39

364 MLA. Waddesdon Bequest, 1898
Bibl. C.H. Read, *The Waddesden Bequest* (London 1902; rev. Dalton 1927), no. 168; Tait 1981, p. 56, col. pl. XIA, B, C; John Stucley, *Sir Bevill Grenville and his times, 1596–1643* (Chichester 1983), p. 149, pl. 3a–b;

Tait 1986, cat. no. 35, col. pl. XXIV–XXV and fig. 170

365 MLA BL3470. Bernal Collection, 1855
Bibl. Tait 1976, no. 301.

366 MLA HG cat. 285

367 MLA 1941.7–7.1
Bibl. Tait 1976, no. 303

368 MLA 1924.3–8.1
Bibl. Tait 1976, no. 302

369 MLA AF2863. Franks Bequest, 1897
Bibl. Tait 1976, no. 297

370 MLA 1957.10–9.1
Bibl. Tait 1976, no. 304

371 OA 1910.12–24.3
Bibl. Tait 1976, no. 305. 16th- and 17th-century examples are illustrated in *Wenwu* 1982.2, pp. 28–33, fig. 11 and *Wenwu* 1982.8, pp. 16–28, pl. 5:5. See also *Kaogu* 1985.6, pp. 540–9, fig. 2:2

372 OA 1938.5–24.247
Bibl. Tait 1976, no. 306; London 1935, no. 716

373 OA 1949.12–13.1–2
Bibl. Tait 1976, no. 309

374 OA 1930.12–17.39
Bibl. Tait 1976, no. 310a. For later Ming jade carving of dragons (17th century) see *Wenwu* 1983.2, pp. 56–64, pl. 5:1

375 OA 1930.12–17.37
Bibl. Tait 1976, no. 310b. See also reference in **374**

376 OA 1930.12–17.34
Bibl. Tait 1976, no. 310c

377 OA 1930.12–17.36
Bibl. Tait 1976, no. 310d. See also reference in **374**

378 OA 1938.5–24.210
Bibl. Tait 1976, no. 281a. For comparable excavated examples see *Wenwu* 1955.10, p. 50, fig. 3; *Wenwu* 1982.2, pp. 34–8, fig. 17; *Wenwu* 1963.1, pp. 50–8, back cover, figs 1–4

379 OA 1938.5–24.264
Bibl. Tait 1976, no. 281b. See also references in **378**

380 OA 1938.5–24.262
Bibl. Tait 1976, no. 311a. See also references in **378**

381 OA 1938.5–24.209
Bibl. Tait 1976, no. 311b. See also references in **378**

382 OA 1938.5–24.273
Bibl. Tait 1976, no. 311c. See also references in **378**

383–7 OA 1981.11–13.15 (bottom right), 16 (top left), 17 (bottom left), 18 (top centre), 19 (top right)
Bibl. For excavated examples see *Wenwu* 1979.4, pp. 54–63, figs 12, 19–21; *Wenwu* 1982.8, pp. 16–28, figs 35–41; *Kaogu* 1985.6, pp. 540–9, fig. 1:3, pl. 7:1

388 OA 2002.5–21.1, ex Carl Kempe collection
Bibl. B. Gyllensvard, *Chinese Gold and Silver in the Carl Kempe Collection*, Stockholm 1953, no. 153 (where it is described as a hairdress)

389 OA Ch.Ptg.Add.173

390–3 OA 1938.5–24.260 (top), 253 (left), 255 (bottom); 1937. 4–16.239 (right)
Bibl. London 1935, no. 711. Compare pins from Qing dynasty in Jilin province; see *Wenwu* 1984.11, pp. 76–84, figs 9, 12, pl. 5–2, 3, 6. For the elaborate filigree work from a Ming tomb in Jiangxi referred to in the Introduction to Chapter 12, see *Wenwu* 1959.1, pp. 48–52

394 OA 1920.9–17.0108

395 OA +14178

396 OA 1961.10–16.3
Bibl. Tait 1976, no. 318

397 Photo courtesy of H.E. Richardson

398 OA 1964.10–15.1
Bibl. Tait 1976, no. 319

399 OA 1905.5–18.77
Bibl. Tait 1976, no. 380

400 OA 1905.5–18.75
Bibl. Tait 1976, no. 320

401 OA 1905.5–31.1
Bibl. Tait 1976, no. 321

402 OA 1903.10–6.12–13
Bibl. Tait 1976, no. 323

403 ETH 1922.3–13.3
Bibl. Tait 1976, no. 324c; P. Ben-Amos, *The Art of Benin* (London 1980)

404 ETH 1910.5–13.2–3
Bibl. Tait 1976, no. 324b. See also **403**

405 ETH 1922.7–14.1
Bibl. Tait 1976, no. 324d. See also **403**

406 ETH 1900.4–27.11 (top)
Bibl. Tait 1976, no. 325a; M.D. McLeod, *The Asante* (London 1981)

407 ETH 1900.4–27.25 (bottom right)
Bibl. Tait 1976, no. 325b. See also **406**

408 ETH 1942.Af 9.1 (bottom left)
Bibl. Tait 1976, no. 325d. See also **406**

409 ETH 56.12–15.1 (circular)
Bibl. Tait 1976, no. 325e. See also **406**

410 ETH 98.6–30.6 (shell)
Bibl. See **409**

411 ETH 1900.4–27.37 (rectangular)
Bibl. See **409**

412 ETH Q74.Af 2922
Bibl. Tait 1976, no. 325h

413 ETH 1900.4–7.44
Bibl. Tait 1976, no. 325f. See also **406**

414 ETH 1900.4–27.44
Bibl. Tait 1976, no. 325g. See also **406**

415 PD 1872–1–13–844
Bibl. Rudoe 2004a

416 MLA HG cat. 13

417 MLA HG cat. 8

418 MLA HG cat. 335

419 MLA HG cat. 147

420 MLA HG cat. 594

421 MLA HG cat. 593

422 MLA HG cat. 598

423 MLA HG cat. 28

424 MLA HG cat. 705
Bibl. Gere and Rudoe 2000, fig. 18

425 MLA HG cat. 654

426 MLA HG cat. 713

427 MLA HG cat. 655

428 MLA HG cat. 689

429 MLA HG cat. 687

430 MLA 2002,3–1,1. Gift of The Hon. Mrs Mary Anna Marten, 2002

431 MLA 1993,2–5,1. Gift of R. C. Kwok, 2002

432 MLA 2003,12–1,1. Gift of R. C. Kwok and the British Museum Friends

433 MLA HG cat. 959

434 MLA HG cat. 983

435 MLA HG cat. 985
Bibl. Rudoe 2004b, fig 6–15

436 MLA HG cat. 953

437 MLA HG, cat. 998

438 MLA HG cat. 1006
Bibl. Gere and Rudoe 2000, fig. 19

439 MLA HG cat. 1018
Bibl. Gere and Rudoe 2000, fig. 20

440 MLA HG cat. 1053
Bibl. Purcell 1999, pp. 200–13

441 MLA HG cat. 1068–9

442 MLA HG cat. 1062

443 MLA HG cat. 1065

444 MLA 2001,3–5,1. Gift of R. C. Kwok

445 MLA HG cat. 1094

446 MLA 1991,7–1,1
Bibl. Rudoe 1994, cat. 373

447 MLA HG cat. 1109

448 MLA HG cat. 1113
Bibl. Gere and Rudoe 2000, fig. 9

449 MLA HG cat. 1115

450 MLA 1991,5–2,1
Bibl. Rudoe 1994, cat. 393

451 MLA 1999,7–5,1

452 MLA 1992,12–3,1

453 MLA 2001,7–9,1

454 MLA 2001,7–9,2

455 MLA 2001,7–9,7. Anonymous gift

456 MLA 2001,11–3,1. Anonymous gift

457 OA. After Beijing 1973

458 OA 1947.7–12.478
Bibl. Tait 1976, no. 326a. For the Shang period compare jade amulets from Fu Hao's tomb at Anyang, Henan province; see Beijing 1980, pls CXXXII–CXLVII. Early Western Zhou examples have come from Rujiazhuang at Baoji in Shaanxi province; see *Wenwu* 1976.4, pp. 34–56, figs 31, 35, pl. 9:3, 4

459 OA 1945.10–17.162
Bibl. Tait 1976, no. 326b. See also **458**

460 OA 1937.4–16.77
Bibl. Tait 1976, no. 326c. See also **458**

461 OA 1945.10–17.37
Bibl. Tait 1976, no. 326d. See also **458**

462 OA 1947.7–12.466
Bibl. Tait 1976, no. 326e. See also **458**

463 OA 1947.7–12.510
Bibl. Tait 1976, no. 327

464 OA 1945.10–17.49
Bibl. Tait 1976, no. 329

465 OA 1947.7–12.516
Bibl. Tait 1976, no. 328

466–8 WAA 126251 (**466**); 126445 (**467**); 126448 (**468**)
Bibl. Tait 1976, no. 332

469–70 WAA 1930.5–8.137–8
Bibl. Tait 1976, no. 333

471 EA 62444
Bibl. Tait 1976, no. 10; Andrews 1981, no. 235

472 EA 14703
Bibl. Tait 1976, no. 334a

473 EA 54747
Bibl. Tait 1976, no. 334b

474 EA 57710
Bibl. Tait 1976, no. 334c

475 EA 57773
Bibl. Tait 1976, no. 334d

476 EA 57803
Bibl. Tait 1976, no. 334e

477 EA 57812
Bibl. Tait 1976, no. 334f

478 EA 24787
Bibl. Tait 1976, no. 338; Andrews 1981, no. 450

479 EA 3077
Bibl. Tait 1976, no. 339; Andrews 1981, no. 414

480 WAA 103057
Bibl. Tait 1976, no. 355

481 EA 30484
Bibl. Tait 1976, no. 341; Andrews 1981, no. 403

482 EA 2572

483 EA 24774
Bibl. Tait 1976, no. 342a; Andrews 1981, no. 397

484 EA 30478
Bibl. Tait 1976, no. 342b; Andrews 1981, no. 399

485 EA 36466
Bibl. Tait 1976, no. 344b

486 WAA 130761
Bibl. Tait 1976, no. 343a

487 WAA 126389
Bibl. Tait 1976, no. 336

488 EA 23426
Bibl. Tait 1976, no. 337b

489 EA 14456
Bibl. Tait 1976, no. 347

490 WAA 51.1–1.18
Bibl. Tait 1976, no. 350

491 EA 59850
Bibl. Tait 1976, no. 349a

492 EA 66620
Bibl. Tait 1976, no. 349b

493 WAA 116228
Bibl. Tait 1976, no. 351

494 WAA 135781
Bibl. Tait 1976, no. 353

495 WAA 56.12–23.789
Bibl. Tait 1976, no. 352

496 PRB 50.6–1.3–5.15–16
Bibl. Tait 1976, no. 169; E. Hawkins, *Archaeological Journal* 8 (1851), pp. 33–44

497 PRB P1983.10–3.1
Bibl. C. Johns, *Antiquaries Journal* 64 (1984), pp. 393–4

498 PRB 1954.12–6.1
Bibl. Tait 1976, no. 354

499 MLA AF351. Franks Bequest, 1897
Bibl. Tait 1976, no. 355

500 MLA AF242. Franks Bequest, 1897
Bibl. Tait 1976, no. 357; Gary Vikan, 'Art, medicine and magic in Early Byzantium', *Dumbarton Oaks Papers* 38 (1984), p. 77

501 MLA 1983.7–4.1
Bibl. Cf. M.C. Ross, 'A Byzantine gold medallion at Dumbarton Oaks', *Dumbarton Oaks Papers* 11 (1957), pp. 247–61

502 MLA AF352. Franks Bequest, 1897
Bibl. Tait 1976, no. 358; Westermann-Angerhausen 1983–4, pp. 25–6, Abb. 11–12, Kat. Nr. 4

503 MLA 1965.6–4.1
Bibl. Tait 1976, no. 359

504 MLA 1926.4–9.1
Bibl. Tait 1976, no. 360; Robin Cormack, *Writing in gold: Byzantine society and its icons* (London 1985), p. 64, fig. 19

505 MLA ML3527. Morel collection

506 MLA AF519. Franks Bequest, 1897
Bibl. A. Roes, 'Talismans Mérovingiens en Pierre', in *Review Archéologique de l'Est et du Centre-Est* XI (Dijon 1960), pp. 32–8

507 AF518. Franks Bequest, 1897
Bibl. As **505**

508 MLA 73.6–2.95
Bibl. Tait 1976, no. 362; Meaney 1981, p. 130

509 MLA 1902.2–10.1
Bibl. Tait 1976, no. 368; F. de Mely, *Exuviae sacrae Constantinopolitanae* III (Paris 1904), p. 321, fig. 36; Sir C. Hercules Read, *Tribute on his retirement from the British Museum* (1921), pl. xv; L. Gonse, *L'Art Gothique* (n.d.), p. 457; O. Dalton, *Guide to Medieval Antiquities* (London 1924), p. 139, fig. 84; M. Campbell, *Apollo* (1980), p. 422; *Les Fastes du Gothique*, (exh. cat., Paris, October 1981 to February 1982), no. 190, pp. 235–6

510 MLA AF1023
Bibl. Tait 1976, no. 370a

511 MLA AF1865, no. 370b

512 MLA AF1930
Bibl. Tait 1976, no. 370c

513 MLA 1925.1–13.1
Bibl. Tait 1976, no. 370d

514 MLA AF897. Franks Bequest, 1897
Bibl. Tait 1976, no. 371

515 MLA 49.3–1.33
Bibl. Tait 1976, no. 369a

516 MLA AF2711. Franks Bequest, 1897
Bibl. Tait 1976, no. 369b

517 MLA 1983.10–2.1

518 MLA 1971.6–3.5
Bibl. Tait 1976, no. 365b

519 MLA 56.7–1.2031
Bibl. B.W. Spencer, 'Medieval pilgrim badges', *Rotterdam Papers* I (1968), pp. 137–53

520 MLA 47.8–29.1
Bibl. Tait 1976, no. 365c

521 MLA AF2765. Franks Bequest, 1897
Bibl. Tait 1976, no. 367

522 MLA 1959.7–6.1
Bibl. Tait 1976, no. 372

523 MLA AF2772. Franks Bequest, 1897
Bibl. Tait 1976, no. 373

524 MLA. On loan from HM The Queen
Bibl. Tait 1976, no. 366

525 MLA 1941.10–7.1
Bibl. Tait 1976, no. 374; Somers Cocks and Truman 1984, p. 90, fig. 1

526 MLA AF2867. Franks Bequest, 1897
Bibl. Tait 1976, no. 375

527 MLA 1965.6–1.1
Bibl. Tait 1976, no .376

528 Convent de Las Descalzas Reales, Madrid (photo MAS, reproduced by permission of the Patrimonio Nacional, Madrid)

529 MLA HG cat. 249

530 MLA HG cat. 577

531 MLA HG cat. 591
Bibl. A. Hull Grundy, 'Victorian Jewellery', *Apollo* 73 (February 1961), pp. 40–4

532 OA 1939.3–13.1
Bibl. See **333**

533 OA 1960.8–1.1
Bibl. Tait 1976, no. 379

534 OA 1964.2–12.2

535 OA 1880–29
Bibl. Tait 1976, no. 378

536 WAA 120598

537 WAA 122720
Bibl. Tait 1976, no. 381

538 GR 476F. Franks Bequest, 1897
Bibl. Tait 1976, no. 384a

539 PRB 1900.11–23.3
Bibl. Tait 1976, no. 384b

540 MLA 1970.3–1.1
Bibl. Tait 1976, no. 385

541 MLA 90.9–1.15. Carlisle Collection
Bibl. Tait 1976, no. 386

542 MLA 99.7–18.2
Bibl. Tait 1976, no. 387; Hackenbroch 1979, p. 23, fig. 38A–B, col. pl. I; Tait 1980, cat. no. 6, p. 47, col. pl.

543 MLA. Payne-Knight Bequest, 1824
Bibl. Tait 1976, no. 388

544 MLA AF2869. Franks Bequest, 1897
Bibl. Tait 1976, no. 389

545 MLA 99.7–19.1
Bibl. Tait 1976, no. 395

546 MLA AF2673. Franks Bequest, 1897
Bibl. Tait 1976, no. 390

547 MLA AF2654. Franks Bequest, 1897
Bibl. Tait 1976, no. 391; Tait 1980, cat. no. 33, p. 58, col. pl.

548 MLA. Sloane Collection, 1753
Bibl. Dalton 1915, no. 187

549 MLA. Sloane Collection, 1753
Bibl. Dalton 1915, no. 488

550 MLA. Carlisle Collection
Bibl. Dalton 1915, no. 340

551 MLA 1984.3–4.1

552 MLA 90.9–1.11. Carlisle Collection
Bibl. Tait 1976, no. 393

553 MLA. Payne-Knight Bequest, 1824
Bibl. Tait 1976, no. 397

554 MLA AF1467. Franks Bequest, 1897
Bibl. Tait 1976, no. 396

555 MLA HG cat. 877
Bibl. Tait and Gere 1978, col. pl. XI

556 MLA HG cat. 898

557 MLA HG cat. 940

558 MLA HG cat. 952
Bibl. O. Scarisbrick, 'Jewelled Tribute to the Past,' *Country Life* (29 January 1981), pp. 244–6, pl. 6

559 MLA Dalton 1915, no. 181

560 MLA HG cat. 913

561 GR 42.7–28.127. Burgon Collection
Bibl. Tait 1976, no. 402

562 GR 1926.4–7.3
Bibl. Tait 1976, no. 409

563 GR 354F. Franks Bequest, 1897
Bibl. Tait 1976, no. 410

564 GR 65.7–12.59
Bibl. Tait 1976, no. 411

565 GR 1929.4–17.1
Bibl. Tait 1976, no. 456

566 GR 802F. Franks Bequest, 1897
Bibl. Tait 1976, no. 459

567 MLA 1829.11–14.1
Bibl. Tait 1976, no. 445; Backhouse, Turner and Webster 1984, cat. no. 9, p. 30

568 MLA AF458. Franks Bequest, 1897
Bibl. Tait 1976, no. 446; Backhouse, Turner and Webster 1984, cat. no. 10, p. 30

569 MLA Ring cat. 184
Bibl. Tait 1976, no. 363a; Meaney 1981, pp. 23–4

570 MLA 55.11–15.1
Bibl. Tait 1976, no. 460; Meaney 1981, p. 174

571 MLA 1955.12–1.1
Bibl. Wilson 1964, pp. 160–1, pl. XXVIII

572 WAA. See **31**

573 WAA 127650
Bibl. Tait 1976, no. 399

574 EA 17897. Blacas Collection
Bibl. Tait 1976, no. 406a

575 EA 65110. Acworth Collection
Bibl. Tait 1976, no. 406b

576 EA 24777
Bibl. Tait 1976, no. 407

577 EA 68868

578 EA 36468
Bibl. Tait 1976, no. 412

579 WAA 136027
Bibl. Tait 1976, no. 408a

580 WAA 136028
Bibl. Tait 1976, no. 408b

581–3 PRB 57.6–30.1–3
Bibl. Tait 1976, no. 413a–c

584 WAA 119353
Bibl. Tait 1976, no. 414

585 MLA AF228. Franks Bequest, 1897
Bibl. Tait 1976, no. 415

586 MLA AF304. Dimitri Collection; Franks Bequest, 1897
Bibl. Tait 1976, no. 436

587 MLA 1937.11–18.1. Guilhou collection
Bibl. Tait 1976, no. 417; M. Deloche, *Etude . . . sur Anneaux Sigillaires* (Paris 1900), pp. 49–50

588 MLA AF480. Franks Bequest, 1897
Bibl. Dalton 1912, p. 27, no. 172, pl. 1

589 MLA 1982.5–1.1
Bibl. E. Fontenay, *Les Bijoux* (1887), 51–2; *Catalogue of the Pichon collection* (1897), lot 55; *Catalogue of the Guilhou collection*, Sothebys, 11 November 1937, lot 590

590 MLA 1982.5–2.1

591 MLA AF783. Franks Bequest, 1897
Bibl. Tait 1976, no. 423

592 MLA AF811. Franks Bequest, 1897
Bibl. Tait 1976, no. 424

593 MLA 56.10–15.1
Bibl. Tait 1976, no. 422; Tait 1986, cat. no. 42, fig. 186

594 MLA. Carlisle Collection
Bibl. Dalton 1912, no. 661, p. 100; Dalton 1915, no. 834

595 MLA 1952.10–2.2
Bibl. Tait 1976, no. 425a

596 MLA 1952.10–2.3
Bibl. Tait 1976, no. 425b

597 MLA AF1491
Bibl. Dalton 1912, no. 1419

598 MLA. Franks Bequest, 1897
Bibl. Dalton 1912, no. 1424

599 OA 1945.10–17.61
Bibl. Tait 1976, no. 426

600 OA AF2383. Franks Bequest, 1897
Bibl. Tait 1976, no. 428

601 MLA AF568. Franks Bequest, 1897
Bibl. Tait 1976, no. 427; Ward *et al.* 1981, no. 144, pp. 69–70

602 PRB. Deposited on permanent loan by HM Ministry of Works in 1947
Bibl. Tait 1976, no. 435

603 PRB P1980.10–1.1
Bibl. C. Johns *Antiquaries Journal* 61 (1981), pp. 343–5

604 PRB 1936.2–4.1
Bibl. Tait 1976, no. 434

605 PRB P1981.2–1.10
Bibl. Johns and Potter 1983, pp. 86–8

606 MLA AF231. Franks Bequest, 1897
Bibl. Tait 1976, no. 437

607 Copyright © 1980 The Metropolitan Museum of Art, New York (Lehmann Collection)

608 MLA AF1075. Franks Bequest, 1897
Bibl. Tait 1976, no. 438; Ward *et al.* 1981, no. 196, p. 84

609 AF1090. Franks Bequest, 1897
Bibl. Tait 1976, no. 439; Ward *et al.* 1981, no. 197, p. 84

610 MLA AF1097. Franks Bequest, 1897
Bibl. Tait 1976, no. 440b; Somers Cocks and Truman 1984, p. 134, fig. 1

611 MLA AF1096, Franks Bequest, 1897
Bibl. Tait 1976, no. 440a; Somers Cocks and Truman 1984, p. 134, fig. 1

612 MLA AF1417. Franks Bequest, 1897
Bibl. Tait 1976, no. 443; Tait 1986, under cat. no. 51

613 MLA AF1411. Franks Bequest, 1897
Bibl. Tait 1976, no. 444; Tait 1986, cat. no. 52, fig. 234

614 MLA AF1155. Franks Bequest, 1897
Bibl. Tait 1976, no. 441a

615 MLA AF1158. Franks Bequest, 1897
Bibl. Tait 1976, no. 441b

616 MLA AF1105. Franks Bequest, 1897
Bibl. Tait 1976, no. 442

617 MLA HG cat. 587

618 MLA HG cat. 306
Bibl. Ward *et al.* 1981, no. 234

619 MLA AF1437. Franks Bequest, 1897
Bibl. Tait 1976, no. 447

620 MLA AF1453. Franks Bequest, 1897
Bibl. Tait 1976, no. 448

621 MLA AF1466. Franks Bequest, 1897
Bibl. Tait 1976, no. 449

622 MLA AF1459. Franks Bequest, 1897
Bibl. Tait 1976, no. 450

623 MLA AF1509. Franks Bequest, 1897
Bibl. Tait 1976, no. 451

624 MLA AF1514. Franks Bequest, 1897
Bibl. Tait 1976, no. 453

625 MLA AF1528. Franks Bequest, 1897
Bibl. Tait 1976, no. 452

626 MLA AF1720. Franks Bequest, 1897
Bibl. Tait 1976, no. 454

627 MLA HG cat. 572
Bibl. Ward *et al.* 1981, pl. 273

628 MLA HG cat. 581

629 MLA HG cat. 583
Bibl. Ward *et al.* 1981, pl. 297

Bibliography

A. References

Andrews, C. 1981. *Catalogue of Egyptian Antiquities in the British Museum, VI: Jewellery I, From the Earliest Times to the Seventeenth Dynasty*. London

Arrhenius, B. 1985. *Merovingian Garnet Jewellery*. Stockholm

Backhouse, J., Turner, D.H. and Webster, L. (eds) 1984. *The Golden Age of Anglo-Saxon Art*. London

Beijing 1958. *Wu sheng chutu zhongyao wenwu zhanlan tutu*. Beijing

Beijing 1959. *Luoyang Zhonzhou Lu*. Beijing

Beijing 1972. *Wenhua dageming qijian chutu wenwu di yi*. Beijing

BMCJ. F.H. Marshall, *Catalogue of the Jewellery, Greek, Etruscan, and Roman in the Departments of Antiquities, British Museum* (London 1911)

Dalton, O.M. 1915. *Catalogue of the Engraved Gems of the Post-Classical Periods in the British Museum*. London

Dalton, O.M. 1926. *The Treasure of the Oxus*. London

Egypt's Golden Age (exh. cat., Museum of Fine Arts, Boston 1982)

Gere, C. and Rudoe, J. 2000. 'Knowledge, money and time: Anne Hull Grundy as a collector of Victorian jewellery', *Journal of the Decorative Arts Society* 24, pp. 80-97

GRJ. R.A. Higgins, *Greek and Roman Jewellery* (2nd edn, London 1980)

Hackenbroch, Y. 1979. *Renaissance Jewellery*. London

Jenyns, R.S. and Watson, W. 1963. *Chinese Art. The Minor Arts I*. London

Johns, C. and Potter, T. 1983. *The Thetford Treasure. Roman Jewellery and Silver*. London

London 1935. Royal Academy of Arts, *International Exhibition of Chinese Art, 1935-6, illustrated supplement to the catalogue*. London

Meaney, A. 1981. *Anglo-Saxon Amulets and Curing Stones*, British Archaeological Reports, British Series 96. Oxford

Purcell, K. 1999. *Falize. A Dynasty of Jewellers*. London

Rudoe, J. 1983/4. 'The Layards, Cortelazzo and Castellani: new information from the diaries of Lady Layard', *Jewellery Studies* 1 (Journal of the Society of Jewellery Historians), pp. 59-82

Rudoe, J. 1994. *Decorative Arts 1850-1950. Catalogue of the British Museum Collection* (2nd edn, London)

Rudoe, J. 1997. *Cartier 1900-1939* (exh. cat.). London

Rudoe, J. 2004a. 'Queen Charlotte's jewellery: reconstructing a lost collection', in *The Wisdom of George the Third*, ed. J. Marsden. London

Rudoe, J. 2004b. 'Micromosaics', in S. Soros and S. Walker (eds), *Castellani and Archaeological Jewelry* (exh. cat.), Bard Graduate Center, New York, pp. 153-80

Somers Cocks, A. and Truman, C. 1984. *Renaissance Jewels, Gold Boxes and Objets de Vertu. The Thyssen-Bornemisza Collection*. London

Stead, I.M. 1984. 'Some notes on imported metalwork in Iron Age Britain', in S. Macready and F.H. Thompson (eds), *Cross-Channel Trade between Gaul and Britain in the Pre-Roman Iron Age*, Society of Antiquaries Occasional Paper, n.s. 4, pp. 43-66

Steingräber, E. 1957. *Antique Jewellery*. London

Tait, H. 1963. 'An anonymous loan to the British Museum, I: Renaissance jewellery', *The Connoisseur*, vol. 154 (November 1963), pp. 147-53

Tait, H. 1974. 'Development of styles and forms', in E.A. and J. Heiniger (eds), *The Great Book of Jewels*. Lausanne

Tait, H. 1980. In A. Somers Cocks (ed.), *Princely Magnificence, Court Jewels of the Renaissance 1500-1630* (exh. cat., Victoria and Albert Museum, London)

Tait, H. 1981. *The Waddesdon Bequest: The Legacy of Baron Ferdinand Rothschild to the British Museum*. London

Tait, H. 1984. C. Gere, J. Rudoe, H. Tait and T. Wilson, *The Art of the Jeweller. A Catalogue of the Hull Grundy Gift to the British Museum: Jewellery, Engraved Gems and Goldsmiths' Work*, ed. H. Tait. London

Tait, H. 1985. 'The girdle-prayer-book or "tablett" ...' , *Jewellery Studies* 2 (Journal of the Society of Jewellery Historians, London), pp. 29-58

Tait, H. 1986. *Catalogue of the Waddesdon Bequest in the British Museum, I: The Jewels*. London

Ward et al. 1981. A. Ward, J. Cherry, C. Gere and B. Cartlidge, *The Ring from Antiquity to the Twentieth Century*. London

Wenwu (before 1959 *Wenwu cankao ziliao*). Beijing 1950–

Westermann-Angerhausen, H. 1983-4. 'Ottonischer Fibelschmuck, neue Funde und Überlegungen', *Jewellery Studies* 1 (Journal of the Society of Jewellery Historians, London)

Wilson, D.M. 1964. *Anglo-Saxon Ornamental Metalwork 700-1000 in the British Museum*. London

Yetts, W.P. 1930. *The George Eumorfopoulos Collection, Catalogue of the Chinese and Korean Bronzes, Sculptures, Jades, Jewellery and Miscellaneous Objects, 2*. London

B. British Museum catalogues with jewellery and related material

Arnold, C.J., *The Anglo-Saxon Cemeteries of the Isle of Wight* (London, 1982)

Bivar, A.D.H., *Catalogue of the Western Asiatic Seals in the British Museum. Stamp Seals II: The Sassanian Dynasty* (London 1969)

Bruce-Mitford, R., *The Sutton Hoo Ship-Burial, II: Arms, Armour and Regalia* (London 1978)

Collon, D., *Catalogue of the Western Asiatic Seals in the British Museum. Cylinder Seals II: Akkadian – Post-Akkadian II – Ur III* (London 1982)

Collon, D., *Catalogue of the Western Asiatic Seals in the British Museum. Cylinder Seals III: Isin-Larsa, Old Babylonian* (London 1986)

Collon, D., *Catalogue of the Western Asiatic Seals in the British Museum. Cylinder Seals V: Neo-Assyrian and Neo-Babylonian Periods* (London 2001)

Cooney, J.D., *Catalogue of Egyptian Antiquities in the British Museum, IV: Glass* (London 1976)

Dalton, O.M., *Catalogue of Early Christian Antiquities in the British Museum* (London 1901)

Dalton, O.M., *Catalogue of the Finger Rings, Early Christian, Byzantine, Teutonic, Medieval and Later in the British Museum* (London 1912)

Graham-Campbell, J., *Viking Artefacts: A Select Catalogue* (London 1980)

Hall, H.R., *Catalogue of Egyptian Scarabs, etc., in the British Museum, I: Royal Scarabs* (London 1915)

Jenkins, I. and Sloan, K., *Vases and Volcanoes: Sir William Hamilton and his Collection* (exh. cat., London 1996)

Johns, C., *The Snettisham Roman Jeweller's Hoard* (London 1997)

Jones, M. (ed.), *Fake? The Art of Deception* (exh. cat., London 1990)

Kinnes, I.A. and Longworth, I.H., *Catalogue of the Excavated Prehistoric and Romano-British Material in the Greenwell Collection* (London 1985)

Marshall, F.H., *Catalogue of the Finger Rings, Greek, Etruscan and Roman in the Departments of Antiquities, British Museum* (London 1907)

Merrillees, P.H., *Catalogue of the Western Asiatic Seals in the British Museum. Cylinder Seals VI: Pre-Achaemenid and Achaemenid Periods* (London 2005)

Michel, S., *Magische Gemmen im Britischen Museum*, ed. P. and H. Zazoff, 2 vols (London 2000)

Rawson, J., *Chinese Jade: From the Neolithic to the Qing* (paperback edn, London 2002)

Shelton, K.J., *The Esquiline Treasure* (London 1981)

Tait, H., *Catalogue of the Waddesdon Bequest in the British Museum, III: The 'Curiosities'* (London 1991)

Walters, H.B., *Catalogue of the Bronzes, Greek, Etruscan and Roman in the Departments of Antiquities, British Museum* (London 1899)

Walters, H.B., *Catalogue of the Engraved Gems and Cameos, Greek, Etruscan and Roman in the Departments of Antiquities, British Museum* (London 1926)

Williams, D. and Ogden, J., *Greek Gold: Jewellery of the Classical World* (exh. cat., London 1994)

Further Reading

In addition to the Bibliography, this selection of books published since 1965 is recommended.

ALDRED, C., *Jewels of the Pharaohs* (London 1971)

ALLAN, J.W., *Nishapur Metalwork of the Early Islamic Period* (New York 1982)

ANDREWS, C., *Amulets of Ancient Egypt* (London 1994)

ANDREWS, C., *Ancient Egyptian Jewellery* (London 1990, paperback edn 1996)

ANTONOVA, I., TOLSTIKOV, V. and TREISTER, M., *The Gold of Troy: Searching for Homer's Fabled City*, consultant ed. Donald Easton (London and New York 1996)

ARNOLD, U., *Die Juwelen Augusts des Starken* (Munich 2001)

ARWAS, V. (ed.), *The Liberty Style* (London 1984)

ASCHENGREEN-PIACENTI, K. (ed.), *The Jewels of the Electress Palatine in the Museo degli Argenti* (Florence 1988)

BALFOUR, I., *Famous Diamonds* (revised edn, Colchester 1992)

BERNAL, I., *The Olmec World* (Berkeley 1969)

BRAILSFORD, J.W., *Early Celtic Masterpieces from Britain in the British Museum* (London 1975)

BRUNEL, F., *Jewellery of India* (New Delhi and Bombay 1972)

BURY, S., *Jewellery 1789-1910: The International Era*, 2 vols (Woodbridge 1991)

COE, M.D., *The Maya* (London 1971)

COLLEDGE, M.A.R., *The Art of Palmyra* (London 1976)

COLLON, D. (ed.), *7000 Years of Seals* (London 1997)

CURTIS, J.E. and TALLIS, N. (eds), *Forgotten Empire: The World of Ancient Persia* (exh. cat. London 2005)

DEPPERT-LIPPITZ, B., *Römischer Goldschmuck des ersten und zweiten Jahrhunderts n. Chr. nach datierten Funden* (Mainz 1970)

DIGBY, A., *Maya Jades* (London 1970)

DONGERKERY, K.S., *Jewellery and Personal Adornment in India* (Delhi 1970)

D'OREY, Leonora, *Five Centuries of Jewellery*, National Museum of Ancient Art, Lisbon (London 1995)

DUVAL, P.-M., *Les Celtes* (Paris 1977)

EVANS, J., *A History of Jewellery 1100-1870* (2nd edn, London 1970)

FISHER, A., *Africa Adorned* (London 1984)

GABARDI, M., *Art Deco Jewelry 1920-1949* (London 1989)

GERE, C., *Victorian Jewellery Design* (London 1972)

GERE, C. and MUNN, G., *Artists' Jewellery: Pre-Raphaelite to Arts and Crafts* (Woodbridge 1989)

GERLACH, M., *Primitive and Folk Jewellery* (Vienna 1906, repr. London and New York 1971)

GREGORIETTI, G., *Jewellery through the Ages* (Milan 1969)

HENIG, M. (ed.), *A Handbook of Roman Art* (Oxford 1983)

HINKS, P., *Nineteenth Century Jewellery* (London 1975)

HINKS, P., *Twentieth Century British Jewellery 1900-1980* (London 1983)

HINTON, D., *Medieval Jewellery from the Eleventh to the Fifteenth Century* (Aylesbury 1982)

HÖPFNER, G. and HAASE, G., *Metallschmuck aus Indien* (Berlin 1978)

JACOBSTHAL, P., *Early Celtic Art* (Oxford 1944, repr. 1969)

JENKINS, M. and KEENE, M., *Islamic Jewellery in the Metropolitan Museum of Art* (New York 1982)

Jewellery Studies, Journal of the Society of Jewellery Historians (London, 1983–)

JOHNS, C., *The Jewellery of Roman Britain: Celtic and Classical Traditions* (London 1996)

JONES, M. (ed.), *Why Fakes Matter: Essays on Problems of Authenticity* (London 1992)

LATIF, M., *Bijoux Moghols*, in French, German and English (Brussels 1982)

LOTH, A.-M., *La vie publique et privée dans l'Inde ancienne, VII: Les bijoux*, 2 fasc. (Paris 1972)

McEWAN, C. (ed.), *Precolumbian Gold: Technology, Style and Iconography* (London 2000)

MACK, J. (ed.), *Ethnic Jewellery* (London 1988)

MARQUARDT, B., *Schmuck, Klassizismus und Biedermeier 1780-1850, Deutschland, Österreich, Schweiz* (Munich 1983)

MAXWELL-HYSLOP, K.R., *Western Asiatic Jewellery c. 3000-612 BC* (London 1971)

MEEN, V.B. and TUSHINGHAM, A.D., *Crown Jewels of Iran* (Toronto 1968)

MEGAW, J.V.S., *Art of the European Iron Age: A Study of the Elusive Image* (Bath 1970)

MOREL, B., *The French Crown Jewels* (Paris 1988)

MULLER, P.M., *Jewels in Spain 1500-1800* (New York 1972)

MUNN, G.C., *Castellani and Giuliano, Revivalist Jewellers of the Nineteeth Century* (London 1984)

NEWMAN, H., *An Illustrated Dictionary of Jewelry* (London 1981)

NICHOLSON, H.B., *The Art of Aztec Mexico: Treasures of Tenochtitlan* (Washington 1983)

OGDEN, J., *Jewellery of the Ancient World* (London 1982)

OGDEN, J., *Interpreting the Past: Ancient Jewellery* (London 1992)

OMAN, C., *British Rings 800-1914* (London 1974)

PRESSMAR, E., *Indische Ringe* (Frankfurt-am-Main 1982)

RUDOE, J., 'Engraved gems: the lost art of antiquity', in K. Sloane (ed.), *Enlightenment: Discovering the World in the Eighteenth Century* (London 2003), pp. 158-65

SCARISBRICK, D., *Jewellery in Britain, 1066-1837: A Documentary, Social, Literary and Artistic Survey* (London 1993)

SCARISBRICK, D., *Rings: Symbols of Wealth, Power and Affection* (London 1993)

SIMPSON, St J. (ed.), *Queen of Sheba: Treasures from Ancient Yemen* (London 2002)

SNOWMAN, K. (ed.), *The Master Jewellers* (London 1990)

SPINK, M. (ed.), *Islamic Jewellery* (London 1986)

STEAD, I.M., *Celtic Art* (2nd edn, London 1996)

STURM, F.X. and WINTER-JENSEN, A., *Bijoux Art Nouveau* (Geneva 1982)

TILLANDER, H., *Diamond Cuts in Historic Jewellery, 1381-1910* (London 1995)

TISSOT, F., *La vie publique et privée dans l'Inde ancienne: Gandhara* (Paris 1985)

TWINING, E.F. (Lord), *A History of the Crown Jewels of Europe* (London 1960)

UNTRACHT, O., *Traditional Jewelry of India* (London 1997)

VEVER, H., *French Jewellery of the Nineteenth Century* (originally published 1908-12; this reprint trans. and ed. K. Purcell, London 2001)

WHITE, J.M. and BUNKER, E.C., *Adornment for Eternity: Status and Rank in Chinese Ornament* (Denver Art Museum 1994)

WILKINSON, A., *Ancient Egyptian Jewellery* (London 1971)

Index

Numbers in italic type refer to the pages on which the captions appear

Abydos (Egypt) 27, 29
Adoration of the Magi 206
Aegina Treasure 38, 38–9
Aemilia Ars 190
Æthelswith (Anglo-Saxon queen) 228
Æthelwulf (Anglo-Saxon king) 228
Africa, West 177–82, 178–81
agate 12, 24–5, 91, 115, 118, 118–19, 119, 167, 208, 208, 211, 217, 224, 232
aigrettes 184, 241
ajouré 33, 34, 193, 241
see also openwork; opus interrasile; pierced work
alabaster 26
Albert, Prince 187
Alexander the Great 224
alloys 127, 128, 130, 133, 176; see also electrum; tumbaga
altarpiece 220
Amarna period 43, 44, 47
amber 14, 40, 48, 74, 113, 114
Amesbury (Wiltshire, England) 230, 232
amethyst 34, 35, 86, 96, 101, 138, 138, 143, 154, 198, 208, 234, 235
Ammenemes IV (Egyptian king) 34
amulet-box/case 33, 174, 175, 203, 204, 214, 215
amulets 11, 27, 27, 32–3, 35, 35, 44, 84, 94, 188, 194, 194, 197–8, 197–8, 200–1, 203–5, 208–9, 211, 213–14, 214–15, 230, 234
Anglo-Saxon period 103, 105, 107, 107–8, 108, 111, 112, 208, 217, 228, 228
animal ornament 53–5, 63, 66, 71, 73, 74, 76, 84, 86, 91, 101, 103, 104, 105, 107, 108, 111, 112, 114, 118, 129, 142, 215, 227
Style I (Germanic) 103, 107; Style II (Germanic) 105, 107
ankh-signs 44, 198, 201, 241
Ankhesenamun 230, 231
anklets 27, 73, 121, 130, 177, 181
Anne, Queen (of England) 239, 240
antelope 93, 94
Anti-Gallican Society 184
Anyang (China) 71
'archaeological' style 20, 183, 189, 223, 224, 226, 241
archers' thumb-rings 234, 234
armbands, see armlets
armlets 15, 42, 55, 56, 66, 73, 76, 78, 80, 97, 137, 148, 174, 178
see also arm-rings; bangles; bracelets
arm-rings 48, 49, 53, 112
armorial bearings 144, 231–4, 233–5, 241, 243
Arpachiyah (Iraq) 11, 28, 229
Art Nouveau 20, 184, 191–2
Arts and Crafts 190, 192
Asante (Ghana) 178, 180–2, 181
Ashurnasirpal II (Assyrian king) 56
Assyrians 55, 56, 58, 66
Astarte (Canaanite goddess) 197–8, 201
Attwood, Mary 241
Atum (Egyptian god) 34
Atys (mythological figure) 98
Augustus (Roman emperor) 224
Augustus the Strong 183
Avars 104, 108
awaw-bangles 43, 43
Aztecs 18, 133

Backworth (Northumberland, England) 204, 205
Badarian Period (Egypt) 26, 26
badge 184

bangles 26, 27, 27, 29, 40, 42–3, 43, 93, 94, 198, 204
see also bracelets
Bastet (Egyptian goddess) 198, 202–3
beads 12, 13, 14, 18, 22–4, 23, 25, 26, 27, 29, 30–1, 34, 34–5, 37, 38, 39, 43–4, 44, 47, 48, 64, 66, 70, 86, 91, 91, 92, 94, 115, 116, 120, 120, 123, 180, 198, 201, 208, 216, 216, 217
bear 197
Belize 121, 123–4
belts 27, 54, 55, 72, 114, 118, 118, 119, 146, 147, 170
belt buckles 71, 96, 103, 105, 118, 142, 144, 146, 154, 167
belt-clasps 89, 90, 91, 118, 140, 192
belt fittings 118, 142, 144, 146
belt-hooks 18, 71, 71, 118
belt-plaques 70, 118–19, 118–19, 142, 144–5, 146, 147, 149, 167, 168, 170
belt set 118, 118, 167
Benin (Nigeria), 177–8, 178
Berini, Antonio 224
Bes (Egyptian god) 68, 198, 202
betrothal ring 231, 234, 236, 236, 238
see also marriage-ring
Bing, Siegfried 191
birds 68, 96, 103, 105, 108, 116, 118, 128, 130, 132, 137, 142, 146, 148, 185, 187, 194, 232, 233
boar 205
Bodh Gaya, Bihar (India) 91
body-chain (Byzantine) 99–100
Bohun, Mary de 140
Boltby Scar (Yorkshire, England) 40
bone 26, 26, 70, 94, 97
botanical jewels 184, 187
Boucheron, Maison 191
Boudicca, Queen 76
Bouvet, René 191
bracelets 26, 27, 27, 31, 35, 37, 44, 47, 48, 52, 53, 55, 56–7, 57, 58, 63, 63, 65, 66, 68, 69, 73, 76, 83, 86, 88, 94, 97, 120, 120, 121, 130, 137, 151, 177, 188, 189, 192, 204, 206, 223
see also armlets; arm-rings; bangles
bracteate 104, 241
brass 78, 177, 178
brass, monumental 138
Brazen Serpent 152
Brazil 183, 188
breast ornaments, see pectoral ornaments
Brogden, John 184
bronze 14, 15, 40, 65, 71, 71–2, 72, 74, 74, 78, 90, 91, 96, 97, 118, 120, 148, 175
Bronze Age 14, 37, 40–1, 48–9, 50–3, 53
brooches 15, 20, 48, 48, 51, 53, 72, 73, 76, 80, 97, 109, 135–6, 151, 185–91, 193, 205–6, 224
amuletic 209, 211; bow 104; crossbow 97; disc 108, 111, 112; disc-on-bow 103; dragonesque 96, 97; 'eye' 214; heart-shaped 138, 143; penannular 109, 113; perambulator 72; quoit 103; radiate-head 105; ring 138, 140; square-headed 103; thistle 109; Tier-fiebeln 72
see also fibulae
brooch-pendant 224
Browning, Elizabeth Barrett 234, 235
Browning, Robert 235
Buckland, Dover (England) 103
buckles 71, 90, 103, 105, 142, 144, 146, 154, 167, 191–2, 208
see also belt-clasps; belt-hooks; belt-plaques; belt set
Buddhism 92, 114, 115, 214, 215, 215
buffalo 194
Bulgari 184
bullae 20, 241
bulls 23, 39, 90, 197, 197, 198, 202, 211, 214
Burma 18, 214
butterflies 87, 187, 189
buttons 154, 154

Byzantine period 16, 87, 89, 97–8, 99–101, 100, 108, 109, 135, 138, 206, 230, 236, 236

cabochon gems 18, 103, 161, 168, 174, 241
Cairo (Egypt) 146
calibré-cutting 20, 193, 241
cameos 16, 98, 151, 206, 216, 217, 218, 219–20, 220, 222–4, 223, 226, 240, 241
Camirus (Rhodes) 60, 60
Campana collection 189
candlestick 184
'Cannington' ring 211
Canosa di Puglia (Italy) 109
cape, gold 48
Capizzucchi, Marchese Camillo 150
carbuncle 208, 211, 241
Carthage Treasure 98
Cartier 184, 193
'Castellani' Brooch 109
Castellani workshop 184, 189, 224
Castle Newe (Scotland) 78
cat's eye (chrysoberyl) 154, 184
cats 34, 36, 198, 203, 203
feline motifs 81, 83
caul 211, 214
Cellini, Benvenuto 154
Celts 15–16, 72–4, 78, 94, 112, 112–13, 114, 205
chains 12, 23, 31, 37, 43, 86, 91, 99–100, 154, 154, 160, 204
chalcedony 31, 86, 162, 220
Chalcis Treasure 140, 142
champlevé enamelling, see enamelling
Charles I, King (of England) 162, 235, 239, 240
Charles V, King (of Spain) 212
Charlotte, Queen 183, 183, 185
chasing 33, 44, 48, 52–3, 55, 69, 76, 78, 80, 90, 92, 98, 101, 128, 147, 148, 168, 170, 180, 181, 224, 227, 232, 241
Cheapside Hoard 154, 160–2
Chessel Down (Isle of Wight) 103
China 16, 16, 18, 70–2, 70–1, 100, 114–15, 115–18, 117–19, 147, 148–9, 167, 170, 173, 194, 194, 197, 234
chip-carving 113, 242
Chi-Rho monogram 205, 205, 241–2
choker 23, 24, 150
Christ 209, 211, 212
Christian motifs 98, 98, 108, 138, 144, 144, 150, 152, 156, 205, 205–6, 209, 209, 211–13, 212, 218, 220, 222, 228, 236, 238–9
chrysoberyl 154
chrysoprase 192
cicada 194
cire-perdue casting 19, 44, 73, 82, 126, 130, 130, 132, 134, 180, 181, 182, 242
Clare Castle (Suffolk) 209, 212
clasps 168, 192
see also belt-clasp; shoulder-clasps
clay 13, 23, 28
clip-brooch 191
cloisonné (inlaid work) 13, 30, 33, 36, 66, 69, 88, 92, 94, 103, 105, 107, 107, 198, 200, 203, 242
see also enamelling, cloisonné
cockerel 190
coins 76, 78, 99, 103–4, 143, 209, 213
collars 14, 27, 32, 34, 42–3, 43, 47, 52, 94, 175, 183
see also necklaces; neck-rings; torcs
Colombia 128, 129–30, 130, 132, 132
Colonna, Edouard 191
comb-fibula 63
combs 18, 114, 115, 117, 119, 147, 186, 191
commemorative finger-rings 235, 239, 240–1
commessi 220, 224
composition, glazed 26, 27, 27, 32, 33, 34–5, 42, 43, 44, 47, 198, 202, 230, 231
see also faience
conch shells 91

Constantinople 16, 100
copper 26, 27, 32, 33, 40, 101, 112–13, 128, 176, 178
coral 15, 72, 175–6, 176, 177, 188, 191, 211, 212, 214
Corbridge (Northumberland, England) 236, 236
Córdoba (Spain) 73, 76
corncockle 47
cornelian 12, 14, 23–4, 25, 27, 29, 30–1, 33, 34, 35, 39, 44, 47, 86, 91, 191, 198, 203, 216, 216–17, 224, 232
etched cornelian beads 24, 92, 216, 216
corsage ornaments 185–6
County Cavan (Ireland) 113
Courtisols (France) 74
Coventry (Warwickshire, England) 140, 211
cowrie-shells 11, 23, 28, 198, 198, 200
cravat-pins 184, 214
crescents 65, 84, 85, 205
Crete 13, 37
Cromwell, Thomas 220
Cross, Descent from 138, 209
crosses, pendant 103, 107, 206, 208, 212, 212
crowns 119, 130, 147, 170
Crucifixion 138, 209, 209, 212
crystal, see rock-crystal
cutting (of jewels) 18, 20, 161, 165, 241, 242, 243

dancers 42, 118
Daniel, Judgement of 152
Dawson, Nelson and Edith 192
deer 59
Desborough (Northamptonshire, England) 107
Des Granges, David 162, 163
Devizes (Wiltshire, England) 209, 213
dextrarum iunctio 236, 236
see also fede-rings
diadems 26, 27, 29, 37, 38, 59, 60, 66, 84, 86, 93, 94, 130, 183
see also headbands; head-dress ornaments; head-dresses
diamonds 88, 140, 154, 156, 161, 163, 165, 183, 183–7, 189, 193, 208, 224, 238, 240, 242, 243
Diana (Roman goddess) 164
Dinnington (Northumberland, England) 50
dog 72
dolphins 80, 96, 188, 227
doves 205, 238
Dowgate Hill (London) 135
dragonflies 192
dragons 71, 96, 167, 168, 170, 170, 173, 175, 190, 194, 197, 234
dress-fastener 53, 54
dress ornaments 68
dress-pins 23, 24, 48, 49, 53, 54
'Dromacius and Betta' ring 231, 233
ducks 55, 55, 69, 72, 72, 73
Dudley, Robert, Earl of Leicester 11, 154
Dunstable Swan Jewel 138, 138, 140

Eady, Thomas 241
eagles 90, 174, 187
ear flares 18, 81, 83, 123, 127, 130
ear ornaments 44, 83, 121, 127, 134
earplugs 42, 43, 44, 123
earrings 12, 16, 18, 23, 24, 31, 36, 36, 38, 39–40, 40, 42–3, 42, 44–6, 48, 50, 59, 63, 65, 65, 66, 84, 86, 88, 93, 94, 98, 99, 104, 119, 132, 133, 146, 151, 162, 183, 188–90, 193
Ecuador 128, 129
Egypt 11, 12, 13, 14, 26, 26–7, 29, 32–3, 33–6, 42–7, 92, 94, 99–100, 146, 146, 198, 200–2, 203–4, 229–30
Egyptian blue 27
electrum 27, 34–5, 46, 76, 78, 81, 198, 242

elephants *178, 182*
Elizabeth I, Queen (of England) *152, 159, 220, 223*
Emanuel, Harry, *188*
embossing, *see* repoussé
emeralds 86, *87*, 88, 96, 98, 99, *140, 154, 160, 163, 166, 184, 193*
enamelling 15–16, 19, 64, 65, *65*, 73, 78, *84*, 86, 88, 96, 97, 109, 112, *112*–13, 135, *135*–7, 138, *138*, 140, *142*–4, 146, *146*, 152, 154, 156, 159, 161, 161, 162, *163*–6, 174, *174*–5, 184, *184*, 187, 189–92, 206, 209, 212, *212*, 220, 222, 223, 224, 235, 238–41, 242
  cloisonné 15, 16, 109, 135, *135*–7, 138, 146, *146, 175*, 190, 206, 242
  champlevé 15–16, 78, 96, 97, 174, *174*, 242
  basse-taille 156, 242
  émail en ronde bosse 138, *138*, 156, 242
  miniature enamel-paintings on enamels 19, 154, 160, *164*–6, 242
filigree *65*, 140, *142, 144*, 212, 223, 242
engraving 19, 65–6, 92, 113, 162, 216, 227, *227*, 229, 230, 231, 232, *234*–6, 242
Enkomi (Cyprus) 38, *39*
Ephesus (Turkey) 60, *60*
Epsom (Surrey, England) 217, 219
Eros 84
Espinasse, G. *191*
etched cornelian beads, *see* cornelian
Etruscans 60, 61–2, 63, *63, 189, 227, 230*
eye 211, *214*; eye of Horus *198, 202, 203*

Fahner, Theodor *192*
faience 13, 14, 23, 28, 64, 91, *197*, 242; *see also* composition, glazed
falcons 27, *92, 94, 198, 198*; *see also* hawks
Falize, Alexis 184, *190*
'fan-holder' *154, 160*
Faras (Egypt) 29
Faunus 96
Faversham (Kent, England) *103*
feathers 170, *184, 188*
fede-rings 234, 236, *238*
Fei, Alessandro 20
felspar 26, 34, 35, 44, 198
fibulae 48, 53, *59*, 60, 63, 94, 242
  comb-fibula *63*
  see also brooches
Figueireido, Joao 226, *240*
filigree 12, 13, 18, 25, 30, 36, 37, 63, 64, *64*–5, 65, 84, 86, 101, *103*–5, 115, 130, *135*–7, 142, *146*, *146*–7, 169, 170, 173, *173*–4, 223, *223*, 227, 239–40, 242
  cast (false) filigree 130, *132*, 133–4, 242
finger-rings 12, 15, 16, 24, 30, 35, 44, *44*–5, 49, 53, 55, 63, 65, 66, 69, 73, 76, 91, 92, 94, 96, 97, 98, 112, *134*, 137, 138, *138, 147*–8, 154, 181, *181*–2, 192, 201–2, 206, 208, 209, 211, 216, 217, 219, 220, 224, 227–31, *227*–8, 232, *233*–4, *234*–6, 236, *236*, 237, 239
  see also betrothal ring, marriage-ring
fish 137, *194, 198, 200, 203*
Fishpool Hoard *140, 143, 233*
Flaxman, John 226
flies 43, 44, *197*
'Flora of Pistrucci' *224*, 226
flowers 148, *161, 167, 170, 187*
Fontenay, Eugène 20, 189
'fool's gold' *185*
forehead ornaments 26, *29*
Fortuna 94, *98*
fox *197*
Framlingham Castle (Suffolk, England) 220, 223
France 182, *184*, 186, 220, 223, 231
Frederick II Hohenstaufen 218
Frederick V of Bohemia *163*
frogs 44, *197, 203*
frontlet, gold *31*

fruit *149, 187*
Fuaraig Glen (Scotland) *50*
'Fuller Brooch' 16, *108*

Gandhara 214–15, *215*
Garden of Eden 239
garlands, imitation 43
garnet 16, 20, 29, 34, *84*, 86, *87*, 96, 101, 103, 105, 107, 154, *215*, 217, 223, 230
George III, King (of England) *183*, 240
Georgia 89, *90, 91*
Germanic peoples 101, *103, 105*, 108
gilding 16, 71, *71*, 101, 103, 111, 112, 114, 117, 146, 149, *215*, 242
  depletion 130, *132*; fire-gilding 16, 242; parcel-gilding 16, *76, 105, 145*, 205, 243
'gimmel' rings 239, *239*
girdles 26, 26, 27, *42*
glass 13, 15, 33, 36, 42, 44, *44*–6, 48, 57, 58, 64, 72, 73, 74, 88, 92, 94, 96, 105, 114, 120, 176, 181, *214*, 229; millefiori *107*, 112, *112*, 242; paste 19–20, *183, 240*
glazed composition, *see* composition
Gloucester (England) 235
Gnadenpfennig 163
goats 31, *55*, 227
gods, goddesses 60, *63, 69, 90*
Godstow (Oxon, England) *238*
gold: Aztec view of *133*; beads 24, 26, 31, *43*, 46, 57, 64, 68, 190, 203; coloured *187*; dust 178, 181; earliest use of 11–12; flowers *91*; foil 26, *101, 103, 113, 116*; Inca use of 127–8; plating 65; sheet 40, 48, 65, 88, *93*, 98, 104, 109, 116, 117–18, 128–9, 130, 137, 170; sources of 40, *84*, 108; wire 27, 30, 44, 48, 51, *93*; wire mesh *173*; working 14, *33*, 36, 114, 128
  see also filigree
gorgeret *150*
Gorgons 217, 219, 223, *226*
Gothic style 184, *190*
Goths 101
Gotland (Sweden) *103*–4, *111*
gourd *169*
Grailly, Jean de *233, 233*
granulation 12, 13, 25, 33, 36, *36*–7, 39, 57, *59*–60, 63, 64, 65, 92, 101, 104, 115, 116, 117, 119, *119*, 137, 146, *146*–7, 147, *199, 201, 203, 223, 227, 233*, 242; false *176*
grapes, amethyst *154, 162*
grasshopper *191*
Great Exhibition 184
Greeks 15, 58, *59*, 64–5, *65*–6, 204, 216, 227, 230
'Grenville' Jewel 162, *163*
Grenville, Sir Bevil 162, *163*
greyhounds *39*
Greymoor Hill, Carlisle (England) 228
griffins 55, 65, 66, 68, *68, 69*, 137, 232
guilds 88, 177
Gundestrup cauldron *74*

hair compartments *185, 235*, 239, 240–1
hair ornaments 12, 16, 18, 23, 37, 87, 114, 115, 147, 167, *167*–8, 176, 184
hairpins 18, 70–1, 88, 94, 114, 115, 116, 147, 149, 160, 167, 169
hair ribbons, gold 23
hair-rings 30, *50*
Hallstatt (Austria) 15, 49, 72–3, *72*
Halton Moor (Lancashire, England) *111*
hands *198, 203*, 211, *212*
Hanley, William 240
harness ornaments 71
Harpocrates 47
hat ornaments 140, 150, 152, 154, *191, 193*
Hawara (Egypt) 88
hawks *36*–7, 60, *198, 203*
  see also falcons

headbands 23, *31*–2, 33, *176*
head-dress ornaments 30, 121, 137, *138*
head-dresses 23, 24, 170, *175*
  see also diadems
Heh (Egyptian god) *198, 204*
Helios *189*
Hellenistic period 63, 65, 84, *84*, 86, *86, 87, 93, 189, 216*
Henry IV, King (of England) 140
Henry VIII, King (of England) 19, 220
Heracles (Hercules) 98, 220
Heracles-knot (reef-knot) 27, 35, *84, 84*, 86, 205
heroes and animals 31, *54*, 229
heron *190*
Hilliard, Nicholas 19, *19*, 154, *161*
Hirtz, L. *191*
Hittites 36, *198, 201*
Holbein, Hans 19, *151*, 151, 154, *190*
Hollingbury Hill (Sussex, England) 49
Holstein (Germany) 48
horn *184, 191*
Horus (Egyptian god) 232
  eye of Horus *198, 202, 203*; falcon of Horus 27
Hoxne (Suffolk, England) 96
Huber, Patriz *192*
humming birds *188*
Hunt & Roskell 186

illuminated MSS, influence of *138*, 209
Inca 127–8
India 18, *91*–2, *193*, 234–5
  see also Mughal India
inlay 12, 16, 20, 25, 27, 30, 32, 33, 36, 44, 47, *59*, 64, 65, 66, 69, 71, *71, 72*, 82, 86, 88, 90, 92, *92*, 101, 103, 105, 107, 113, 114, 115, *116*, 198, *200, 203, 224*
Inquisition 166
inscriptions 98, 138, *138*, 140, *140, 143*, 146, *147*, 150, 152, 160, *198, 201*, 206, 208, 209, *209*, 211, *211*–13, *215*, 219, *224*, *228*–9, 231–6, 238–40, 239
  Insignia of the Garter 156
intaglio 98, *165*–6, 230
Ipswich (Suffolk) 78
Iran 53–5, *54*–6, 68, 68, 89, 90
  see also Persia
Iraq 11, 12, 23–5, *197*, 198, 202, 229
Ireland *50*, 53, 112, *112*–13, 114
iron 72, *73*, 74, 94, 97
Iron Age 72–4, *72*–4, 76, 78, 94
Isis (Egyptian goddess) 232
Islam 16, 145–6, *147*, 214, 215, *215*
Italy 150, 150, 189, 222, 231
ivory 26, 27, 29, 57, 177, *178, 178, 187*, 212, 230

jacinth 208, 242
'Jacobite' rings 239
jade 16, 18, 70, 71, 81, 118, 119, 121, *123*, *124*–6, *133*, 167, *167*–9, 194, *197*, *197*, 234, *234*
jadeite 29, 70, 81, *194*
Jaipur (India) 174
James I, King (of England) 154, *161*
Japan 18, 20, 119–120, *120*, 184, 214
'Japanese taste' *190*–1
jasper 26, 34, 35, 44, 47, *198, 198*
java *148*
jet 14, 40, 41, 94, *97*
Joseph in the Well 156
Jugendstil 184, *192*

Kennard, John 244
Kiev 16, *137, 138*
Kolts 137
Korea 119, *119*, 147, *148*–9
Kouklia (Cyprus) 15
Kourion Karloriziki (Cyprus) 15
Kyme (Turkey) 86

'labrets' *126, 133*
lacquer *192*
Lalique, René 184, *191*

Lama (goddess) 197, *200*
Lamashtu (Mesopotamian demon) *198, 202*
Lamb of God *189*
landscapes *164*
lapidaries 208
lapis lazuli 12–13, *23*–5, 26, *30*–1, 34, 35, 47, *115, 175*, 176, 197, 198, 202, 229, *229*
Lark Hill hoard 16, *138*
latchet *112*
La Tène 15, 72–3, *73, 74*–6, 227
'Leda and the Swan' 220
leg *198, 203*
leopards *191*
Liberty and Co. 20, *193*
Li Jingxun 115, *115*
lions 54, *55, 59*, 60, 68, 69, 98, *191, 198*
lip-pieces 18
lip-plugs (labrets) 121, *126*
lizard *169*
lockets 162, *163*–4, *190*, 220, 235
  see also 'Lyte' Jewel
'lock-ring' *50*
Lombardic period *105, 208*
'Londesborough' Brooch *113*
loop-in-loop chains 12, 31, 37, 43, 98, 242
lost-wax casting, *see* cire-perdue
lotus flowers, *33, 47, 198*
Louis XIV, King (of France) 224
Lucius Verus (Roman emperor) 222
lunula 14, 40, 41, *42*
Luristan (Iran) 53–4, *54*
'Lyte' Jewel 19, *19*, 154, *160*–1
Lyte, Thomas 154, *160*–1

magatama 119, 120, *120*
Maidum (Egypt) 32
Maintenon, Mme de 223, *224*
malachite 29
mano cornuta 211, *212*
marcasite *185*
Marchesini, Niccola 187
Marchi, Luigi *190*
Maria I, Queen (of Portugal) 226, *240*
marriage-rings 228, 233, 234, 236, *236*, 239, *239*
  Jewish 239, *239*
Mary I, Queen (of England) 239
Mary, Queen of Scots 234, *235*
Mary, Virgin *138*, 206, *212, 213*
masks 81, *82*, 129, 130, *130*
Matmar (Egypt) 27, *32*
Maya 18, 121–3, *123*–6
medals 163
medallions 184, *206*
Medici, Lorenzo de' *218*, 219
medieval style *189, 190*
  see also Gothic
Medusa 217, *219*, 223, *226*
Melfort (Scotland) 14, *41*
Melillo, Giacinto 189
Melos 60, *84, 86*
memento mori 222, *240*, 242
merchant's mark 234, *235*
Merovingian period *208*, 231, *233*
Mesoamerica 121, *123*–6, 127–34, *129*–30, 132–4
Mesopotamia, *see* Iraq
message jewellery *185, 187*
Mexico 81–2, *81*, 123, *126, 134*
Michelsen, A. *192*
micromosaic *189*
millefiori, *see* glass
Minerva 98
miniatures 19, *19*, 154, 160, *161*, 162, *163*–4, *173*, 174, *183*, 184
Minoans 13–14, 15, 37, 38, *38*–9, 227, 229
Mixtecs 133–4, *134*
Mochica 81–2, *83*
Mold (Wales) 48
Mongolia 176, *176*
monkeys *39, 83*
monsters 54, *137, 138, 140*

Morawe, C. F. 192
Moray Firth (Scotland) 97
Morvah (Cornwall, England) 52
mosaic 12, 82–3, 189, 224
Mostagedda (Egypt) 26–7, 29, 198
mother of pearl 28, 191
mould (for casting a ring) 227
mourning rings 239
mouth-mask 83
mouthpieces 38
musicians 42, 118
Mughal India 18, 173–4, 173–4, 234, 234
Mulsanne (France) 233
Mürrle Bennett 192
Mycenaeans 14, 15, 37, 38, 39, 58, 60, 227, 227

Nanchang (China) 173
Napoleon I, Emperor 235, 239
Naqada cultures (Egypt) 26
Nassaro, Matteo dal 219, 222
Nature god 38
Nazca people 82, 82
necklaces 12, 14, 16, 20, 23, 23, 27, 28–9, 36, 36, 39, 40, 41, 47, 57, 58, 63, 63–4, 65, 66, 68, 74, 84, 86, 86–8, 92, 94, 98, 99, 100, 107, 115, 115, 119, 121, 123, 130, 138, 150, 164–5, 174, 175, 177, 188–9, 191, 193, 198, 198, 203–4
necklets 40
neck-rings 48, 74, 111, 112
see also collars; torcs
nefer-signs 44, 243
nekhaw 200, 203–4
nephrite 70, 81, 194
Netherlands 160, 164–5
niello 16, 88, 97, 98, 101, 103, 108, 111, 137–8, 138, 140, 140, 144–5, 146, 206, 215, 228, 232, 234, 236, 243
Nihavand (Persia) 145, 146, 215
Nilgiri Hills (India) 91, 91
Nineveh (Iraq) 197, 197
'Noah' Cameo 218, 219
Nofret (Egyptian queen) 32
Northampton, William, 1st Earl of 156
nose ornaments 18, 83, 129–30, 133
nose pins 121, 126
Nubkheperre Inyotef (Egyptian king) 35
nuggets, gold 181

oak leaves 186
obsidian 11, 13, 23, 28, 126
Okorág (Hungary) 80
Olmec 18, 80–1, 81
Omphale 220
onyx 98, 165–6, 216, 217–18, 219, 220, 222–4, 240, 242
opals 163, 211, 222
fire-opal 193
openwork 33, 34, 44, 69, 90, 97, 111, 119, 133, 142, 148, 154, 168, 169, 170, 173, 202, 211, 220, 222, 223, 224
see also ajouré; opus interrasile; pierced work
opus interrasile ('pierced work') 88, 98, 99–100, 236, 243
Ordos region (China) 70
Orpheus 232
Ottonian period 136, 138, 206
Oxus Treasure 55, 56, 66, 66, 68, 68–9
oyster-shells 33, 34, 203

padlocks 143, 185
paintings 11, 14, 16, 34, 36, 42, 94, 114, 115, 151, 154, 160, 167, 170, 173, 194, 194, 212, 213, 223, 237
Palmyra (Syria) 89
Pan, see Faunus
Panpocun (China) 70
Park Brow (Sussex, England) 76
parrot 174
Parthia 89, 90, 91
Pasargadae (Iran) 65
paste-set jewellery 19–20, 183, 240

Payne-Knight, Richard 224, 226
Pazuzu (Mesopotamian demon) 198, 202
peacocks 170, 205, 206, 215, 228
pearls 20, 68, 68, 87, 98–9, 101, 109, 115, 115, 135–6, 140, 151, 154, 169, 176, 183–5, 187, 190–1
'baroque' 159, 193, 240
pectoral ornaments 18, 38, 51, 60, 92, 94, 124, 129, 130, 134, 181, 243
Pelican in her Piety 140
pendants 11, 18, 20, 23, 24–5, 26, 28, 31–3, 33, 36, 36–9, 38, 44, 47, 51, 55, 58, 65, 66, 68, 70, 81, 81, 82, 84, 84, 86, 86–8, 91, 99, 101, 103–4, 114, 119, 119, 121, 124–6, 130, 132, 134, 137, 144, 146, 154, 154, 156, 159, 160, 166, 174–5, 190–2, 194, 194, 197, 197, 198, 198, 200–1, 203, 204, 208, 208, 209, 211, 211, 219, 220, 222–3, 229, 229
brooch-pendants 224
Penrith (Cumbria, England) 109
Pentney (Norfolk, England) 111, 112
Perient, Joan 138
Persia 16, 66, 68, 69, 145, 146, 215
Peru 81–2, 82–3, 128
Peterborough (Northamptonshire, England) 228
Petrus Christus 237
Phillips Brothers 184, 190
Philostratus 16
Phoenicians 57–8, 57, 198, 203, 230, 232
'Phoenix' Jewel 159
Phoenixes 159, 169, 170
pierced work 97, 170, 206
see also ajouré; openwork; opus interrasile
Pierrepont, Evelyn 240
Pierret, Ernesto 189
Pietà 220
pietra dura 224, 243
pig 197
pilgrim badges 208, 211
pins 15, 53–4, 133, 147
see also dress-pins; hairpins
Pistrucci, Benedetto 223, 224
Pitkelloney Farm (Scotland) 78
plaques 34, 60, 70, 71, 72, 118, 118, 145, 147, 148, 168, 170, 173, 174, 198
see also belt-plaques
plasma 98, 243
platinum 20, 193
Pleurs (France) 75
Pomanders 151, 154, 166, 243
'Pompeiian' style 189
pony see horses
porcelain 84, 192
posies 140
Poslingford (Suffolk, England) 228, 229
prayer-book, girdle 151, 151–2, 154
prayers, inscribed 209
prophylactic charms 209, 211, 211–14, 215
Pu-Abi (Sumerian queen) 12, 30, 227
puzzle rings 238

Quercia, Janvier 191
Quran 215, 215

Rahotep (Egyptian prince) 32
rams 56, 69, 72, 197
Ramsgate (Kent, England) 49
Ravenscroft family 235
reef knot see Heracles-knot
regalia 101, 181
relics 208–9, 209, 212
reliquaries 138, 206, 208, 209, 212–13
Renaissance 150–1, 154, 184, 190, 219, 224
repoussé 13, 32, 33, 39–40, 48, 58, 65, 69, 82, 83, 90, 100, 101, 101, 103–4, 128, 128, 134, 145, 152, 170, 180, 181, 201, 215, 227, 239, 243
ribbon slide 165, 166

Richard II, King (of England) 138
Richborough (Kent, England) 236, 236
'ring-money' 50
rings see finger-rings; hair-rings; toe-rings
rock-crystal 20, 115, 138, 148, 184, 208, 208, 209, 220, 233–4, 235
Roman Britain 94, 94, 96, 230, 236, 236
Romans 16, 86–9, 87, 205, 205, 217, 219, 222, 227, 230, 231, 233, 234, 236
Romulus and Remus 232, 233
rosette, gold 59
runes 208, 228, 228
Rubbiani, Alfonso 190
ruby 140, 143, 154, 160, 163, 185, 187, 193, 211, 220, 224, 233
Russia 137, 138

St Demetrios 206
St George 206
St Paul, the Conversion of 150
saints 135, 211, 238
Samaria, woman of 152
Sandoz, G. 192
sapphire 87, 88, 91, 98–9, 138, 140, 143, 154, 162, 163, 165, 208, 211, 241
sard 227, 243
sardonyx 216, 217, 227, 227, 230
Sarre (Kent, England) 103
Sasanians 91, 232
satyr 96
Saulini, Tommaso 223, 226
scarabs 33, 34–5, 36, 44, 44, 47, 63, 198, 201, 203, 229–30, 232, 243
scaraboid 232, 243
scent-bottle 161, 162
sceptre 15
scorpions 44, 182, 198
scrolling 176, 176
sculptures 43, 56, 89, 92, 215
sea-battle, scene of 164
sea-dragon 159
seals 24, 31, 66, 115, 197, 205, 229, 229
seed-pearls 20, 86, 146
Selby (Yorkshire, England) 233
Senses, the Five 108
serekhs 27, 27, 30
Serpent, Brazen, see Brazen Serpent
serpentine 81
serpents, see snakes
Shah Jahan 173, 174, 174, 234
shale 40, 48
shebyu-collar 14, 43, 43
shells 11, 23, 23, 26, 28–9, 82, 124, 126
shibuichi 20, 243
shoulder-clasps 107
shrines 208–9, 211
siege, scene of 164
signet-rings 44, 66, 91, 143, 216, 227, 228, 229–31, 231–2, 233–4, 234–5
silver 12, 14, 16, 23, 24, 27, 32, 33, 35, 55, 70, 72, 73, 74, 76, 80, 94, 94, 103–5, 108–11, 112, 117, 137–8, 142, 144–5, 146, 170, 176, 181, 184, 192, 205–6, 208, 211, 231; gilt 35, 113, 116–17, 142, 144, 146, 149, 170, 191, 211, 235, 240
Sintra (Portugal) 52
sirens 63, 65
skull and crossbones 240
Slavs 104, 108
sleeve-fastener 50, 53
snakes 19, 58, 73, 76, 88, 93, 198, 205
Snettisham Treasure 73, 74, 76, 78
Sobkemsaf II (Egyptian king) 35
Sobkemsaf (Egyptian queen) 34
Society of Jesus 222
solidus 99, 103–4
Solomon, judgement of 152
spacer-bars 27, 27, 30, 34, 34–5, 36
spacer-beads 26, 26, 57
spacer-plate necklaces 40
Spain 19, 73, 75, 78, 166
Speke, Lady Philippa 152, 159
sphinxes 60, 68, 227, 232
spinel 140, 243

stamped ornament 104
stags 55, 194, 232
steatite 13, 26, 26, 44, 227
'stilettos', jade 81
stone 11, 26, 36, 119–20, 120, 197, 198, 198, 203
banded 216, 217
strap-necklace 63
Strass, Georges-Frédéric 19
Streeter, E. W. 190
Sully Moors, nr Cardiff (Wales) 217, 219
Sumerians 12–13, 12, 23–5, 23, 53, 216, 216
'Sussex loop' arm-ring 53
Sutton Hoo (Suffolk, England) 101, 107
Susanna accused by the Elders 152
swans 138, 138, 140, 206
swastika 59
swivel-settings 44, 45, 230, 232
sword harness mounts 107
Székesfehérvár (Hungary) 80

Talisman box 92
see also amulet-boxes
Taormina (Sicily) 84
Tara Hill (Ireland) 50
Tarentum (Italy) 64
Tassie, James & William 226, 240
Taxila (India) 92
Taylor, Ebenezer 241
Tell Brak (Syria) 197, 197
Tell-el'Ajjul (Palestine) 36, 37, 198
Teotihuacan (Mexico) 125
Tepe Nūsh-i Jān (Iran) 55
Tharros (Sardinia) 57, 57, 198, 203
Thetford (Norfolk, England) 96, 97, 236
Thomsen, Christian 192
Thorn Reliquary, Holy 138, 209, 209
Three Kings 209
thumb-rings 173, 234, 234
tiara 186, 188
Tibet 174, 174–5, 176, 214, 215
Tiffany & Co 20, 184, 190
Tikal (Guatemala) 125
tinctures, heraldic 232–3, 235, 243
toadstone 208, 211
toe-rings 73, 181, 182
toggle-pins 24, 30
tooth pendants 208, 208
topaze 185
torcs 15, 46, 48, 50, 53, 66, 69, 74, 74–6, 76, 78, 243
tortoiseshell 186
Toscana (Italy) 105
Toutin, Henri 154, 164
'Townley' Brooch 136
'Trewhiddle' Style 111
Trezzo, Jacopo de 219
Troy (Turkey) 13
tumbaga 132
Tunis (N. Africa) 87
turquoise 18, 26, 29, 34, 35, 69, 71, 90, 143, 174–6, 176, 185, 187, 198
turtle 198, 198

Ukraine 103–4, 137
Ur (Iraq) 12, 12, 23–5, 23–5, 28, 30–1, 33, 36, 37, 216, 216–17, 227, 229, 229
uraei 44, 201, 202, 203, 243
Uruk (Iraq) 198, 202
Usküdar (Turkey) 232

Vandal period 104
Varna (Bulgaria) 40
Venus 94, 226
Victoria, Queen 187
Victory, figures of 84, 86, 183, 205
Vikings 109, 111, 112, 114

waist-clasp, see clasp
wands 204
wedding-rings, see marriage-rings

Wedgwood, Josiah 226
Wentworth, Thomas, 2nd Baron 154
wesekh-collars *14, 27, 32, 34, 34, 42, 47,*
 243
Wièse, J. and L. 184, *190*
wheel pendants *204,* 205
Wigber Low (Derbyshire, England)
 208
'willow-pattern' dish *184*
Wilton Diptych 138
Wittersham (Kent, England) *138*
woodpeckers 96
Woolley, Sir Leonard 23
workshops, jewellers'/goldsmiths'
 13, *14, 20, 34,* 36, *237*
wreaths, gold 63, *63,* 65, 66
Writtle (Essex, England) 138, *138*
Wyatt, Sir Thomas 151, *151*

Ziwiye (Iran) *55*